Principles of Global Security

Principles of Global Security

JOHN D. STEINBRUNER

BROOKINGS INSTITUTION PRESS
Washington, D.C.

Library of Congress Cataloging-in-Publication data
Steinbruner, John D., 1941–
Principles of global security / John Steinbruner.
p. cm.
Includes bibliographical references and index.
ISBN 0-8157-8096-6 (cloth : alk. paper) —
ISBN 0-8157-8095-8 (paper : alk. paper)
1. Security, International. 2. International economic relations.
I. Title.
JZ6005 .S74 2000 99-050913
327.1'72—dc21 CIP

9 8 7 6 5 4 3 2 1

The paper used in this publication meets minimum requirements of the American National Standard for Information Sciences—Permanence of Paper for Printed Library Materials: ANSI Z39.48-1984.

Typeset in Sabon

Composition by Cynthia Stock
Silver Spring, Maryland

Printed by R. R. Donnelley and Sons
Harrisonburg, Virginia

THE BROOKINGS INSTITUTION

The Brookings Institution is an independent organization devoted to nonpartisan research, education, and publication in economics, government, foreign policy, and the social sciences generally. Its principal purposes are to aid in the development of sound public policies and to promote public understanding of issues of national importance.

The Institution was founded on December 8, 1927, to merge the activities of the Institute for Government Research, founded in 1916, the Institute of Economics, founded in 1922, and the Robert Brookings Graduate School of Economics and Government, founded in 1924.

The general administration of the Institution is the responsibility of a Board of Trustees charged with safeguarding the independence of the staff and fostering the most favorable conditions for scientific research and publication. The immediate direction of the policies, program, and staff is vested in the president, assisted by an advisory committee of the officers and staff.

In publishing a study, the Institution presents it as a competent treatment of a subject worthy of public consideration. The interpretations or conclusions in such publications are those of the author or authors and do not necessarily reflect the views of the other staff members, officers, or trustees of the Brookings Institution.

For Cris, who sustained the effort,

and for David, Greg, and Gretchen,
whose generation inherits the issues

Foreword

ALTHOUGH A FAMILIAR proverb holds the pen to be mightier than the sword, when it comes down to practical circumstances the two generally work together. The quality of a nation's national security policy is affected both by the capacity of military forces and by the purposes to which they are directed. A major defect in either dimension is likely to cause serious trouble, however robust the other may be.

For the United States and its allies, military capacity as traditionally conceived far exceeds that of any potential opponent, but the consequence of that fact is nonetheless an open question. Moreover, the circumstances under which military forces operate are changing substantially.

This book explores major revisions that may be necessary in the configuration and operational practices of military forces and in the basic relationships among historical opponents in order to achieve security throughout the world. It suggests that the stronger have a much greater practical stake in the security of the weaker than has yet been recognized for reasons that have not yet been fully understood. If that proves to be true, it has the potential to eventually transform the practice of international security. At the outset of that process, it is important to consider the reasons why it might be true.

The author wishes to express his gratitude to the many colleagues whose knowledge and ideas have shaped this work without implicating them in the specific arguments made. Among Brookings Institution research staff members that includes particularly Robert Axtell, Bruce Blair, Roberta Cohen, Francis Deng, Joshua Epstein, Kenneth Flamm, Clifford Gaddy, Raymond Garthoff, Carol Graham, Jerry Hough, William Kaufmann, Catherine McArdle Kelleher, Lawrence Korb, Nicholas Lardy, Edward Lincoln, Nora Lustig, Terrence Lyons, Michael MccGwire, Thomas McNaugher, Michael Mochizuki, Janne Nolan, Michael O'Hanlon, Wolfgang Reinicke, Yahya Sadowski, Stephen Schwartz, Paul Stares, Shibley Telhami, Susan Woodward, and Peyton Young. The work has origins in the cooperative security project jointly conducted with William Perry and Ashton Carter as well as Brookings colleague Janne Nolan and in the 2050 project with particularly direct influence from Allen Hammond and Bruce Murray. The book has been strongly affected by members of the Committee on International Security and Arms Control of the National Academy of Sciences chaired by John Holdren and directed by Jo Husbands. It has also been influenced by members of the Carnegie Commission on Preventing Deadly Conflict jointly chaired by David Hamburg and Cyrus Vance and directed by Jane Holl. A draft of the manuscript was reviewed by members of the Committee on International Security Studies of the American Academy of Arts and Sciences chaired by Carl Kaysen, and direct comments on the text provided by Abram Chayes, Antonia Chayes, Carl Kaysen, Michael Klare, Robert Pastor, Barry Posen, Judith Reppy, and Bruce Russet resulted in a number of important corrections and improvements, as did similar comments independently provided by William Kaufmann and Leon Sigal.

Jason Forrester has provided the primary research assistance for the book and his contribution has been especially substantial. Research assistance in the early phases of preparing the manuscript was also provided by Melanie Allen, Brian Finlay, and Susan Hardesty. Staff assistance was provided by Mica Kreutz, Rebecca Over, and Elizabeth Pelletreau. The manuscript was edited by Elizabeth Forsyth under editorial direction of Janet Walker and was verified by Susan Jackson assisted by Mohammed Sulaiman. Carlotta Ribar proofread the pages, and Julia Petrakis provided an index.

The author also wishes to express special gratitude to his wife, Cris, whose personal support was indispensable.

Financial support for the project was provided by the John D. and Catherine T. MacArthur Foundation, the Carnegie Corporation of New York, and the W. Alton Jones Foundation. Both the author and the

Brookings Institution are grateful for that support. Program officers from those foundations, Ruth Adams, Kennette Benedict, George Perkovich, and David Speedie, individually made substantive contributions to the project, as did Jane Wales. Throughout the writing of the manuscript the author held the Sydney Stein Jr. Chair in International Security at Brookings.

The views expressed here are those of the author and should not be ascribed to any of the persons whose assistance is acknowledged above, or to the trustees, officers, or other staff members of the Brookings Institution.

MICHAEL H. ARMACOST
President

Washington, D.C.
February 2000

Contents

Principles of Global Security

CHAPTER ONE

Contending Presumptions

In the fall of 1991, David Hamburg, then president of the Carnegie Corporation of New York, and Sam Nunn, then a U.S. senator from Georgia, convened a series of meetings to discuss the future of international security. They were impressed, as everyone was, by the precipitous ending of the cold war—just then being confirmed by the imminent dissolution of the Soviet Union—but they were already concerned about the aftermath. They were particularly concerned that the diffusion of the accumulated weapons arsenals and of their embedded technologies might produce a dangerous pattern of conflict. They believed that the United States would have a strong interest in controlling the dangers of weapons proliferation and would have to bear primary responsibility for doing so. They wanted to consider the implications.

In one of the many meetings held, an argument was advanced that the specific problems of proliferation could not be isolated from the general conditions of international security and that fundamental revisions of established practice would have to be contemplated as a new era emerged. The reasoning was that the historical pattern of belligerent confrontation between the major states could not continue indefinitely, not only because the inexorable spread of advanced technology would increase the risk to civilian society but also because the globalization of economic activity was altering the nature of the security problem. Diffuse violence, it was suggested, posed a greater threat than traditional forms of mass aggression, driving even the most reluctant states into intricate collaboration for mutual protection. Classic notions of balancing power by means of active military deployments would have to be overlaid by more refined concepts of cooperation. Unavoidable disparities in raw military capacity would have to be constrained by explicit principles of equity, and those principles would have to be reinforced by agreed rules of procedure for force operations, rules that would be continuously practiced and actively monitored. The doctrine of deterrence—the major policy product of the cold war—would have to be subordinated to the countervailing idea of reassurance.

This argument envisaged a major shift in the organizing principles of international security. Under the established deterrent arrangement, security is based primarily on the active confrontation of military forces. If reassurance were to be established as the predominant principle, the active confrontation of deployed forces would be replaced by the continuous enforcement of collaborative rules designed to preclude military forces from being mobilized into an immediately threatening configuration. Deterrence as currently practiced involves the continuous presentation of an active threat. Reassurance would involve comprehensive restraint on such threats continuously documented in convincing detail. A shift in the degree of reliance on these basic principles would have to be undertaken, the argument maintained, not only to control proliferation but also to assure all other aspects of security under drastically altered circumstances.

In response to that argument, Senator Nunn, with a wry choice of phrasing, posed a skeptical question. "Well," he said, "you have human nature and all of history going against you there. What have you got going for you?"

The argument in question actually did not contradict all the results of history or every aspect of human nature. Strands of cooperation are deeply implanted in both, and indeed one could hardly have a major war without elaborate forms of cooperation within the military establishments of the opposing parties. Cooperation is arguably as integral to the human experience as battle. It is reasonable to consider how the balance of these different activities and the scope of their application might shift with changing circumstances. Nonetheless Senator Nunn's question undoubtedly reflected where the burden of proof did then and does continue to lie. Most of those engaged with the subject of international security, whether as direct participants or as attentive citizens, are acutely sensitive to the possibility of willful attack. A solid majority in most societies is convinced that active preparation of national military forces provides the only reliable means of protection. This attitude is formulated in the self-labeled realist school of thought, which holds that security necessarily depends on the organized power of the nation-state and that states by their very nature compete with one another in the development of power to the extent they are able.[1] As a result, the staunch realists contend, any form of arranged security cooperation is less reliable than national military power.[2] Those who hold that view concede that the passing of the cold war produced many important changes in circumstance, but they do not believe that those changes altered the fundamental character of nation-states or of the security problems they generate. As a practical matter, that is the prevailing presumption, and it is up to those who question it to make a convincing case.

On broad questions of this sort, assigning the burden of proof is nearly always decisive as far as prevailing opinion is concerned. Those who are made to carry it generally lose the argument. In this instance it clearly would be extremely difficult to overturn the entrenched presumptions of the realist school whose origins can be traced, if not literally to all of human history, then certainly to prominent features extending back as far as there is documented testimony. From the earliest records of human societies, warfare has been both an organizing focus and a prime source of political motivation. The binding power of common threat and the closely associated impulse to control territory have had much to do with the rise of states, the justification of their governments, the genesis of armies, the development of technology, the evolution of manufacturing capability, and formation of the human attitudes that have accompanied all of these. Countless battles have been fought in the course of colonizing the planet. Hundreds of millions of individual lives have been expended. The experience has created a legacy of military confrontation that many people consider immutable, as the senator's question implied. Since preparations for war and the occasional conduct of it have been central preoccupations for virtually all the major states throughout their existence, it is widely assumed that the pattern is rooted in human nature and that it will endure indefinitely.

But security practices clearly are not immutable in every important respect. And as consequential as prevailing opinion unquestionably is, it is not the only consideration of importance. Although the full implications are still obscure, it is increasingly apparent that contemporary societies are encountering a major deflection in the course of their development, as illustrated dramatically by the manner in which the cold war ended. That was largely a spontaneous event, surprising virtually everyone who experienced it, including the political leaders most intimately involved. No one seriously anticipated the reunification of Germany, the dissolution of the Warsaw Treaty Organization, or the dismemberment of the Soviet Union until just before those events occurred. In the aftermath there has been a natural inclination, particularly in the United States, to interpret this good fortune as an episode in the triumphant extension of market democracy, but it is prudent to question whether that will prove to be the full story. Since no one could anticipate either the timing or the scope of what happened, no one can claim to grasp all of the consequences either. The massive transformation that has engulfed the Soviet Union and its Central European allies suggests the workings of very large forces capable of doing far more than settling an ideological quarrel. If that can happen in one part of the world, it may be happening in all of it, and the process may be far from complete. The specific security implications presumably will not overturn all that history has done, but they might well prove to be far more extensive than currently imagined, especially by adherents of the realist perspective. Exploring that possibility is appropriate, even urgent, and it is the central purpose of this book.

Discontinuity

For those willing to undertake such an exploration, the hint of a general transformation in progress is a natural place to begin, and there are some strong clues about the underlying forces that might be driving such a process.[3] It has something to do, one can surmise, with trends in the capacity for violence. In absolute terms the past century has been the most destructive in history, with more than 100 million people killed and a commensurate amount of physical damage done through various forms of warfare.[4] But that record is eclipsed by the technical potential for destruction, which already has reached unprecedented magnitude and is on the verge of reaching unprecedented intrusiveness. As the principal activity of the cold war, military forces were developed to the point at which they could directly slaughter tens of millions of people within a few hours and so devastate the infrastructure of major societies that hundreds of millions and perhaps billions of other people would be at grave risk. Political attitudes have so accommodated that development that it is not now considered remarkable and, with the proclaimed passing of the cold war, not even especially relevant. The capacity for rapid destruction on that scale imposes relentless pressures on fallible human institutions, however, and simple common sense suggests that the cold war pattern of nuclear weapons deployments cannot be sustained in a safe manner indefinitely. Some major transformation in the handling of this capability can eventually be expected.

The potential for mass destruction is not the only source of unusual pressure, moreover. The capacity for precise attack at very long range is developing to the point that forms of coercion could be undertaken that have never been feasible before. In all of history up to this point, killing a king and sacking his headquarters first required defeating his protective armies. It will soon be feasible to accomplish this directly at any moment from any location. If that capability matures to its full potential and diffuses throughout the world, critical assets of all societies will be continuously exposed to dedicated attack from anonymous sources. Even the possibility of this threat means that advanced rules of restraint will have to be devised if normal daily life is to be protected.

But the enhanced capacity for violence is not the only and probably not even the primary agent of social transformation. It is based on a technical revolution with implications much broader than the conduct of warfare. It also is set in the context of what necessarily will be a unique moment in history—an unprecedented surge in the total human population. Whatever else might be happening, the combined effects of technology and population dynamics are altering some of the critical operating conditions of human societies, are creating unusual pressures within them, and appear to be inducing a new pattern of interaction among them. One of the many consequences of this situation is the emergence of fundamentally different security problems. Correspondingly fundamental changes in the practice of war, or what is now more politely called international security, can be expected to follow.

Technology

A sense of historical discontinuity produced by radical technical change was, of course, a prominent feature of the cold war itself. That sense emerged with the revelation in the final stages of World War II of what were then called atomic weapons, and it became a continuous theme in the extensive effort to comprehend their implications. The point was forcefully expressed in a memorandum written on September 11, 1945, by U.S. Secretary of War Henry L. Stimson to President Harry S. Truman:

> If the atomic bomb were merely another though more devastating military weapon to be assimilated into our pattern of international relations, it would be one thing. We could then follow the old custom of secrecy and nationalistic military superiority relying on international caution to prescribe the future use of the weapon as we did with gas. But I think the bomb instead constitutes merely a first step in a new control by man over the forces of nature too revolutionary and dangerous to fit into the old concepts. I think it really caps the climax of the race between man's growing technical power for destructiveness and his psychological power of self-control and group control—his moral power.[5]

The same thought was summarized two decades later by Albert Einstein in one of his most widely noted remarks: "The unleashing of the power of the atom has changed everything but our modes of thinking, and thus we drift toward unparalleled catastrophes."[6]

The "everything" that Einstein had in mind concerned the energy densities that his conceptual advances had enabled. With mastery of the contributing technologies, it became possible over a two-decade period to increase the explosive yield of a given amount of weapons material by a factor of a million. With the mastery of ballistic missile technology, it became possible to deliver nuclear explosives over intercontinental ranges at speeds more than forty times greater than the aircraft of World War II were able to achieve and to do so with sufficient precision to bring the destructive effects to bear on intended targets with very high confidence.[7] But contrary to Stimson's plea, those accomplishments were applied to standard missions of warfare and were assimilated to the traditional pattern of international relations. Two contending alliances arose, each imagining that the other might use the new technology to initiate a massive assault without notice. Each alliance spent large sums preparing to apply the new weapons to the massive ground assaults and strategic bombardments characteristic of World War II. The physical calculations that supported the technical achievements made it possible to measure the destructive implications of these more advanced forms of warfare with enough precision to provide an indisputable and riveting depiction of threat. The clarity and the magnitude of nuclear weapons effects crystallized a conception of international security based on a confrontational balance of opposing forces, and that conception became the organizing formulation of international security.

If nuclear weapons and ballistic missiles were the most prominent and most destructive technical developments of the period, however, they were not the most radical. Intertwined in their development was a series of even greater technical advances involving the efficient handling of information. Over a five-decade span, the costs of storing a unit of information, processing it in some useful application, and transmitting it over long distances have declined by factors of up to 100 million or more and are projected to continue declining for at least another decade.[8] In the earliest stages these achievements were driven by weapons applications, but the primary impetus shifted rapidly to the development of consumer products and a wide range of commercial services. The consequences of the technologies themselves and of their distinctive pattern of development are more diffuse and much less readily calculated than the consequences of a millionfold increase in the energy density of explosives, but they clearly have much broader scope. In fact they affect virtually all forms of organized human activity.

Although the literature dedicated to information technology articulates a strong sense of historical discontinuity that could be assimilated readily to Einstein's remark, as yet no crystallizing image of threat or of any other identifiable consequence has provided the organizing focus for policy that nuclear weapons effects provided for the cold war era. Nonetheless it is evident that massive efficiency gains in the handling of information are capable of bringing about truly fundamental changes in core activities of human societies, and it is plausible that they will actually do so. Vastly facilitated information flows make it feasible, for example, to organize basic economic functions on a global scale, and market forces appear to be mandating it. That is most evident to date in the operations of capital markets whose accelerating international growth in recent years gives evidence of historical discontinuity. Discontinuity is less evident in the figures for trade and for direct foreign investment, but these indicators do show a trend of increasing activity across national boundaries. If basic manufacturing and the provision of services are eventually driven to global scale to the extent that is technically feasible, then a progressively integrated international economy will emerge with properties that diverge sharply from past experience.

Rapid shifts in the structure of employment would be expected to occur in such an economy as individuals and firms learn how to use information technology. The national identity of all economies would also be diluted as the leading entrepreneurs adapt to the imperatives of organizing across cultural divisions. National governments would not be able to prevent these effects without disrupting economic performance, nor would they be able to stimulate or regulate economic performance by the standard methods of macroeconomic management. Since a spontaneously integrating international economy would generate universal incentives and would require universal operating rules, it would drive national governments into ever more intricate forms of collaboration in an effort to pursue national economic objectives. It also would disperse access to products, information, and technology of all sorts—some of them distinctly dangerous—and would intensify interactions among separate cultures. In general it would tie everyone's fate to everyone else's to an extent never experienced before.

At the moment it cannot be indisputably demonstrated that a global economy of this sort is actually emerging, but that is certainly a strong possibility.[9] The sheer efficiency with which information is handled makes it so.

Population Dynamics

The companion phenomenon of population dynamics has not captured strategic imagination to the extent that nuclear weapons and information technology have, but its significance is at least as great if not more so. In the aftermath of World War II the overall size of the human population began a process of accelerated increase typically associated with an exponential growth sequence before reaching some limiting condition. Although substantial uncertainties are involved, standard estimates suggest that the total number of human beings alive on earth first reached 1 billion around 1800; that is, it had required all of human history up to that point to generate a total population of that size. The second billion was added about 125 years later, the third thirty years after that, the fourth fourteen years later, the fifth thirteen years later, and the sixth twelve years later in 1999.[10] As Nobel laureate nuclear physicist Murray Gell-Mann has pointed out, this sequence can be fitted to a parabolic curve that explodes to infinity in the year 2025.[11] We know that limiting conditions will be encountered well before that happens, and the limiting process is already visible. Birth rates are declining in most parts of the world. The demographic momentum that has been established, however, will sustain for several more decades the surge in growth that began around 1950. Barring some cataclysm, about 8 billion people will be alive in 2025, an increase of 1 billion people every fourteen to fifteen years over that span of time.[12] The trajectory thereafter is more speculative, but United Nations mid-range estimates—the best approximation of consensus on the subject—suggest eventual stabilization at the level of 10 billion or so.[13]

The composition of this population surge is as important as its magnitude. The increases are not occurring proportionately across the spectrum of income and wealth. Virtually all of the projected increase is expected to occur in the poorest segments of the population—those falling in the lowest 20 percent of the distribution of income and wealth.[14] That pattern differentiates the more advanced economies—members of the Organization for Economic Cooperation and Development (OECD)—from all of the others, but the same pattern also occurs within the developed economies. Throughout the world the wealthier populations are already at or below replacement levels of fertility, and the net increases are occurring almost entirely among the lowest-income groups.[15] In addition to altering the income distribution, this phenomenon also affects the age structure of the population, generating disproportionately large age cohorts that produce a corresponding pattern of surge and decline in the demand for basic requirements—education, housing, employment, consumer durables, and eventually health and retirement benefits—as they move through the life cycle. Sharp differences have emerged in the age structures of different societies, with the populations of the developing economies as a whole significantly younger than those of the industrial economies.[16]

The potential consequences of these distributional patterns are very large indeed, particularly in interaction with the consequences of information technology. So far it appears that the process of economic growth associated with the adaptation to information technology is concentrated in the leading sectors of the advanced economies, as would be expected. Those who are more sophisticated and have greater access to capital are undertaking the technical advances and are learning more rapidly how to capture the economic advantages provided. That appears to be the case in the United States, at least, which also appears to be the society that is farthest along in the process of adaptation. For more than two decades, the benefits of economic growth in the United States have been concentrated at the top of the income spectrum. There has been stagnation in the middle parts of the spectrum and decline at the bottom. Between 1979 and 1996 the average annual income of males in the lowest 20 percent of the wage distribution in the United States declined 19 percent, while wage income of the top decile increased 10 percent.[17] Comparable figures for family wages over the same seventeen-year period declined 11 percent for the bottom quintile and increased 14 percent for the top quintile.[18] Experience over this period has been roughly comparable in the other OECD countries as well. It may be that, as the process of adjustment to technical change proceeds, the economic benefits will become more widely distributed. If that does not occur naturally, there will be exceedingly strong pressures to make it happen by design. It is difficult to imagine that social coherence could be preserved decade after decade with economic growth occurring at the top of the prosperity pyramid and population growth at the bottom. Those societies that do not produce a more equitable pattern of development will be in serious trouble, and the world as a whole will be in serious trouble if too many societies fail to achieve whatever standards of equity are necessary to preserve their coherence.

The economic implications of this fundamental requirement are extremely demanding. Simple redistribution policies could not achieve an acceptable outcome. There are too few rich and too many poor for any feasible amount of generosity in the form of income or wealth transfers to solve the problem. Adequate standards of equity will have to be achieved through broadly distributed growth, and some imposing numbers can be derived from that fact. Improving standards of living in the rapidly expanding population base will require a tripling of energy production over five decades even if unprecedentedly large efficiency gains are realized. It also will require a doubling of food production. Both accomplishments will have to be done in an environmentally tractable manner, at least in the minimum sense that the effects are not locally so rapacious as to preclude the production increases required or globally so destructive as to make the consequences intolerable. In some regions with large population concentrations—China and India in particular—it is doubtful that even that minimum standard can be achieved on the basis of current technology. The investment required to develop alternatives within the time period required is not in place. Neither of these societies could manage an investment of that pace and magnitude with its own resources exclusively, and a global process of investment that responds to the problem has not yet been organized.

This, then, is the new strategic environment. Human societies are undergoing a monumental transformation affecting their most basic features. That transformation will have major implications for most areas of public policy, indeed most organized activity of any sort. But as one of the more prominent of the expected consequences, the ancient art of war embellished by the modern practice of security will probably blend into yet larger subjects—the pursuit of global economic prosperity, the provision of social welfare, the general management of violence, and the engagement with the fundamental processes of nature. By implication, the effective protection of any society against various forms of violent assault and the broader defense of its interests will involve more than the deployment of standard military forces to perform traditional missions. The performance of these missions will be affected more directly by matters that historically have been considered background circumstances—education, commercial investment, and public health, for example—and anything else on which basic social coherence might depend. New issues of security can be expected to arise, and to the extent that they are genuinely new they will be difficult to anticipate. The long-recognized issues of security that can be anticipated will be profoundly altered. Necessary adjustments to deeply established security practices may well prove to be even more difficult than accommodation to the entirely unfamiliar. Both the scope and the time scale of consequence in this emerging situation are substantially greater than they have ever been, and that fact creates a mismatch with the capabilities of human institutions as they have evolved to date. We simply do not understand the full implications of the momentum that human societies have acquired. As one of the many reflections of that fact, no decisionmaking mechanisms operate with the multiple-decade, substantively integrated perspective necessary to visualize either the major strategic dangers or a comprehensively desirable outcome. The human enterprise is largely blind to the destiny it is creating.

Given this massive uncertainty, a valid and broadly accepted conceptualization of international security probably will not emerge to replace the cold war formulation for quite some time, if ever. But that, of course, will not suspend the process of transformation. Even in a complete vacuum of conscious purpose, that process can be expected to reshape the legacies of the cold war and of the deeper history of warfare in general, perhaps as profoundly as glaciers reconfigure the earth's surface or as internal convection moves the continents around.

Unsustainable Legacies

It is not a trivial matter to determine what the most consequential of these legacies are or to judge which of them will be subjected to the greatest pressure in the emerging situation. That task involves disputable interpretation rather than simple observation. Moreover, it is much easier to recognize an evolutionary adaptation after it has occurred than to predict it in advance. Nevertheless, there are some fairly obvious presumptions, and the obvious is not always wrong. The cold war process produced a volatile configuration of military forces with embedded dangers that were suppressed in the heat of confrontation. It also produced an inequitable distribution of military power and a process of technical diffusion capable of generating some unmanageably perverse effects. These three conditions cannot be sustained simultaneously and indefinitely. One can anticipate that a volatile and inequitable international security arrangement will be eroded by the process of technical diffusion and eventually will have to be redesigned.

Volatility was a natural consequence of technical development, but not an entirely inevitable or irreversible one. Nuclear weapons, jet aircraft, ballistic missiles, and information technology gave tremendous impulse and global reach to offensive military operations. When assimilated to the aggressive blitzkrieg doctrine that Germany had used so effectively in World War II, these innovations led quite naturally to a pattern of deployment in which the major military establishments continuously prepared for large-scale operations on very short notice. The underlying supposition was that the primary threat originated from aggressive intent and that advanced technology would enable decisive results to be achieved by surprise attack. The lesson derived from World War II was not that the aggressors ultimately were defeated, but rather that they nearly won in the initial phase.

This line of development produced a new phenomenon in the history of warfare. Prior to World War II military establishments were preserved in skeletal form in peacetime and mobilized their combat capabilities only in the case of immediately intended use. As the cold war configuration emerged, they set, and largely achieved, a much higher standard of preparation. For ground force and naval units, it could be argued, the more advanced pattern was an evolutionary extension of what counterpart forces had accomplished prior to World War I, but there clearly was no precedent for the degree of readiness embodied in nuclear weapons operations or in the most advanced tactical air units. Contemporary nuclear forces are prepared to initiate an attack on thousands of targets at intercontinental range within half an hour of receiving an authoritative order to do so and to complete the attack within a few hours. Under routine conditions, contemporary tactical air units are prepared to act in a matter of days rather than hours, but for most of the locations where a serious military engagement could occur, that would be a small number of days. This ability yields an intimidating deterrent but also a threatening offense poised for assault. This configuration of forces discourages deliberate aggression quite decisively but also enables a massive accident to occur. This possibility is a problem serious enough to induce a substantial change in operational practice, whether or not an accident does occur.

The issue of equity became far more visible in the aftermath of the cold war than it was during the course of it. With the advantage of retrospect, it seems evident that it was a major factor from the outset. The two contending alliances that waged the central confrontation did not at any time have a stable balance of assets or exposure. The Soviet Union was pitted against all of the industrial democracies but could not match their combined economic and technical base. By virtue of geography it also was much more vulnerable to conventional arms engagements, dramatically so in comparison with the United States. It managed to compete in the development and deployment of nuclear weapons, ballistic missiles, and to a lesser extent tactical aircraft. It did not keep pace in the critical area of information technology, however, and fell progressively behind in the derived capacity to perform the more sophisticated command functions and to engage in high-precision operations. Moreover, the burden of the Soviet defense effort seriously distorted the composition of the economy and contributed to the crisis of economic performance that ultimately undermined the entire political system.[19]

With the dismemberment of the Soviet Union, an obvious and overwhelming imbalance in assets emerged. As indicated in table 1-1, the levels of annual investment in military equipment sustained by the United States and its principal allies far exceed even the most generous estimates of what the other major military establishments allocate to that purpose. As a result, members of the U.S. alliance system have a capacity to perform traditional military missions that no outside military establishment can match. In those terms, at least, they enjoy a higher standard of security than the rest of the world.

By contrast, a tremendous security burden was imposed on Russia, as an assertive heir to the major part of the Soviet military establishment, including the entire nuclear weapons component, and as a much more reluctant heir to Soviet political history. Russia absorbed an oversized, poorly maintained, and inappropriately configured military force that had to be relocated from the territory of former allies and other Soviet successor states. Along with that inheritance came the residue of antagonism and suspicion that the Soviet Union had inspired, the most significant con-

Table 1-1. *Annual Investment in Military Capability, 1998*

Country	*Annual investment (billions of U.S. dollars)*
United States	90.3
NATO (without United States), Japan, and South Korea	61.9
Russia	4.8–15.0
China	3.7–15.0
Iraq	< 1.0
North Korea	< 1.0

Source: Author's estimates based on International Institute for Strategic Studies, *The Military Balance, 1998–1999* (Oxford University Press, 1998), and John D. Steinbruner and William W. Kaufmann, "International Security Reconsidered," in Robert D. Reischauer, ed., *Setting National Priorities: Budget Choices for the Next Century* (Brookings, 1997), p. 158. Figures for U.S. investment are from International Institute for Strategic Studies, *The Military Balance,* p. 15. NATO (without the United States), Japanese, and South Korean investment is estimated to be 30 percent of total defense spending. For Chinese and Russian investment, a range is listed because of the great discrepancy between official military budget figures and international estimates. The range of Russian investment is drawn from International Institute for Strategic Studies, *The Military Balance,* pp. 104–05. For China, the low-end figure is 33.7 percent of the official defense budget (derived by assuming that China matches the percentage of the U.S. military budget devoted to investment). The high-end Chinese figure comes from Steinbruner and Kaufmann, "International Security Reconsidered," p. 158. The estimates for Iraqi and North Korean investment are from International Institute for Strategic Studies, *The Military Balance*. For either country, it is implausible to imagine military investment figures over $1 billion.

sequence of which was a deeply established presumption that Russia would not be eligible to join the predominant alliance system. Caught up in a massive economic transformation of overriding priority, Russia has not been able to finance its inherited military establishment at the rate that would be required to sustain it, let alone make it competitive.[20] As a consequence, its capacity to perform legitimate military missions is deteriorating, as is its ability to assure managerial coherence. The internal deterioration of the Russian military establishment laboring under conditions of inferiority poses dangers that are distinctly different and much greater than any residual inclination or capacity it might have for external aggression. Those dangers are a new, unavoidable, and as yet unresolved problem of international security. They are not confined solely to the Russian military establishment.

The third troublesome legacy—the process of technical diffusion—always has been a feature of military interactions, but one that clearly is being enhanced not only by the effects of information technology but also more generally by the remarkable surge of modern science as a whole. Weapons developments emerge from basic science. The fundamentals of science are necessarily accessible to all human societies and in principle to all individuals. The methods used to control access to specific weapons applications—security classification, export licensing, and similar regulatory restrictions—can be effective for some period of time, but they do not establish impermeable barriers. The inventions of any society eventually can be emulated or appropriated by any other society that makes a dedicated effort to do so, and the process of globalization clearly is diminishing the amount of time and effort required. Enhanced information flows, the extensive commercialization of basic technical development, and the competitive efforts of weapons producers to export their products have facilitated access to advanced weapons technology to the point that, in principle, any major innovation can be expected to be broadly available within a decade or so. Policies of restriction and disparities in the magnitude of investment undoubtedly can sustain for longer periods of time the advantages in the scale of advanced weapons deployment that the United States and its allies have established. But they cannot preserve an absolute qualitative monopoly. Nuclear explosives, biological pathogens, lethal toxins, chemical agents, and the basic components of precision delivery all can be acquired by smaller states and other organizations that would not have the capacity to develop them independently. This access and the incentive to use it to offset the advantages of the preponderant military establishments create pressures that in principle could force substantial innovation in the practice of international security.

Formative Problems

The extreme difficulty of deriving a valid and broadly accepted strategic conception for the new set of circumstances probably means that the process of adaptation will occur gradually in the course of dealing with specific problems whose immediate implications are evident, even if their extended consequences are not. As a practical matter the problems that come to play this formative role are likely to have a significant effect on the ultimate outcome. Some of these are predictable. Others will emerge from events that cannot be anticipated. Basic understanding of the process of adaptation and efforts to shape it both rest, somewhat precariously, on the more predictable and more enduring of these specific problems.

Sustaining Traditional Missions

The most predictable of these problems has to do with continuation of the basic military missions that were the focus of investment throughout the cold war era. These can be summarized broadly as deterring nuclear war, preventing hostile incursion into sovereign territory or air space, and protecting legitimate use of the seas. Most of the effort of the major military establishments—the design and purchase of equipment, the organization of units, the pattern of deployment, the training of personnel, the development of operational doctrine, and the integration of all these components into readily available combat capability—is designed to perform these core missions and to do so on short notice against a comparably configured opponent. The central principle of countervailing military power directed against deliberately calculated mass aggression survives the end of the cold war and is supported by the political emotions and institutional commitments derived from historical experience. Within the United States, which operates the most capable military establishment and thereby sets the standard for the rest of the world, the official defense plan projects an indefinite continuation of this basic pattern.[21] The resources to do so clearly are available, if the political will to spend them in this way is itself sustained. Entrenched as it is, however, that commitment will be subjected to the corrosive effects of the new strategic circumstances.

The primary fact is that there is no plausible opponent to justify advanced states of readiness for undertaking traditional missions on a large scale and with short notice. It would require at least two decades of investment and probably more for any military establishment outside the U.S. system of alliances to match the capabilities of the United States alone. No country is attempting such an effort, and despite continuing rhetorical popularity of great power logic, there is very little reason to do so. The massive assaults that underlie mission conceptions derived from the major wars of this century have lost much of the incentive that once motivated them. Quite apart from the high probability of ruinous defeat, major exercises to seize and hold territory and to impose jurisdiction by force cannot be consolidated in a globalizing economy and an increasingly interactive culture. Basically it is too expensive to rule principally by force, and political jurisdiction therefore depends on establishing legitimacy. In instances of divided societies where the affected population might conceivably ratify political jurisdiction acquired by force—on the Korean peninsula, for example, or Taiwan—active vigilance clearly is justified and is being practiced. But the sum total of these instances is not sufficient to sustain a general pattern of confrontation. The overriding incentive for the major military establishments and their supporting societies is to preserve their traditional mission capabilities at less expense in order to direct investment to the newer and broader dimensions of security. The concern for greater efficiency mainly affects the United States, Russia, China, and, to a somewhat lesser extent, India. These countries are emerging from the experience of the century with the largest military establishments operating in a pattern of implicit confrontation. They have strong reasons to establish the forms of collaboration that would enable the traditional missions to be performed reliably at lower levels of force deployment.

When translated into practical terms, this incentive for greater efficiency intersects the independent interest in establishing an inherently safer and less volatile pattern of deployment. Even though the traditional military missions are universally articulated in terms of defensive intent and even though there is no reason to doubt the sincerity of those intentions, the configuration of forces that has emerged from the cold war era overwhelmingly emphasizes offensive operations. This fact is embodied most prominently in the U.S. military establishment, which, again, sets the international standard. Facing no conventional threat of significant size to the United States itself, American forces are organized to project power on a global scale. They are deployed in defense of allied territory, and it is unlikely that they would initiate an unprovoked massive assault against any other country. Nonetheless, in any major engagement in which they are involved, they would conduct extensive tactical air attacks against the entire infrastructure of an opponent's military capability, as demonstrated during the 1991 Persian Gulf war and the 1999 air campaign against Yugoslavia. In conducting limited tactical air attacks against Libya in 1986 and against Afghanistan and the Sudan in 1998, the United States established its willingness to engage in unilateral reprisal against states judged to have sponsored terrorist actions.[22] Air strikes against Iraq in 1993 and 1998 extended the doctrine of reprisal to political provocations not involving immediate acts of violence.[23] The combined-arms assault on Panama in 1989 was essentially a military operation to enforce U.S. drug laws.

This record of assertive military action creates an incentive for countries outside the U.S. alliance to develop some form of countervailing capability. Unable to match or defend themselves against U.S. offensive operations, countries that are or might be entangled in any serious political dispute have reason to seek a countervailing deterrent, and the inexorable diffusion of technology provides ample scope of opportunity. Nuclear explosives and precision strike technology both provide feasible means of disrupting the offensive operations of a superior military establishment. The implications of that fact are likely to shape the evolution of security relationships with the smaller dissident states such as Iran, Iraq, Libya, and North Korea and potentially with larger ones as well. The process of globalization would appear to encourage changes in conception and in policy on both sides in all of these confrontational relationships.

The dangerous dynamics generated by unbalanced deterrent relationships can be alleviated if those caught up in them concede the legitimate defensive objectives of the other party and systematically reassure each other that those purposes will not be contested. Over the course of the cold war the United States became adept at the practice of systematic reassurance as it transformed its World War II enemies into major allies. The emerging situation gives powerful incentive to extend that legacy both to the major cold war enemies and to the smaller dissident states—an implication resisted in practice but feasible in principle. One of the most fundamental implications of globalization is a shift in the balance of reliance in security policy from deterrence to reassurance, from active confrontation to cooperative engagement, as envisaged in the argument that provoked Senator Nunn's question.[24] The incentives to undertake this shift are realistic in character, and they operate across the entire spectrum of cultural and political inclination. Quite apart from rhetorical labels, it is unrealistic to imagine that any of the national military forces could provide reliable security without relying on any formal cooperation whatsoever. Not even the strongest states, including specifically the United States, have ever had or could plausibly acquire sufficient capacity to operate under that extreme formula. Various forms of organized cooperation always have been a necessary element of state security, and the most secure states are the ones that systematically have developed that aspect of the practice. The practical issue is the relative balance of self-reliance and cooperation.

Containing Civil Conflict

It is prudent to expect that civil violence will become a more serious international security concern under the new strategic circumstances than it has been. Since World War II many more people have been killed in internal conflicts than in the type of engagements between states that have been the principal focus of security policy and active military preparation. Since this form of violence has occurred largely in societies that have been relatively isolated from the developing international economy and has not spread visibly beyond those societies, it has not been considered a matter of primary concern for the international community as a whole. Mass violence resulting from the political separation of India and Pakistan, for example, from internal repression in Mao's China and Pol Pot's Cambodia, from protracted civil wars in Afghanistan, Angola, El Salvador, Mozambique, and the Sudan, and from the disintegration of coherent government in Bosnia, Kosovo, Rwanda, and Somalia has been treated as a local tragedy rather than a general threat. These and other episodes have reflected a presumption of tolerance that probably will be revised significantly as the consequences of globalization are better appreciated, even if it is not reversed. Intensifying economic interactions and the pattern of inequitably distributed growth associated with them increase the possibility that major instances of sustained civil violence will themselves interact more consequentially. In particular, some critical number of these instances occurring simultaneously might undermine the basic legal standards necessary to operate the globalizing economy. The killing that occurs in episodes of massive civil violence is done by organizations operating outside the bounds of normal legal standards, and those organizations are themselves increasingly capable of extending their operations on a broader scale. What they do to arm and finance themselves stimulates criminal activity generally, and the international community will have to be more concerned with this effect than it historically has been.

The spectrum of concern in this regard runs from overt civil conflicts in which organized militia equipped with conventional military weapons prey on civilian populations that are not protected by any regular military establishment to terrorist campaigns directed against populations whose military protection can be penetrated clandestinely. There are many variations within the spectrum, but the unifying fact is that spontaneous violence emerging from the sustained breakdown of a legal system and organized violence undertaken by intensely disaffected political groups both can cause mass casualties comparable to those caused by formal warfare. The potential to do so appears to be increasing, moreover, with the diffusion of weapons technology and the weakening of basic social coherence in many parts of the world. A military establishment prepared for traditional forms of warfare can readily suppress any particular militia operation, if it chooses to do so. With a more difficult and more sustained effort, it eventually can control any given terrorist operation as well. A global epidemic of either type of violence would be completely unmanageable, however, and that possibility cannot be dismissed in a world of intensifying interaction. As even the leading societies are forced to contend with the threat of civil violence, the weight of effort in international security can be expected to shift from the practice of deterrent confrontation devised for traditional military engagements to the methods of systematic prevention that are the only feasible means of containing the epidemic potential of such violence.

Managing Interactions with Nature

It seems apparent, however, that the most extensive reformulation of security interest eventually will emerge from the need to contend with the environmental consequences of expanding human activity. Even before the population surge has run its course, the aggregate effects of human production have reached levels that conceivably might affect the most fundamental operations of nature necessary to sustain life. The composition of the atmosphere, for example, is not in stable equilibrium and might be altered dramatically by catalytic changes that human beings as a whole unwittingly introduce. Similarly the pattern of ocean currents to which climate conditions in Northern Europe are especially sensitive is susceptible to radical shifts that also might be triggered by small changes in critical parameters. As yet no specific phenomenon of this sort has been demonstrated with the compelling clarity attributed to nuclear weapons effects, but the potential consequences are even greater. Although nature is not a calculating enemy capable of organizing deliberate aggression, it occasionally produces cataclysmic events capable of devastation far beyond what any form of warfare might do.

To date the most prominent concern about global environmental effects has centered on the anticipated phenomenon of global warming—an increase in average temperature at the earth's surface caused by an accumulation of those gases in the atmosphere that absorb and re-emit radiated energy. It is well established that two of the compounds that have this effect—carbon dioxide and methane—have increased more than 30 and 100 percent, respectively, since 1800, the point at which large-scale human industrial activity began to develop.[25] Since carbon dioxide is retained in the atmosphere for lengthy periods of time and since substantial rates of emission are certain to continue through the decades of rapid population growth, human society will generate some warming effect on the earth's atmosphere for more than a century to come. The net magnitude of the effect is uncertain and hotly disputed, as are the expected consequences. The officially estimated range, however, is comparable in size and ten times more rapid than the temperature shift associated with the last Ice Age some 18,000 years ago.[26]

This fact alone has tremendous strategic significance. It provides direct evidence that aggregate human activity has reached the historical juncture at which cataclysmic shifts in global environmental processes might be triggered. And that possibility, in turn, imposes what promises to be the central dilemma of the era: if human societies wait until decisive evidence of global environmental danger has accumulated, it probably will be too late to avoid; if they act in mistaken anticipation, they could seriously misdirect their efforts. An unresolved tension between these potential errors of judgment stands in the background of many specific issues. Were the balance to be shifted by some scientific result or crystallization of opinion, a new formulation of international security could rapidly emerge. If a global environmental threat is ever visualized with sufficient clarity, either validly or otherwise, it could have an organizing influence comparable to or greater than that of nuclear weapons.

It also is possible, and even more likely, that environmental interactions in particularly sensitive regions will acquire an organizing significance comparable to the major points of conventional force engagement that provided the basic contingencies for military planning during the cold war. In some areas of the world, high population densities are seriously burdening local soil and water resources—northern China and East Africa in particular.[27] Those areas will experience earliest and most intensely the problems of managing resource scarcity that, with the general population surge, will be related increasingly to the problem of preventing civil violence. Although the connection among resource scarcity, economic austerity, and civil violence is difficult to demonstrate with historical evidence and involves subtle interactions that are not yet fully understood, the violence that engulfed the Great Lakes region of Africa following the outbreak of mass murder in Rwanda in 1994 suggests that something more fundamental was at work than the political personalities who dominated most of the news reports.[28] The interaction between resource scarcity and principles of equitable allocation is one of the most likely to occur. To the extent that a general problem is recognized, the leading instances will command systematic attention.

Implications

In summary, then, there is good reason to believe that the evolving practice of international security will not be a simple, not necessarily even a recognizable, extension of historical experience, as weighty as that experience has been. Sharp discontinuities in the determining conditions of human societies and in the nature of the problems being presented can be expected to induce fundamental revisions in all of the major elements of the topic—in the guiding principles of strategy, in the deployment patterns and operational configuration of military forces, in the principal missions to which they are directed, in the alliance arrangements that set the basic patterns of allegiance, and in the methods used to regulate the diffusion of weapons. And the ability to undertake the necessary adjustments will be a test of the viability of all forms of government, especially the ascendant democracies. These are not matters that can be settled by an anointed few acting in secrecy. They require broadly based judgments from entire political systems, and the systems primarily in question are being driven by the process of globalization into degrees of engagement and forms of collaboration that none of them is prepared to welcome. It is a human drama in the broadest sense of the term.

Since it will not be possible to understand the full implications of globalization anytime soon, the drama will unfold as a story of partial but, one hopes, evolving comprehension. Whatever adaptive comprehension eventually is achieved doubtless will be embedded in many unresolved arguments and probably will be obscured by sustained misconceptions that only come to be recognized with the advantage of very distant retrospect. It is too early to project ultimate outcomes with any confidence, but it is possible to identify some of the major security problems that will drive the process of adjustment and some of the basic principles that are likely to shape it. The central purpose of the chapters that follow is to identify formative problems and organizing principles relating to the predictable issues of security. They examine in sequence how the configuration of nuclear and conventional forces might be affected, how the problems of communal violence and the dangers of technical proliferation might be managed, and how security relationships among the major states might be altered. Many other issues might arise, but one can be reasonably sure that the state of international security in the globalizing environment will be determined in large part by how these issues evolve. This discussion aspires simply to stimulate productive thinking, as distinct from attempting to reach settled conclusions. As Søren Kierkegaard once observed, life is understood backward but lived forward. Thinking forward under uncharted circumstances is risky, confusing, and contentious but must nonetheless be attempted.

CHAPTER TWO

Managing Deterrent Operations

EVEN WITH THE POTENTIAL for a major strategic engagement with nature looming in the background, the pattern of nuclear weapons deployment remains the largest and most imminent physical threat to any and all human societies. As an enduring consequence of cold war military development, tens of millions of lives and tens of trillions of dollars worth of physical infrastructure are held daily at risk for the declared purpose of deterring large-scale war. Were that central purpose to fail and the operationally prepared threats executed, the full effects would be more devastating than even those imposing figures suggest. Core assets of the globalizing economy are at stake in this hostage arrangement. Their massive and sudden loss would reverberate far beyond the specific locations of attack.

This situation does not inspire the fear or command the attention that it did during the cold war. Opinion polls register a clear decline in the expressed concern about a full nuclear war, and political leaders generally articulate a sense of receding danger. In one of the more prominent efforts to reinforce that impression, President William Clinton and President Boris Yeltsin announced in January 1994 an agreement to remove the designated targets from their respective nuclear forces and stated that the forces would be operated day-to-day in a manner that did not presume they were enemies.[1] The following day President Clinton addressed the American people from Moscow, declaring categorically, "We no longer live in the shadow of nuclear annihilation."[2] The official statement of U.S. national security strategy issued three years later mentions weapons of mass destruction third and last on the list of threats, but the text refers to the danger of these weapons in the hands of terrorists, criminal organizations, and "outlaw states."[3] The document never refers to the massive nuclear engagement that the deterrent forces are in fact prepared to conduct.

This dramatic change in political presumption is an important development, but it does not fundamentally alter either the basic pattern or the potential consequences of nuclear weapons operations. The target assignments that were removed by agreement in 1994 can be restored within a minute or so. Whatever the declared presumption might be, the United States and Russia still maintain continuously available opposing forces that are directed primarily at each other and would be virtually as lethal as they were at the height of the cold war, as summarized in tables 2-1 through 2-4. The tables array the respective forces as they were at the peak of cold war deployment in 1987 and a decade later in 1998. As a rough indication of their destructive potential, the tables display the total area that each force could subject to blast overpressure with an efficient delivery pattern.[4] Based on data from Hiroshima and Nagasaki, it is assumed that blast overpressures of 12 pounds per square inch would kill 98 percent of the people in the affected area and that 5 pounds per square inch would kill 50 percent. The population distribution profiles of Russia and the United States differ somewhat, but not enough to produce a substantially different state of vulnerability. In 1998 some 78 million people were living in the central cities of the United States, encompassing an area just under 28,000 square miles, an average density of 2,800 people per square mile. The 1998 Russian force could cover this area with lethal effects using only about 40 percent of its full capability. That would kill more than 75 million people at an average rate of about 30,000 people per warhead. Any additional attack would have to be allocated to metropolitan areas that are ten times less densely populated than the central cities, and the fatalities per warhead would also be nearly ten times lower. In Russia 67 million people are living in cities of 100,000 people or more, with an average density somewhat higher than in the United States. Of these, 65 million could be killed with about one-third of the available American forces, at a rate exceeding 30,000 per warhead. Thereafter the rate of fatalities per warhead would decline by a factor of more than ten.

The level of American and Russian nuclear forces will decline further as a result of both unilateral actions and formal agreement, but these reductions will not remove the threat to urban population concentrations and associated industrial capacity. Nor will they affect the capabilities of the other national nuclear forces. Britain, France, and China also operate rapidly available forces that are capable of destruction exceeding any historical war. Israel, India, and Pakistan are widely believed to have prepared tens and perhaps hundreds of weapons that are not observably deployed but could be directed against a regional opponent within a few days or weeks. Many other industrial countries, if they so chose, could develop and apply nuclear weapons in the course of a year or so. Full use of even the smallest of these national arsenals would be catastrophic, and every single weapon that has been manufactured represents a threat of strategic proportions—the possibility of instantaneous personal, social, and physical destruction on a scale that cannot be deliberately produced by any other means.

This situation has a practical implication that is substantially independent of political sentiment, whatever it might be. Because of the magnitude and imminence of the threat entailed, the pattern of nuclear weapons deployment is the single most important objective determinant of security for all countries whether or not they participate directly in the activities involved. The scale of destruction that has been operationally prepared, especially by the American and the Russian forces, is global in significance. The confrontation that persists at the level of daily operations between those two forces sets a general condition of international security that cannot be bypassed by any compensating means. Whether that pattern will continue is necessarily the first question in assessing the process of adjustment to new conditions: Is the practice of active deterrence to be maintained indefinitely as the central feature defining international security, or is it to be transformed in the course of establishing a fundamentally different arrangement?

That question engages intense feelings and deep convictions. Over the course of the cold war, deterrence became a thoroughly internalized rationale—a reigning doctrine with broad acceptance and emotional resonance buttressed by political and institutional commitments that would be very difficult to dislodge. Moreover, since the knowledge of how to make nuclear weapons cannot be eradicated, a natural deterrent effect emanating from that knowledge undoubtedly will be an enduring element of international security regardless of the adjustments that new circumstances might in-

Table 2-1. *U.S. Strategic Nuclear Forces, 1987*

Type of weapon	*Number deployed*	*Number of warheads*	*Yield per warhead (kilotons)*	*Total yield (kilotons)*	*Area at 12 pounds per square inch per warhead*[a]	*Total area at 12 pounds per square inch*[a]	*Area at 5 pounds per square inch per warhead*[a]	*Total area at 5 pounds per square inch*[a]
Intercontinental ballistic missiles (ICBMs)								
MX (W87)	30	300	300	90,000	9.74	2,922	22.08	6,623
Minuteman III (Mk-12 with W62)	220	660	170	112,200	5.49	3,623	13.58	8,963
Minuteman III (Mk-12A with W78)	300	900	335	301,500	9.61	8,649	23.42	21,078
Minuteman II (W56)	450	440	1,200	528,000	25.23	11,103	48.18	21,199
ICBM total	1,000	2,300	...	1,031,700	...	26,297	...	57,863
Submarine-launched ballistic missiles (SLBMs)								
Poseidon (C-3) (Mk-3 with W68)	256	2,560	45	115,200	3.41	8,730	5.52	14,131
Poseidon (C-4) (Mk-4 with W76)	192	1,536	100	153,600	4.76	7,311	9.12	14,008
Trident I (C-4) (Mk-4 with W76)	192	1,536	100	153,600	4.76	7,311	9.12	14,008
SLBM total	640	5,632	...	422,400	...	23,352	...	42,147

Bombers								
B-52 Stratofortress	241							
FB-111A	56							
B-1B Lancer	64							
B-2								
Bomber weapons (force loadings)								
SRAM (AGM-69A)		1,140	250	285,000	8.43	9,610	19.03	21,700
ALCM (AGM-86B)		1,614	150	242,100	6.00	9,687	12.42	20,042
Bombs		2,999	650	1,949,350	17.88	53,626	34.89	104,632
Bombers total	361	5,723	. . .	1,949,350	. . .	72,923	. . .	146,374
Grand total	2,001	13,655	. . .	3,403,450	. . .	122,572	. . .	246,384

Source: Natural Resources Defense Council Nuclear Program, "Nuclear Data for United States and Russia Strategic Nuclear Forces," www.nrdc.org/nrdcpro/nudb/datainx.html [accessed November 1999]: see "U.S. ICBM Forces, 1959–1996," "U.S. Ballistic Missile Submarine Forces, 1960–1996,"and "U.S. Strategic Bomber Forces, 1945–1996." For yields of ICBM and SLBM, Stephen Schwartz, ed., *Atomic Audit: The Costs and Consequences of U.S. Nuclear Weapons since 1940* (Brookings, 1998), table 1.3, pp. 86–91. For yields of bomber bombs, Natural Resources Defense Council Nuclear Program, "Table of U.S. Strategic Nuclear Forces, End 1996," www.nrdc.org/nrdcpro/nudb/datab11.html [accessed November 1999]. Calculations for area per warhead (at 12 and 5 pounds per square inch) were derived using the Rand Corporation's Bomb Damage Effect Computer. Figures for total area may not be exact due to rounding.

. . . Not applicable.

a. In square miles, 600-foot airburst.

Table 2-2. *U.S. Strategic Nuclear Forces, 1998*

Type of weapon	*Number deployed*	*Number of war-heads*	*Yield per war-head (kilotons)*	*Total yield (kilotons)*	*Area at 12 pounds per square inch per warhead*[a]	*Total area at 12 pounds per square inch*[a]	*Area at 5 pounds per square inch per warhead*[a]	*Total area at 5 pounds per square inch*[a]
Intercontinental ballistic missiles (ICBMs)								
MX (W87)	50	500	300	150,000	9.74	4,871	22.08	11,038
Minuteman III (Mk-12 with W62)	200	600	170	102,000	5.49	3,294	13.58	8,148
Minuteman III (Mk-12A with W78)	300	900	335	301,500	9.61	8,649	23.42	21,078
ICBM total	550	2,000	. . .	553,500	. . .	16,814	. . .	40,264
Submarine-launched ballistic missiles (SLBMs)								
Trident I (C-4) (Mk-4 with W76)	192	1,536	100	153,600	4.76	7,311	11.26	17,295
Trident II (D-5) (Mk-4 with W76)	192	1,536	100	153,600	4.76	7,311	11.26	17,295
Trident II (D-5) (Mk-5 with W88)	48	384	475	182,400	10.04	3,855	29.59	11,363
SLBM total	432	3,456	. . .	489,600	. . .	18,477	. . .	45,953

Bombers								
B-2 Spirit	21/9							
B-52H Stratofortress	71/44							
Bomber warheads								
ALCM/W80	. . .	400	250	100,000	7.95	3,180	18.74	7,497
ACM/W80	. . .	400	150	60,000	6.00	2,400	12.42	4,968
B61-7/B61-11, B83 bombs	. . .	1,000	650	650,000	12.42	12,420	34.49	34,490
Bombers total	92/53	1,800	. . .	810,000	. . .	18,000	. . .	46,955
Grand total	1,074	7,256	. . .	1,853,100	. . .	53,291	. . .	133,172

Source: William M. Arkin, Robert S. Norris, and Joshua Handler, *Taking Stock: Worldwide Nuclear Deployments 1998* (Natural Resources Defense Council Nuclear Program, March 1998), p. 14; Natural Resources Defense Council Nuclear Program, "Nuclear Data for United States and Russia Strategic Nuclear Forces," www.nrdc.org/nrdcpro/nudb/datainx.html [accessed November 1999]: see "U.S. ICBM Forces, 1959–1996," "U.S. Ballistic Missile Submarine Forces, 1960–1996,"and "U.S. Strategic Bomber Forces, 1945–1996." For yields of bomber bombs, Natural Resources Defense Council Nuclear Program, "Table of U.S. Strategic Nuclear Forces, End 1996," www.nrdc.org/nrdcpro/nudb/datab11.html [accessed November 1999]. Calculations for area per warhead (at 12 and 5 pounds per square inch) were derived using the Rand Corporation's Bomb Damage Effect Computer. Figures for total area may not be exact due to rounding.

. . . Not applicable.

a. In square miles, 600-foot airburst.

Table 2-3. *Soviet Union Strategic Nuclear Forces, 1987*

Type of weapon	*Number deployed*	*Number of war-heads*	*Yield per war-head (kilotons)*	*Total yield (kilotons)*	*Area at 12 pounds per square inch per warhead*[a]	*Total area at 12 pounds per square inch*[a]	*Area at 5 pounds per square inch per warhead*[a]	*Total area at 5 pounds per square inch*[a]
Intercontinental ballistic missiles (ICBMs)								
SS-11 Sego M2 and M3	420	420	725	304,500	19.18	8,057	37.72	15,844
SS-13 Savage M1 and M2	60	60	600	36,000	17.04	1,022	32.93	1,976
SS-17 Spanker M3	139	556	750	417,000	19.63	10,912	38.55	21.434
SS-18 Satan M4	308	3,080	500	1,540,000	14.64	45,084	29.02	89,922
SS-19 Stiletto M3	360	2,160	550	1,188,000	15.95	34,452	31.04	67,040
SS-24 Scalpel M1	5	50	500	25,000	14.64	732	29.20	1,460
SS-25 Sickle	126	126	500	63,000	14.64	1,845	29.20	3,679
ICBM total	1,279	5,896	. . .	3,573,500	. . .	102,104	. . .	201,355
Submarine-launched ballistic missiles (SLBMs)								
SS-N-5 Golf II Serb	39	39	1,000	39,000	22.71	886	45.50	1,775
SS-N-6 Golf IV Sewfly	272	272	700	190,400	18.74	5,098	36.90	10,037
SS-N-8 Hotel III Sewfly	6	6	800	4,800	20.22	121	40.23	241
SS-N-8 Delta I	216	216	800	172,800	20.22	4,368	40.23	8,690
SS-N-8 Delta II	64	64	800	51,200	20.22	1,294	40.23	2,575

SS-N-17 Yankee II	12	12	350	4,200	11.04	132	24.01	288
SS-N-18 Delta III Stingray	224	672	250	168,000	8.43	5,663	19.03	12,791
SS-N-20 Typhoon Sturgeon	80	800	100	80,000	4.76	3,807	17.60	14,079
SS-N-23 Delta IV Skiff	48	192	100	19,200	4.76	914	9.12	1,751
SLBM total	961	2,273	. . .	729,600	. . .	22,151	. . .	52,227
Bombers								
Tu-95 Bear A	30	60	250	15,000	8.43	506	19.03	1,142
Tu-95 Bear B/C	30	120	250	30,000	8.43	1,101	19.03	2,284
Tu-95 Bear G	40	240	250	60,000	8.43	2,023	19.03	4,568
Tu-95M Bear-H6	5	30	250	7,500	8.43	253	19.03	571
Bombers total	105	450	. . .	112,500	. . .	3,883	. . .	8,565
Grand total	2,345	8,619	. . .	4,860,900	. . .	100,661	. . .	276,162

Source: Natural Resources Defense Council Nuclear Program, "Nuclear Data for United States and Russia Strategic Nuclear Forces," www.nrdc.org/nrdcpro/nudb/datainx.html [accessed November 1999]: see "USSR/Russian ICBM Forces, 1960–1996," "USSR/Russian Strategic Bomber Forces, 1956–1996," and "USSR/Russian Ballistic Missile Submarine Forces, 1958–1996." For some information on ICBMs and SLBMs, Barton Wright, "Table 1: Best Estimates of the Characteristics of Soviet Nuclear Ballistic Missiles," *World Weapons Database,* vol. 1: *Soviet Missiles* (Brookline, Mass.: Institute for Defense and Disarmament Studies, 1986), pp. 50–51. For yields of bomber bombs, Natural Resources Defense Council Nuclear Program, "Table of Russian Strategic Forces, End 1996," www.nrdc.org/nrdcpro/nudb/datab14.html [accessed November 1999]. Calculations for area per warhead (at 12 and 5 pounds per square inch) were derived using the Rand Corporation's Bomb Damage Effect Computer. Figures for total area may not be exact due to rounding.

. . . Not applicable.

a. In square miles, 600-foot airburst.

Table 2-4. *Russian Strategic Nuclear Forces, 1998*

Type of weapon	*Number deployed*	*Number of war-heads*	*Yield per war-head (kilotons)*	*Total yield (kilotons)*	*Area at 12 pounds per square inch per warhead*[a]	*Total area at 12 pounds per square inch*[a]	*Area at 5 pounds per square inch per warhead*[a]	*Total area at 5 pounds per square inch*[a]
Intercontinental ballistic missiles (ICBMs)								
SS-17 Spanker M3	10	100	750	25,000	19.63	1,963	38.55	3,855
SS-18 Satan M4	180	1,800	650	1,170,000	17.88	32,184	34.89	62,800
SS-19 Stiletto M3	165	990	550	544,500	15.95	15,791	31.04	30,727
SS-24 Scalpel M1	36	360	550	198,000	15.95	5,742	31.04	11,173
SS-24 Scalpel M2	10	100	550	55,000	15.95	1,595	31.04	3,104
SS-25 Sickle	360	360	550	198,000	15.95	5,742	31.04	11,173
ICBM total	761	3,710	. . .	2,240,500	. . .	63,017	. . .	122,832
Submarine-launched ballistic missiles (SLBMs)								
SS-N-18 Delta III Stingray	192	576	500	288,000	14.64	8,431	29.20	16,817
SS-N-20 Golf V Sturgeon	80	800	200	160,000	7.21	5,767	15.68	12,546
SS-N-23 Delta IV Skiff	112	448	100	44,800	4.76	2,132	9.12	4,087
SLBM total	384	1,824	. . .	492,800	. . .	16,330	. . .	33,450

Bombers								
Tu-95M Bear-H6	29	174	250	43,500	8.43	1,466	19.03	3,312
Tu-95M Bear-H16	35	560	250	140,000	8.43	4,719	19.03	10,659
Tu-160 Blackjack	6	72	250	18,000	8.43	607	19.03	1,371
Bomber total	70	806	. . .	201,500	. . .	6,792	. . .	15,342
Grand total	1,215	6,340	. . .	2,934,800	. . .	86,139	. . .	171,624

Source: William M. Arkin, Robert S. Norris, and Joshua Handler, *Taking Stock: Worldwide Nuclear Deployments 1998* (Natural Resources Defense Council Nuclear Program, March 1998), p. 27; Natural Resources Defense Council Nuclear Program, "Nuclear Data for United States and Russia Strategic Nuclear Forces," www.nrdc.org/nrdcpro/nudb/datainx.html [accessed November 1999]: see "USSR/Russian ICBM Forces, 1960–1996," "USSR/Russian Strategic Bomber Forces, 1956–1996," and "USSR/Russian Ballistic Missile Submarine Forces, 1958–1996." For some information on ICBMs and SLBMs, Barton Wright, "Table 1: Best Estimates of the Characteristics of Soviet Nuclear Ballistic Missiles," *World Weapons Database,* vol. 1: *Soviet Missiles* (Brookline, Mass.: Institute for Defense and Disarmament Studies, 1986), pp. 50–51. For yields of bomber bombs, Natural Resources Defense Council Nuclear Program, "Table of Russian Strategic Forces, End 1996," www.nrdc.org/nrdcpro/nudb/datab14.html [accessed November 1999]. Calculations for area per warhead (at 12 and 5 pounds per square inch) were derived using the Rand Corporation's Bomb Damage Effect Computer. Figures for total area may not be exact due to rounding.

. . . Not applicable.

a. In square miles, 600-foot airburst.

duce. The prevailing pattern of deployment is not immutable, however. There are feasible changes in nuclear weapons operations that would sustain the core deterrent effect at a much higher standard of overall safety. Developing these changes systematically would create a meaningfully different international security arrangement.

The distinction between deterrence and safety is a conceptual refinement that can be expected to emerge with increasing prominence as security policies throughout the world struggle to cope with a new set of demands. To a degree that was not recognized in the cold war formulation, these are competing objectives, and there are insistent reasons for shifting the balance between them that was established in the original pattern of deployment. Whatever the ultimate outcome, this balance will be one of the driving forces of the emerging era.

Active Deterrence

The basic idea of deterrence—to prevent attack by threatening retaliation—is readily detected in traditional military writings and is presumably as old as war itself. The specific word, however, and the strategic conceptualization that now accompanies it emerged as the justifying rationale for the deployment of nuclear weapons.[5]

That process was hardly an exercise in deductive logic. It is apparent from the historical record that the concept of deterrence did not inspire the development of nuclear weapons in the first place. That initially was done in pursuit of technical opportunity and for the implicit purpose of using nuclear weapons to prevail in a global war already being conducted. Nor did the concept directly determine either the technical elaboration or the deployment configuration that evolved over the two decades following World War II. The size and technical composition of the two major arsenals emerged in a series of political decisions that prominently featured nationalist sentiment and ideological rivalry but made very little reference to the strategic rationale subsequently developed to explain the outcomes.[6]

The rationale has assumed major practical importance, however, even though it is more a product than a determinant of the original decisions. The single word *deterrence* has been widely accepted as a summary statement of the most fundamental national security objective and indeed as the central pillar of foreign policy generally. Within the United States, at least, it is clearly one of the most solidly established elements of political consensus and one of the least disputed functions of national government. It provides the organizing conception of purpose necessary to coordinate disparate actions of the many individuals and formal units involved in nuclear weapons operations. As a concept that has come to be generally understood and broadly accepted, it is a primary means of preserving organizational coherence, an aspiration that never is fully accomplished and therefore always is a continuing concern.

Mission Commitments

There is by now an extensive literature tracing the genesis of official deterrence doctrine, documenting its content, and discussing its conceptual underpinnings.[7] The full account reflects the rich diversity and unresolved argument that one would expect of a topic so deeply entangled in historical experience. But, as with any concept that has organizing powers, the basic idea is simple. It begins with a practical fact that, for all its unwelcome implications, cannot be denied: the array of technologies involved in nuclear weapons is much more readily applied to offensive than to defensive applications, so much so that a devastating assault cannot be physically precluded and therefore has to be convincingly dissuaded.[8] For the first time in history a society cannot be protected by interposing a barrier of military forces against potential sources of aggression, even if the society in question enjoys superior assets. In recognition of that fact the central purpose of nuclear weapons is to prevent the use of other nuclear weapons and, by extension, any form of mass aggression by assuring intimidating punishment. That basic precept has spawned variations whereby the deterrent effect is to be directed against lesser provocations by more measured means, not necessarily involving nuclear weapons. The core principle nonetheless rests on the massive destructiveness of a large nuclear arsenal ostentatiously displayed, and the variations are generally considered to be supplements to rather than substitutes for the main effect.

The logic of this arrangement rests on a theory of human behavior. It presumes that major wars are generated by a process of reasoned calculation and can be prevented by the same means. Admitting wide latitude for the calculations that the most belligerent leaders might consider rational, the concept of deterrence requires that the countervailing threat of retaliation be large enough and be conveyed with sufficient assurance to negate any conceivable benefit that a willful aggressor might anticipate. Since the net deterrent effect is presumed to be a product of magnitude and probability, it has been considered prudent to maintain a large force immediately prepared to act in order to establish a reliable deterrent against the most extreme opponent. It is acknowledged to be absolutely vital, however, that a deployed deterrent force be protected against preemptive destruction. A vulnerable deterrent effort would be defeated by its own logic—it would provoke attack from a calculating opponent rather than prevent it.

In practical application, this basic logic has encountered significant qualification. Although the initial inclination was to believe or, at any rate, to hope that all forms of aggression could be suppressed by the destructive power of nuclear weapons, it quickly became apparent that major limitations would be derived from basic rules of proportionality. For the same reason that one would not attempt to use a sledgehammer against a fly, the credibility of the deterrent effect depends on some reasonable relationship between the provocation and the response and on some plausible comparison of alternative means. Thus deterrence has proved to be more credible between opponents of comparable capability than between unbalanced adversaries. It also has been more effective against massive attack than against limited forms of aggression. The historical record indicates that the use of nuclear weapons has been considered on most of the occasions when a military force that possesses them has encountered a significant combat problem.[9] Since the attacks on Hiroshima and Nagasaki in the final stages of World War II, however, these thoughts usually have been rejected quickly and never implemented. The United States endured major agonies in Korea and in Vietnam, fighting against opponents that did not possess nuclear weapons, without attempting to use them. The Soviet Union wrote a similar record in Afghanistan.

Official articulation of deterrence doctrine has not been entirely candid about these qualifications, but when declaratory statements are read in the context of deployment patterns, a reasonably clear picture emerges. The principal deployments of deterrent force have been located and managed in a manner that signals a primary commitment to the defense of national territory against a large-scale nuclear attack. The main forces are based largely on national territory and are not associated with any particular point of engagement or any special theater of operations. Submarine patrols have been developed both in broad ocean areas and in more protected waters in order to assure invulnerability to preemptive attack, but they are not subordinated to regional commanders. The operational preparations of these deployments have emphasized large-scale retaliation undertaken in rapid reaction to the initial stages of an opponent's attack. Both the stated doctrine and the operational pattern have provided enough flexibility to scale the deterrent response down to fit a limited attack, but it is evident that the primary commitment has been directed to deterring a massive assault by massive means. That extreme mission has been taken a great deal more seriously than any of the lesser or extended variations.

The main forces designed to perform this core deterrent mission also can be used to underwrite its principal extensions—the positive guarantees offered to formally allied countries that their territory will be defended not only against nuclear assault but against conventional invasion as well. In fact if these guarantees ever had to be acted on, operational realities would almost certainly require the use of the main deterrent forces, largely because they are better protected and more carefully managed than other forces. In the course of developing the original nuclear weapons deployments and the accompanying deterrence doctrine, however, a distinction was drawn between the core deterrent effect as applied to a nuclear assault on national territory and the same effect extended either to allies or to other types of threat.[10] In the course of several formative episodes, it was suggested repeatedly that both types of extension were less credible than the core commitment and that admission of doubt was embodied in special deployment arrangements. In the most prominent of these, the United States deployed nuclear forces in the Azores (Portugal), Belgium, Bermuda, Canada, Cuba (Guantanamo), France, Greece, Greenland (Denmark), Italy, Netherlands, Okinawa (Japan), Philippines, South Korea, Spain, Turkey, United Kingdom, West Germany, and Taiwan with accompanying procedures that gave the host countries a direct, although not a fully determining, role in the operations of those forces.[11] The resulting deployments were smaller, distinctly more vulnerable, technically less capable, and operationally more cumbersome than the main force. They frequently are referred to as tactical rather than strategic forces, and they are not integrated into the intricate target allocation and delivery schedules that are applied to operations of the main force. Clearly the extended deterrent missions—extended to allies and to conventional threats—are taken seriously, but they are not accorded the same stature as the core mission.

There also have been declaratory suggestions that nuclear weapons might have application even beyond formally extended deterrence, despite a series of treaty commitments intended to constrain such extensions.[12] U.S. officials, for example, consistently have reserved the right to consider the use of nuclear weapons in retaliation against any use of lethal chemicals or biological organisms as agents of mass destruction or indeed against any especially egregious form of conventional aggression. Statements of this sort are intended to bolster the probability term of the deterrence equation—to undermine any calculation that the threat of lethal retaliation would never be applied to acts of violence not encompassed in the core and extended deterrence missions. The declaratory statements have not substantially affected the prevailing conditions of deployment, however, and are not consistent with the record of restraint in responding to lesser provocation. They are significant in considering a transformation of nuclear weapons operations, but they have not been a major influence on the historical pattern. The principal issues of operational safety are posed by deployments designed to perform the core and the extended deterrence missions.

Inherent Problems

The attempt to harmonize the evolving logic of deterrence with the technical and operational details of weapons deployment encountered several notable problems that have strongly affected the circumstances of international security.

In the first instance, this had to do with the size of the arsenals that were developed. In the heat of cold war competition, the number of nuclear weapons that were manufactured by the United States and the Soviet Union far exceeded the levels that any concept of deterrence would plausibly require. Assuming that the weapons were to be distributed with reasonable efficiency, no more than 2,000 weapons at most could rationally be used for deterrence against even the largest national opponent.[13] Beyond that point, so much damage would have been done that further attack would be physically wasteful and increasingly ineffective, since most of the industrial and population concentrations already would have suffered extensive damage. For example, only 700–800 typical weapons efficiently directed against either the United States or Russia would directly kill 35–45 percent of their respective populations and destroy 60–65 percent of their industrial capacity.[14] Doubling or tripling the number of weapons used would extend those bands of expected damage by only a few percentage points. If the deterrent threat is not effective at the level of 2,000 delivered weapons, there is no reason to believe that it would be effective at any higher multiple of that number. Nonetheless the two main protagonists fabricated a combined total of more than 100,000 nuclear weapons between 1950 and 1990, and each maintained tens of thousands of these in active deployment.

This excessive capability initially was justified as a prudent measure of protection. If only a fraction of the deployed force was needed to embody the deterrent effect, then the rest of it was said to be assurance that the irreducible minimum would be available even after suffering the heavy attrition of an initial strike. It became apparent, however, that the redundant capacity was not being held in protected reserve to assure coverage of those targets most directly associated with the core deterrent effect. Rather it was placed in active deployment and was directed largely against the specific nuclear weapons locations of the opposing force. This interaction was difficult to reconcile with the strict logic of deterrence. It projected an inclination to initiate attack rather than merely to retaliate; it suggested an intention to prosecute a nuclear war rather than to prevent it. Obviously it makes no sense to retaliate against installations—ballistic missile locations in particular—whose weapons already have been fired.[15]

That ambiguity was compounded in the later phases of nuclear weapons development by the introduction of high-quality, multiple-warhead systems of ballistic missiles in fixed locations. At least in principle, that configuration allows a single nuclear weapon to destroy as many of the opponent's weapons as had been concentrated within an area matching its radius of destruction—up to 10 in the case of the isolated missile silos, 192 in the case of a fully equipped submarine in port, and more than 500 for cruise missile storage sites.

Efforts have been made to eliminate these anomalies by formal agreement. The Strategic Arms Reduction Treaty (START II treaty), whose ratification and implementation is still pending, provides for the reduction of deployed forces to levels that more nearly match plausible deterrent requirements and the complete elimination of multiple-warhead missiles in fixed locations. Even full realization of that agreement, however, and of the additional reductions officially envisaged would not remove or even diminish the underlying problem. The most critical and most vulnerable asset of the deterrent forces is not their dispersed weapons launchers but rather their central command systems. There is safety in numbers and in mobility for the individual weapons, but with each weapon being an item of strategic significance deterrent forces cannot be allowed to operate with full autonomy and in fact have not been so allowed. The authority to order the firing of a nuclear weapon has been centralized at the highest political level in all of the countries that maintain active deployments, and that provision has been embodied in physical and procedural arrangements intended to assure that it is preserved under all circumstances. Those arrangements are themselves vulnerable to attack, and their capabilities can be seriously degraded with a few tens of weapons. The interaction that arises from that fact is the most significant problem of vulnerability for the individual deterrent forces and the most dangerous source of volatility for the overall practice of deterrence. It creates a possibility that active deterrent operations might be self-destructive under certain conditions—that is, they might become the prime cause of a massive war rather than the reliable means of prevention they are intended to be.

The problem is not the deterrent effect itself. Large force deployments continuously held in an immediately available state of readiness certainly do provide a decisive countervailing threat against even the most aggressive calculating opponent. No assessment of vulnerability would provide a rational incentive to initiate attack under the prevailing and projected configuration of forces. Sufficient numbers of weapons can be expected to survive an initial attack to perform the core deterrent mission, and the respective command systems can be expected to operate well enough to provide the necessary authorization and coordination. Those critical standards of protection have been achieved, however, by a combination of methods—dispersed deployment, prior coordination, and rapid reaction—that imposes severe operational demands susceptible to inadvertent failure.

Dispersed deployment—the practice of locating weapons launchers in widely separated places—is the basic means of protecting the deterrent forces from preemptive destruction. It is designed to assure that no opponent could expect to achieve the timing and precision necessary to destroy all of the launcher positions rapidly enough to preclude retaliation. As a consequence of that pattern, local weapons commanders encounter substantially different circumstances. Those in hardened, isolated sites have little in the immediate vicinity to concern them, but those conducting mobile operations are potentially enmeshed in tactical engagements or at any rate changing circumstances that require command decisions. The formal authority and physical ability to fire the weapons are balanced between local commanders responsive to these varying circumstances and central command authorities charged with managing the overall strategic situation. Although initiative is formally vested in the central authorities, one of the major reasons for having local commanders is to assure that the deterrent force could operate if the more concentrated and less numerous central figures were destroyed. This means that under some circumstances local commanders would have to fire their weapons on the basis of implied rather than immediately provided authority. It is difficult to specify those circumstances precisely, however, without undermining the control of central authorities.

In order to minimize this dilemma and to manage the burdens of coordination, the command systems have worked out in detail how they would respond to a nuclear attack. They have assigned specific targets to the dispersed forces and have instructed them to attack these designated targets within a specified time interval following the moment that authorization is provided. Adherence to a designated target allocation and scheduling plan is important in assuring coordinated retaliation, since the command systems could not expect to be able to perform this function after suffering the damage of an initial attack. Recognizing this fact, the command systems are configured to provide authorization for response and designation of a preestablished attack plan within the very short period of time—twenty minutes or so—available before the critical units of authority and the communication links they rely on could, in principle, be destroyed.

The resulting operational pattern is quite elaborate. In an effort to preserve an appropriate balance of initiative, coordination, and timing, significant judgmental demands are imposed on thousands of participants who perform functions of major consequence. The people who operate space satellites and radar installations must continuously monitor the data they provide and combine them with other sources of information to determine without error whether an attack is or is not in progress. Other people must continuously maintain communication links to political leaders and to the military command channels that provide training, maintenance, and logistical support for the dispersed forces as well as coordinated target assignments. Still others operate the physical mechanisms for firing the deployed weapons. It simply is not possible to assure that the logic of deterrence will absolutely determine all that these people do under all circumstances or that their individual interpretations of its specific requirements will be entirely consistent. The actions of a large, dispersed human organization of this sort cannot be determined exactly by any calculated logic, no matter how compelling.

Operational Safety

The problems of control inherent in active deterrent operations were recognized during the cold war and taken quite seriously. Throughout the period, technical development programs were directed to making nuclear weapons not only more destructive but also better protected against accidental or unauthorized detonation. In the more advanced weapons designs, for example, the firing sequence cannot be initiated unless an authorization code has been supplied and internal sensors have determined that the intended process of delivery—a ballistic missile trajectory or an aircraft flight plan—has been completed. Additional features provide for the disabling of weapons if tampering is detected, if invalid codes are entered, or if an unspecified delivery pattern occurs. These features are reinforced by an extensive system of organizational checks and balances that regulates physical access to nuclear weapons and operational management of their delivery systems. In the U.S. forces, at least, no single individual of whatever degree of authority is ever given exclusive custody or complete operational control of a nuclear weapon, and the authorized teams that do perform these functions are subjected to continuous monitoring by others who are instructed to block any unauthorized action. These layered precautions generally are considered to have made it extremely unlikely that a nuclear weapon of advanced design ever would explode entirely by accident or that such a weapon could be used by people not authorized to do so.

The historical record to date supports this judgment. Active deterrent operations have been maintained for nearly half a century without a catastrophic breakdown or even a single incident involving the explosion or unauthorized seizure of a nuclear weapon. A number of serious accidents have occurred, including a January 1961 plane crash in North Carolina in which five of the six safety devices designed to prevent accidental detonation of the nuclear weapon failed.[16] But each of the major episodes and countless minor ones have inspired corrective reactions, and this adaptive process appears to have produced cumulative improvement over time in the reliability of nuclear weapons operations.

The assurance of safety is nonetheless well short of decisive. Even if accidental or completely unauthorized use of the advanced weapons systems is virtually impossible for physical reasons, weapons of earlier design do not meet the same standard, and their disposition is not yet fully determined. Even more serious, the relevance of prevailing safety provisions and the operational record to date is limited by two basic circumstances. First, for all its belligerent display, the cold war period never produced an immediate confrontation between the two major establishments at their more advanced state of development. The most serious episodes—the crises over Berlin in 1961 and over Cuba in 1962—occurred before the Soviet Union in particular had fielded much of its ultimate intercontinental-range force, and those events did not test the full crisis interactions between mature forces. What they did reveal about crisis behavior suggests the potential fragility of deterrent practices.[17] And, second, the precipitous dissolution of the Soviet Union has imposed a potentially unmanageable burden on the deterrent force that Russia inherited. Despite formal agreements that equate the basic levels of deployment, it is evident that the force now operated by Russia is in a substantially weaker position than that of the United States. It is technically less capable, financially more restricted, and geographically more vulnerable. It also is embedded in a military establishment whose conventional capabilities are even more seriously deficient. Active deterrent practices at currently projected levels of force deployment require rates of investment that Russia has not yet been able to establish and may not be able to establish under the pressure of other priorities. Without adequate investment, the mechanisms of control in an active deterrent force are subject to deterioration.

To an extent that was obscured by the political antagonism of the cold war, reliance on active deterrence as the core principle of international security requires an intricate partnership between the main protagonists if high standards of operational safety are to be preserved. This is problematic enough when their capacities are equitably balanced. When one of the parties is both unable and disinclined to sustain the burdens of this form of partnership, the entire arrangement needs to be revisited.

The Inherent Problem

In abstract terms justification of active deterrent practices requires a comparison of two probabilities—on the one hand, the chances of deliberate aggression preventable only by countervailing threats of the magnitude that have been prepared and, on the other, the chances of an inadvertent triggering of those deterrent threats. In principle, with the stakes so high, each of these probabilities should be measured exactly, and the continuation of active deterrence should rest on a reliable determination that the first probability is larger than the second. In fact, neither can be measured objectively at all, and the comparison rests on disputable judgment. In giving overriding priority to the preservation of a massive and immediately available deterrent capability, current practice necessarily assumes, without definitive proof, that the ratio of these probabilities is positive and that the chances of an inadvertent breakdown are tolerably small.[18]

As a matter of practical politics, those assumptions have been established as the standard for routine operations between opposing forces of comparable capability. Although the secrecy that envelops nuclear weapons operations precludes full public accounting, the safety precautions that have been devised and the operational record that has been demonstrated are good enough to sustain the judgment under normal circumstances. Neither the precautions designed nor the actual record can be extended to the circumstances of a direct military confrontation, however. Since the protective configuration of the active deterrent forces relies heavily on rapid reaction to the first stages of attack, the command systems are designed to undergo a subtle but consequential shift in response to circumstances indicating that a serious military engagement might be imminent. Because of that fact, their routine behavior does not necessarily correspond to their crisis reactions.

Under normal circumstances the operational presumption within a strategic command system is that deterrence prevails and that an attack is not imminent despite the readily available capability to undertake it. The forces operate with an overriding bias for negative control—that is, to deny authorization to fire nuclear weapons. Ambiguities are resolved under the dominant influence of that assumption. In situations where a military engagement appears imminent, the operational logic requires the command system to lean toward positive control—that is, to assure that authorized retaliation will be executed. At some point in a truly serious crisis, the burden of proof would shift. The peacetime command system, which requires definitive evidence that an attack is occurring in order to authorize retaliation, would give way to a wartime mentality, which requires proof that an attack is not occurring in order to withhold the commitment to deterrent missions.

The nature of this presumption matters tremendously for a nuclear weapons command system.[19] The dispersed operations of active forces, many elements of which are integrated into the operations of conventional forces, cannot be monitored in exact detail from any single location. Even under routinely benign conditions, the location and behavior of the opposition and the status of the national forces cannot be known completely and instantaneously. Command decisions necessarily depend on the prevailing presumption to fill in what is not specifically known. That dependence both increases and becomes more troublesome in any situation where an immediate military engagement appears possible. Military forces alter the details of their normal operation quite dramatically when they begin to prepare for an engagement. They cease routine training and begin initial preparations for the missions they might have to undertake. In the process they generate large flows of information very different from accustomed patterns, and they impose on their opponents the burden of distinguishing actions motivated by reasonable precaution from actions reflecting aggressive intent. As a practical matter the prevailing presumption is critical to resolving the uncertainties involved in making that judgment in a coherent manner across the dispersed activities of an active deterrent force.

It is not possible to simulate the shift in internal presumption that a strategic command system would have to undergo in moving from routine deterrent operations to the execution of prepared missions. It would be wildly irresponsible to subject nuclear weapons commanders to a training exercise that they did not know to be a training exercise. Despite the secrecy that surrounds such activities, it is reasonably apparent that such a test has never been attempted. At any rate, it would require the full complicity of worldwide news organizations to produce a genuinely credible simulation, and fortunately that cannot be arranged. Nor has any event since the Cuban crisis in 1962 put nuclear weapons operations into a situation where that internal shift might begin to occur. In a few recorded incidents, one of the forces unexpectedly encountered what appeared to be evidence of an immediately impending attack and began to execute the procedures for authorizing retaliation.[20] None of these incidents occurred in a context of events threatening enough to alter the presumption of negative control, however, and all were resolved quickly under the sway of that presumption. No incident of this sort has provoked the American and the Russian command systems at the same time. Therefore the viability of active deterrent operations has not been tested under the conditions that appear to be the most likely to produce a catastrophic breakdown—a circumstance in which the two opposing forces simultaneously began to shift their internal presumption in reaction to a crisis confrontation. Neither has been able to calibrate itself in that situation or to undergo the process of continuous adaptive improvement that applies to normal peacetime operations.

And therein lies the fundamental problem of operational safety. There are coherent reasons to doubt whether nuclear weapons command systems could withstand the pressures that a spontaneously arising crisis confrontation appears capable of generating, in particular whether the opposing forces could preserve the critical distinction between initiation and retaliation with absolute reliability. The ability to prove that an attack is not occurring under peacetime presumptions does not demonstrate the ability to do so when there are immediate reasons to fear it and both sides have departed from their normal operational patterns. The experience of the cold war and of the more benign aftermath indicates that those latter conditions are now less likely to occur but does not establish that they are categorically impossible. Once any degree of possibility is accepted, then in conceptual terms at least there is an undeniable problem. It is a problem that has strategic significance, moreover, because of the magnitude of potential consequence associated with it.

The problem is difficult to bring into practical focus in part because it defies measurement and in part because it runs against the natural grain of imagination. In the many scenarios for the breakdown of deterrence that have been advanced in both the professional and the popular literature, most of the speculation has centered on deranged individuals, vicious conspiracies, or conscious malfeasance of some sort—situations that might subvert the purpose of deterrence but preserve the critical assumption that outcomes are controlled by formulated intentions. It has not been popular to imagine that, despite all the precautions taken, a colossal catastrophe might be generated by overburdened individuals acting in what they sincerely consider to be a responsible manner. Exactly that, however, is the implication of the two historical events that provide perhaps the closest available analog for the breakdown of deterrence—the nuclear power reactor accidents that occurred at the Three Mile Island facility in the United States in 1979 and at Chernobyl in 1986 in what was then part of the Soviet Union.

In the Three Mile Island incident the sequence of events that produced a partial meltdown of the reactor core, a hydrogen explosion within its containment building, and a small release of radioactive material was initiated by a series of technical failures featuring a pressure release valve in the maze of pipes and tanks that circulated pressurized coolant water through the reactor core. The valve stuck in an open position and drained water from the reactor core—long recognized as the gravest threat to safety—for more than two hours before anyone discovered that fact. During that time, emergency pumps designed to compensate automatically for a loss of coolant water were throttled back by reactor operators misinterpreting the problem they were encountering.[21]

In the Chernobyl incident, by far the most serious in the history of nuclear power, two internal explosions destroyed the core of the reactor, killing thirty people immediately and dispersing nearly 12 trillion international units of radioactivity (becquerels) into the environment. The portion of this material that was injected into the earth's atmosphere was much greater than the amount generated by the atomic weapon used on Hiroshima in 1945. It forced an exclusion zone of 4,300 square kilometers around the site and the permanent evacuation of hundreds of thousands of people. The exact nature of the explosions is subject to differing interpretation, but they are known to have been triggered by two uncontrollable surges of reactivity, one driving the reactor to something like 100 times its maximum rated capacity and the other to 400 or 500 times that level. The sequence that led to these events was initiated by the immediate operators of the reactor who were testing what they understood to be a safety procedure. It is evident that they did not understand basic physical features of the reactor that made their operational experiment exceedingly dangerous. If someone did understand the magnitude of the danger, that person was not on the scene and had not conveyed the insight.[22]

Of course, many details are unique to each of these two incidents, but there is a message in the similarities. Both of the installations were protected by layered precautions—physical design features and operational rules—that were believed to render extremely unlikely the damage to the reactor and the release of radiation that occurred. In both instances the immediate operators of the reactors overrode safety mechanisms that would have prevented the accident because they misperceived the situation, and those who might have corrected their misjudgments were too remote and not well enough informed to do so. In both instances the design of the facilities gave operators very little time to discover and correct their misjudgments. One can question the relevance of these incidents to the management of deterrent force operations, but one cannot entirely dismiss the warning.

The Russian Case

The potentially catastrophic coupling of active deterrent forces rigged for rapid reaction was sustained through the latter stages of the cold war on the unspoken judgment that a more refined arrangement was not necessary in strategic terms and not feasible in political terms. The Soviet Union and the United States accepted each other as responsible partners in the arrangement, as formal opponents internally capable of preserving strict standards of negative control and not so belligerent as to drive deterrent force operations to the point of serious danger. The confrontation was pursued within tolerable limits and used on both sides as the organizing focus of national security policy. Neither side ever became alarmed enough about the dangers of a crisis engagement to be seriously interested in an alternative.

The emergence of Russia clearly presents a different situation. In a precipitous process that was not anticipated or systematically planned, the Russian Federation inherited about 16 percent of the Soviet military establishment, including in the end all of its nuclear weapons, but nothing like the same security position.[23] At the beginning of 1989, the Soviet Union had thirty ground force divisions; one air army, 300 Su-24 aircraft; eighteen ground attack fighter regiments; twelve fighter regiments; and one reconnaissance squadron stationed in forward positions in Central Europe with a structure of bases to support them.[24] These were the most capable units in its inventory. If they could not undertake the decisive assault that the members of the North Atlantic Treaty Organization (NATO) feared, they could prevent the reverse from happening and could exercise meaningful influence on the behavior of NATO's forces. They were a buffer that mitigated pressure on the Soviet Union itself, including especially threats to sensitive assets of the strategic command system that might emanate from Western Europe. Russia did not inherit this buffer and could not aspire to recreate it. In the first years of its independent existence, Russia had to move all of the Soviet Union's military units out of Central Europe while leaving the supporting infrastructure behind. It also ceded control over the military installations and most of the force units that had been located in the Baltic republics, Belarus, and Ukraine. That amounted to the most extensive reconfiguration that any major military establishment had undergone since the immediate aftermath of World War II, and it had to be done as Russia's economy, its political system, and the fundamental elements of its policy were all were being radically revised.

Russia has not yet completed the strategic realignment that these circumstances ultimately will require. A process of that scope almost certainly will be measured in decades, and Russia itself cannot control all of the determinants. Even in advance of the eventual outcome, however, it is evident that Russia is not in position to reproduce and sustain the comprehensive military confrontation that proved to be an unmanageable burden for the Soviet Union. Russia's borders encompass both the European and the Asian theaters of military engagement. A fully developed confrontational defense of those borders overlaid with a global deterrent operation would require Russia to balance the military assets of the entire U.S. alliance system plus China as well. Russia's economic base is a small fraction of that array of potential opponents—roughly less than 1 percent—and its technical capacity, although well developed in some areas, cannot match the scope of the industrial democracies aligned with the United States.[25] It is not remotely feasible for Russia to be independently competitive in traditional military terms anytime soon, and even the problem of sustaining the inherited position imposes severe burdens.

Although required to deactivate the intercontinental-range systems that had been located in Belarus, Kazakhstan, and Ukraine, Russian nuclear forces have a sufficient amount of raw firepower to perform the core deterrent mission, and their command system benefits from the large investment in physical protection that the Soviet Union made. Their early-warning system is seriously deficient, however, and they are barely able to maintain ballistic missile submarine operations. Their overall deterrent capability meets basic requirements but does not match the standard set by U.S. forces. In particular, according to the measure of relative capacity used during the cold war, the number of Russian nuclear weapons that would be expected to survive an initial strike under a policy of strict retaliation is substantially less than the number of survivable U.S. nuclear weapons. The actual number is a matter of highly uncertain speculation in both cases, but Russian military planners have to consider the possibility that under very adverse but conceivable circumstances only a few tens of weapons might survive. American military planners can be confident of a much larger force—hundreds of weapons—under the worst of imaginable circumstances.

The consequence of that apparently arcane comparison is more than a matter of abstract prestige. In operational terms it almost certainly means that Russian deterrent forces rely on rapid reaction more than Soviet forces did, even though they are less able to provide the technical requirements. In their strongest form, rapid reaction policies require the command system to authorize retaliation before the attacking weapons have exploded and therefore to act on evidence of ballistic missiles in flight.[26] Cold war rules of prudence required that missile launches be confirmed by two independent means before retaliation would be authorized, but it is evident that Russia cannot reliably uphold that rule. The constellation of satellites and ground radar installations acquired from the Soviet Union has gaps in coverage and would at any rate require substantial technical improvement.

The technical capabilities of Russian conventional forces are even farther from the leading American standard. The major weapons components—tanks, tactical aircraft, artillery, helicopters, and tracked vehicles—are of credible if not fully comparable design, but in all the many aspects involved in using advanced information technology, the Soviet Union did not match the effort of the United States, and Russia has been even less able to do so. Because they are more numerous, conventional forces impose the heaviest demands on investment. In general, with economic regeneration necessarily being its primary concern, Russia has redirected investment away from the military establishment and has not provided the resources that would be necessary to sustain it, let alone make it competitive. It would require annual expenditures in excess of $100 billion to preserve a military establishment of the size that Russia currently aspires to maintain—on the order of 1.2 million people—and an additional amount in the range of $20 billion to $40 billion a year to make up for its technical deficiencies. Although the exact flow of resources is difficult to assess, the annual defense budgets appropriated by the Russian State Duma have been below $20 billion. It is unlikely that the true figure has been more than double that amount and extremely unlikely that it has reached the requirements for sustainability.[27]

These stark facts have imposed a virtually intractable planning problem on the Russian military. In order to meet a bare bones conception of traditional military missions—global deterrence against the United States and territorial defense against the potential opposition of NATO's tactical air forces in the west and China's ground forces in the east—Russia would have to not only preserve but substantially upgrade the 1.2 million–person establishment set as a planning goal. Over a period of time measured in at least a decade, however, Russia will not be able to meet the financial requirements of that aspiration and will have to pursue economic reform policies that are difficult to reconcile with it—most notably, market-driven investment and economic integration with most of the countries that represent the putative opposition. Attempting to uphold traditional military requirements virtually assures the internal deterioration of Russian forces that results from gross underfinancing. Reducing the inherited establishment to levels that could be supported financially over the next decade or so—probably less that 300,000 people—might halt the internal deterioration but also would preclude indefinitely the ability to perform basic missions against quality opposition. The relatively well-disciplined military planning system of the Soviet Union attempted to resolve the dilemma by giving overriding priority to military requirements and eventually failed in the effort. Russia has jettisoned the Soviet planning system and has redirected investment but has not yet embraced a policy that would assure military inferiority. It would be difficult for even the most dedicated reformers to cut the Russian establishment to manageable size without much more substantial international reassurance than has in fact been offered.

With no decisive resolution of this dilemma in sight, Russian military planners have been driven into a reluctant triage among basic military objectives. Predictably enough their response has emphasized residual reliance on nuclear weapons to compensate for the glaring weakness of their conventional forces. In 1994 in the initial statement of Russian military doctrine, a long-standing Soviet pledge not to initiate the use of nuclear weapons was withdrawn and replaced by a pledge only to refrain from using nuclear weapons against non-nuclear states.[28] Subsequent elaborations of the document have indicated that nuclear weapons would be evoked in response to virtually any serious assault against Russian territory. The practical effect of these declarations on military operations is not immediately evident, but the implications are troublesome from the perspective of safety. If, on the one hand, primary reliance is placed on shorter-range nuclear weapons systems integrated into conventional forces operations, the potential for variations in judgment across the dispersed forces will be increased sharply and central coordination almost certainly will be weakened. The possibility of legitimate misjudgment by a local commander or completely unauthorized action will be increased. If, on the other hand, reliance is placed on the more centrally managed systems that also perform the main deterrent missions, then localized circumstances will be coupled more strongly with the core deterrent operations, and the possibility that a minor event will trigger a massive interaction will be increased. These dilemmas will be imposed, moreover, not only on distant interactions with the United States and its formal allies but also on the more immediate and potentially more volatile interactions with neighboring countries.

Since it has never been possible either to measure directly or to simulate validly the probability of command system failures, it also is not possible to measure the effect of intensifying the pressure on Russia. It is qualitatively apparent, however, that the objective conditions of operational safety have degraded from whatever they were during the course of the cold war and will continue to degrade as Russia struggles with an extremely demanding strategic adjustment and the general process of internal reform. The fragility of control within the overburdened Russian military establishment poses a problem of safety in managing both the global coupling of Russian and U.S. deterrent operations and the more localized interaction of forces along a lengthy and turbulent border. The ultimate nightmare is that an unstable relationship between the main deterrent forces will become entangled in intense local disputes not assumed to be relevant until some operational circumstance suddenly proves them to be. An extension of that nightmare is that deterioration within Russia drives a process of proliferation to the point at which other states along the turbulent border initiate their own deterrent operations.

The Logic of Safety First

At the level of basic common sense, a logical adjustment to this situation appears to be compelling. The active deterrent operations that evolved over the cold war are directed primarily to extreme instances of deliberate and massive aggression, and the unmeasurable risk of a catastrophic breakdown has been accepted in order to prepare operations designed against that threat. Deterrence of mass attack has been the dominant objective and safety an important but subordinate consideration. It now seems obvious that deliberately initiated mass aggression is not the exclusive or even the primary problem it once was believed to be. The ideological confrontation that was presumed to motivate it has dissolved. No military establishment outside the United States is prepared to initiate mass aggression, and Russia in particular is not. For virtually all foreseeable circumstances, it can be assumed, any deterrent threat required need not and should not be massive. For the very unlikely few where an effective threat might have to be large, it need not and should not be enacted rapidly. This implies two basic revisions of the cold war priorities: first, safety should be made the primary objective, and the preservation of deterrence should be made a subordinate consideration rather than the other way around; and second, the deterrent effect being preserved should be directed more to the center of the spectrum of threat than to its extreme edge. This is a policy of safety first.

As its primary purpose, such a policy would set higher standards of protection against the most consequential danger—the inadvertent triggering of massive deterrent operations under crisis pressures that are unmanageable to one or both of the coupled strategic forces. That protection would be achieved largely by replacing the prevailing commitments to massive retaliation and rapid reaction with operating rules designed to prepare small-scale deterrent missions—a single weapon or a very few. These small-scale missions would be planned in deliberated reaction to the specific circumstances judged to require them rather than be programmed in advance. Forces configured for limited missions tailored to specific circumstances would be safer for two reasons: they would not generate the large flows of ambiguous information that inevitably emerge from the extensive crisis reactions of active deterrent forces, and any highly alerted capability they did display would be more readily distinguished from the force levels required for a preemptive disarming attack. Moreover, under a fully developed operational design, those natural effects would be enhanced by measures devised to convey reassurance in proportion to any immediately activated deterrent threat—a necessary balance that is not explicitly recognized or systematically prepared under prevailing practice. Residual capabilities to undertake large attacks would be preserved, but they would be generated on a schedule of days to weeks rather than of minutes to hours. The central operating principle of the revised configuration would be that massive attack capabilities are to be kept permanently in the background and never activated for immediate use unless that is the determined intention.

To be considered acceptable even under the rule of safety first, these operational adjustments would have to be enacted mutually by U.S. and Russian forces on an agreed schedule, and the resulting configuration would have to guarantee protection for both sides against a potential preemptive attack. If those conditions were met, however, the reconfigured forces could claim to preserve virtually the same deterrent effect against mass attack and to enhance deterrence against the more limited threats most likely to be encountered. In the esoteric calculus of attributed probability, it might be conceded that the time delay and more robust protection against inadvertent failure might marginally diminish a particularly willful aggressor's perception of risk.[29] But that would be a calculus of intention rather than capability, and it always has been assumed that capability is the more consequential determinant of the deterrent effect. Actual capability for massive reaction, were it to be required, would be essentially undiminished by the operational adjustments. Moreover, with the risk of inadvertent breakdown better contained, the reconfigured forces would be better able to bring a precisely tailored deterrent effect to bear in any circumstance that demanded it. If it were possible to measure these things, common sense would say, the gains to operational safety and to tailored deterrence surely would outweigh any reduction in the effect of massive deterrence associated with a safety first policy.

At the level of operational practice, however, that logic has radical implications. In reversing the established commitment to massive counterattack rapidly enacted, a fully developed policy of safety first would uproot three of the core procedures that have defined the character of deterrent force operations as they have historically evolved. It would terminate the practice of preparing large coordinated attack plans, it would remove deployed weapons from continuous alert status, and it would preclude the initiation of retaliation in response to the first evidence of an impending attack. Those operational changes also would significantly affect the basis for protection against preemptive attack, which has relied heavily on rapid reaction to independently acquired warning information. Such a program would amount to a complete redesign of deterrent operations, a revolution of apparently monumental proportions when viewed from the internal perspective of the military organizations that conduct them.

It is notoriously difficult for any mature organization of demonstrated competence to undergo a fundamental internal reconfiguration. Usually adaptation is marginal in character and is designed to preserve rather than replace core procedures. For that reason, a successful organization can be in grave danger if its operating environment changes swiftly and dramatically. Military organizations certainly are no exception to this rule. There is an interesting question, however, as to how deeply large-scale nuclear weapons operations have been incorporated in the two principal establishments that conduct them. Since the immense destructiveness of nuclear weapons has been extremely difficult to assimilate to military traditions, the logic of restraint involved in a policy of safety first might encounter less-entrenched institutional resistance than expected. At any rate, the dangers of active deterrent operations combined with internal pressures within Russia are subjecting the military establishments of the two countries to pressures capable of transforming their operations. Active deterrent policies cannot be sustained indefinitely without eventually generating issues of operational safety too menacing to be tolerated, and those most intimately involved may be among the first to realize that fact.[30] Even if the responses to the unfolding situation prove to be more marginal than fundamental in character, the visualization of a stark alternative is likely to be important in inducing any adjustment at all.

Radical Transformation

The core argument for a stark alternative asserts that only a fundamental redesign of deterrent force operations can prevent the catastrophe that an inadvertent triggering of mass attack plans would produce. It is impossible to demonstrate and unrealistic to believe, the argument holds, that the situational judgment of American and Russian officials could control the adversarial momentum that active deterrent forces would generate in a serious crisis engagement. The practice of maintaining comprehensive retaliatory capabilities routinely activated connects extreme consequences to any immediate issue serious enough to produce a military confrontation, whether or not the specific circumstances seem to require it. Any issue that produced even a modest military confrontation in Central Europe, for example, would entangle the deterrent forces because of the proximity of strategic assets vital to Russia. No declaration of limited intention issued in the course of such a dispute could decisively disengage those forces. Moreover, the argument maintains, no exercise of judicious authority could compensate fully for the imbalance in capability that has emerged. As a practical fact the operational capacities of the Russian and the U.S. forces are sufficiently different that the outcome of an engagement might be substantially affected by fine details of timing—a riveting concern for Russia that would reverberate back on the United States in an acute crisis. As long as the pattern of active deployment is maintained, the argument asserts, there will be a substantial and unjustified risk that some localized action might generate an uncontrollable conflagration. The only effective means of removing this possibility is to eliminate the operational practices that create it.

This argument is as speculative as the theory of deterrence itself. It rests on judgments that cannot be measured well enough either to be proved or to be refuted in any definitive manner. Speculation of this sort is unlikely to overturn the established doctrine, but it does offer some protection against widely accepted presumptions that might harbor a fatal flaw. In particular it serves to remind that the construction of history advanced by the deterrence rationale provides a highly simplified conception of how nuclear weapons deployments evolved and are managed. The preservation of deterrence and the prevention of war are not the same thing.

The Consequence of Operational History

As with the concept of deterrence used to justify it, the operational configuration of deterrent forces emerged more as a result than as a determinant of the original pattern of nuclear weapons deployment, at least in the better-documented evolution of U.S. forces. In the immediate aftermath of World War II, the nuclear weapons arsenal that the United States exclusively possessed was small and not actively deployed. As a natural extension of the Manhattan project arrangements, the weapons were held in guarded storage under civilian control and were not dispersed to the military services that would use them in warfare, if it ever came to that. As of 1949 the United States possessed a total of 235 fabricated nuclear weapons, and none of them was immediately associated with a delivery system.[31] That arrangement was contested by the military services, however, which perceived nuclear explosives to be a technology that would dominate the future of warfare. The military services were devoted to acquiring the rights of custody over the weapons, and they staged a concerted campaign to do so, involving an especially spirited competition between the navy and the newly formed air force.

Before there was a fully considered national judgment about the intrinsic merits of protected storage or active deployment, the issue was decided in response to the surprising onset of the Korean war in 1950—the event that crystallized a presumption of global confrontation with the Soviet Union. The U.S. defense budget was tripled and directed not merely to conducting the war in Korea but to preparing a defense in Western Europe against a massive ground assault. As a central element of those preparations, financing was provided for a substantial expansion of the nuclear weapons arsenal, and the military services were granted physical custody and operational planning authority over the thousands of weapons of various types that rapidly emerged from the expanded effort. The weapons were dispersed to force commanders with the idea that they would be integrated into virtually all of the combat missions being contemplated. That sequence set the basic conditions for subsequent deterrent operations. It provided political authorization and dedicated financing for a large standing force directed against the military capacities of the Soviet Union.

It did not produce a coherent operational design, however. The projected pattern of nuclear weapons use that resulted from this initial surge of deployment clearly was not planned according to any systematic strategic conception, and it quickly proved to be both wasteful and self-destructive. The operations separately prepared by dispersed commanders produced a redundant concentration of firepower directed at prominent locations and also programmed conflicts in delivery schedules that made the participating forces dangerous to each other. In addition the deployment pattern was exceedingly volatile since it set a strong predisposition to initiate the use of nuclear weapons in virtually any serious military engagement. By 1960 these problems were recognized, and corrective measures were initiated.[32] The pattern of extensive and widely dispersed deployment was not questioned, but the need for coordinated planning and for more robust operational discipline was accepted. Strategic deterrent missions were distinguished more sharply from localized application of nuclear weapons, and their priority was defined more clearly. Responsibility for determining target assignments and delivery schedules for all forces contributing to the U.S. strategic deterrent missions was vested in a staff unit subordinated to the principal air force commander located at Omaha, Nebraska. Operational control of the navy's strategic weapons was exercised by fleet commanders located elsewhere, but it was agreed that mission assignments would be determined jointly at Omaha in order to assure systematic coverage of targets and to minimize chances that one American weapon would destroy another. This assurance was especially important for bomber crews flying through areas subjected to missile attack, and a major purpose of the planning exercise was to clear routes for the bombers through the opposing air defense system by means of prior missile attack. Bomber missions were the principal commitment of the U.S. Air Force at the time.

Under the planning procedures that evolved at Omaha, coordinated target assignments and delivery schedules were worked out for all of the individual weapons that were maintained on active deployment status and were expected to contribute to core deterrent missions. This was done by developing a list of specific locations whose destruction would diminish the military capacity of the presumed enemy—the Soviet Union and the various states considered to be aligned with it. Tens of thousands of these locations were identified and assigned to broad categories of significance—nuclear weapons deployment sites, conventional forces installations, known locations of political and military leaders, industrial facilities, and concentrations of general population. Each location was distinguished further according to its relative importance within the category, and its susceptibility to damage was assessed. Criteria were then set for the expected damage to be achieved for each target, reflecting its intrinsic importance, its susceptibility to weapons effects, and the probability of successfully delivering a single weapon against it. Corresponding weapons aiming points were then determined, taking into account the fact that some of the targets were close enough to one another to be destroyed by a single explosion, while others were well enough protected for the determined criteria of damage to require multiple explosions. Aim points were allocated to deployed weapons in order to achieve the individual target damage criteria with high confidence, and delivery schedules were defined in relation to a reference time that would be specified at the moment when execution of the plan was authorized. The schedules were designed to minimize the risk that one of the participating weapons would destroy another, but some degree of risk was accepted in order to meet the timing requirements of bomber operations. Since bombers on the ground at their operating bases would be exceedingly vulnerable to preemptive destruction, they had to be launched at the first indication of attack in order to survive. Once launched, they had a limited amount of time, measured in hours, either to complete their missions or to return to their base areas. In the process of returning and immediately thereafter, they would be exceedingly vulnerable.

These procedures generated an intricate pattern of operational assignments whose details always have been protected from independent scrutiny by extremely restrictive security classification. Knowledge of the details is not required, however, to discern the most notable implication for operational safety. It is evident that the method of coordination maintained throughout the cold war institutionalized a powerful inclination to conduct deterrent missions on a very large scale, if at all. The process of specifically allocating target assignments and delivery schedules was time-consuming and could not be adapted readily to changing circumstances. The primary purpose was to produce a coherent pattern across all of the individual weapons that might participate in deterrent operations, and the complexities of making all the determinations meant that a single basic plan provided target and schedule assignments for all of the available weapons. As their operational status changed from day to day, individual weapons could be either committed or removed from a given assignment, but the array of assignments was difficult to alter. Variations of the basic plan could be created by withholding specified blocks of target and schedule assignments, but the planning system was acutely aware that the coherence of the pattern of allocation, which was directed predominantly against the military capacity of the presumed opponent, would be degraded by any extensive withholding of assignments, particularly those relating to the nuclear forces of the opponent. The operational planning system did not attempt to judge the efficient level of retaliation required to preserve the deterrent effect; rather it allocated most of its available assets to reduce the weight of attack that it would experience should deterrence ever fail and an actual war occur.[33] As a result, most of the assets had to be used immediately if they were to be used at all, and this mitigated strongly against lesser variations of the basic plan created by withholding target and schedule assignments.

The process of giving strategic direction to the operational planning process and of exercising political authority over the execution of deterrent missions is itself highly protected by rules of secrecy, and no public account has been given as to how this process works.[34] It nonetheless is evident that up through the end of the cold war the officials who exercised formal authority—the elected president and appointed military chain of command—did not attempt to alter the basic character of nuclear weapons operations. They issued general guidance documents to the planning staff in charge of allocating target and schedule assignments, and it is reasonable to presume that dedicated efforts were made to implement the instructions. The terms of guidance used, however, were only loosely connected to the technical details that dictate weapons assignments, and it does not appear that the guidance documents attempted to contest the most important features of the process—the practice of creating an integrated plan encompassing most of the available weapons, the presumption that the Soviet Union would be the principal opponent, and the principle that the primary weight of attack should be directed against both the conventional and the nuclear weapons capabilities of the opposing military establishment. In effect those critical political decisions were made in the original sequence of deployments when authorization was given for large-scale deployments held on active status. Those determinations were made over the course of the Truman and Eisenhower administrations in a process that involved the American political system as a whole, setting boundaries on the practical authority of subsequent presidents and military commanders.

The formative experience and established precedent that form these boundaries are natural features of most human institutions, but they also are reinforced procedurally by the U.S. Constitution. The divided powers and legal protections of the American political system that are meant to prevent the misuse of power have had major consequence for nuclear weapons operations. This is true despite legitimate fears that these principles are severely compromised by the formal centralization of command authority and by the elaborate secrecy that protects from critical public scrutiny the actions of those who exercise it.[35] The autonomy that has been granted to the anointed few is limited. The weapons design features and the operational rules that are used to prevent accidents or unauthorized actions serve to contain the apex of national authority—the president and the top military commanders—as well as the dispersed units that operate the delivery systems. Those who hold formal authority can exercise it only within the framework of presumption that is broadly accepted. No individual or bureaucratic committee within the American system can change the basic parameters of nuclear weapons deployment without engaging the political process as a whole.

As U.S. nuclear forces evolved beyond the original sequence of deployment, command directives were issued that sounded like fundamental revisions of the operational posture. Shortly after James Schlesinger became secretary of defense in 1973, revised instructions were issued mandating greater emphasis on the preparation of limited options, but this exercise did not alter the practice of embedding those options in a single comprehensive plan. In October 1980 the Carter administration directed attention to the political leadership of the Soviet Union on the theory that this would be the most effective deterrent threat, and that appears to have expanded deliberate targeting of the leadership structure.[36] That set of targets was included under previous instructions, however. In 1981 President Ronald Reagan formally instructed the nuclear forces to prepare to fight and win a protracted nuclear war—an instruction that was ideologically construed to be a more decisive mission than the traditional conception of deterrence. By the time that directive was translated into the details of target and schedule assignments, however, which had to acknowledge the physical limits of what could and could not be accomplished, it did not materially alter the established operational pattern. President Reagan himself publicly recanted the basic notion at the Geneva summit with the Soviet leader Mikhail Gorbachev in November 1985 when he declared, "A nuclear war cannot be won and must not be fought."[37] The formal directive was not officially withdrawn until 1997, but by that time it was widely conceded that the instruction never could have been implemented.

In the aftermath of the cold war and in anticipation of the agreed reductions in force deployments, the number of targets associated with the core deterrent mission was reduced from the 10,000–15,000 range at the peak of the cold war to the 3,000 range of the projected force levels, and the planning system became more willing to contemplate limited missions against opponents other than Russia. As the only plausible source of a large nuclear threat, Russia nonetheless remained the predominant focus of planning, and the net change in circumstance enhanced rather than diminished the ingrained operational logic. The smaller size and greater fragility of Russian forces make it more feasible for the United States to limit damage to itself by attacking Russian weapons before they are launched. Over the course of four decades, that was the principal commitment, and it is prudent to assume that it remains so despite the adjustments that have been made in official declarations and deployments. As a practical matter, it would be difficult to divert U.S. forces to a different opponent or a different conception of their mission, and it would be especially difficult to initiate any such operation. But it would be even more difficult to prevent the execution of established commitment if a provocation occurred that was perceived to fit the critical pattern. Wisely or otherwise, the weight of history is likely to override the situational judgment and practical authority of any president or military commander.

For all the obvious uncertainty involved in assessing Russian deterrent forces, it is apparent that they have a corresponding operational configuration. Unfortunately, there is reason to worry that their net capacity to prevent unauthorized actions or to manage crisis pressures may be substantially less, and those are meaningful differences.[38] But their posture is similar. Although they rely more heavily on land-based missile forces than the United States does and did not inherit a comparable commitment to bomber operations, they have endeavored to preserve an alert force of comparable size. One can reasonably infer a coordinated attack plan responsive to the same technical considerations that have driven the American attack plan. It is evident that the United States is the presumed enemy. It also is evident that the operational doctrine calls for rapid reaction to evidence of an impending attack. It is possible that the central figures in the Soviet system did wield more authority than their American counterparts, as was the prevailing belief during the cold war period, but it is questionable whether that authority conferred a fundamentally greater ability either to initiate an attack or to prevent programmed retaliation. The internal control procedures embedded in the Soviet force are quite similar to those developed in the United States, and the emerging pattern of authority in Russia is not as centralized as it was in the Soviet Union. The Russian force, it must be presumed, also has been configured in the course of its historical evolution to undertake extensive operations against the United States in a rapidly enacted reaction to evidence of an impending attack.

Within the logic of deterrence, the coupling of these historical legacies does not appear to be a problem. It is presumed that the central commanders of the respective forces would always be in sufficient control of their own intentions and would wield sufficient authority over dispersed operations to be able to prevent the initiation of attack under any circumstance. If the forces are seen as organizations with distributed power, in which the capacity for making command decisions cannot be and has not been absolutely centralized, then there is a considerable problem. It is questionable whether two adversarial deterrent forces with distributed decisionmaking capacity, both of which are configured to react extremely rapidly to impending attack, could distinguish between initiation and retaliation at the point of imminent engagement. The issue would be not a matter of formulated intention, but rather the aggregate effect of specific actions taken at dispersed locations. And the process of initiation would be not a single event occurring at an instant in time, but rather a spectrum of events over a period of time. In a world of constrained authority and distributed power, the historical configuration of deterrent forces allows for a cataclysmic war between the United States and Russia that no one intended to initiate and in which it would be impossible to determine who actually did.

The Elements of Inherent Safety

In order to set a higher standard of protection against this possibility, it would be necessary to alter both the scope and the timing of the operations of the deterrent forces. The inadvertent triggering of massive attack plans cannot be prevented unless routinely deployed forces are disengaged assertively and completely from those plans. And because of potential vulnerability to preemptive attack, that process of disengagement cannot occur unless the conditions of force deployment prevent large-scale operations from being undertaken rapidly. The core problem of safety emerges from a strong interaction between scope and timing. It is the planning of large-scale operations that has driven a commitment to rapid reaction and vice versa. The advanced practice of safety requires that both elements of this interaction be strictly controlled.

In principle, individual weapons on active deployed status can be disengaged from a preestablished attack plan by changing the method of assigning targets and schedules. Rather than providing each deployed weapon with a repertoire of alternative assignments derived from the centrally coordinated attack plan, as historically has been done, an individual weapon on deployed status would literally have no target assignment and therefore would not be prepared to conduct any immediate mission. As the standard operating rule, target assignments would be authorized for a deployed weapon only at the point that an actual attack is authorized, and that authorization would be provided for each weapon individually rather than for the deterrent force as a whole. The planning system would be instructed to prepare itself for constructing mission assignments in single-weapon increments in response to specific instructions under specific circumstances. A large-scale retaliation that might have to be implemented too rapidly to be planned in individual-weapon increments would be covered by statistical procedures for coordinating multiple-weapon operations. In preparing for this contingency, the planning system would be instructed simply to make a list of single targets, weighted by priority, accessible to each of the weapons deployed. In the event that large-scale, immediate retaliation was judged to be necessary, then a statistical routine would be released allowing the deployed weapons to select from the list of targets in a manner that would assure an appropriate distribution of targets among whatever weapons were authorized for use. Arrangements of this sort have been termed adaptive targeting to distinguish them from the historical process of coordinated attack planning.

Substantial adjustments in the technical configuration of deterrent forces would be required in order to make adaptive targeting the exclusive method of coordination. All multiple-warhead deployments would have to be eliminated, for example, since that configuration violates the rule of planning missions in single-weapon increments. Significant adjustments in guidance system software and in the support services associated with target planning also would be required. A complete transition to adaptive targeting would make a substantial difference in the organizational inclination of deterrent operations. It would focus operational efforts away from the optimization of mass assaults, which never would be appropriate toward the limited, precisely tailored operations that conceivably might be appropriate. It would improve efficiency as well as safety.

In withholding specified assignments from deployed weapons, adaptive targeting procedures would remove them automatically from the advanced alert status that has been characteristic of active deterrent operations. That alone would not be a sufficient restraint on timing, however, since it would not preclude the clandestine preparation and sudden implementation of a massive attack plan. If distributed target and schedule assignments were the only element missing, advanced alert status could be restored rapidly. An inherently safer operational configuration therefore requires more systematic restraints on the timing of the operations that deterrent forces can undertake. The relevant measures involve physical provisions and operational procedures that would compel any deployed weapon to undergo observable preparations before executing a mission. The preparations would require an amount of time sufficient to relieve the opposing command system of the intense pressures that can develop under active deterrent practices.

Provisions of this sort, broadly known as de-alerting, were initiated on a limited basis in reaction to the end of the cold war and have been discussed with increasing prominence ever since. In September 1991, President George Bush unilaterally announced a series of changes in the deployment status of U.S. nuclear forces featuring the deactivation of most of the short-range systems and termination of the routine ground alert posture for bombers that had been maintained for more than three decades.[39] He also canceled two new ballistic missile development programs, truncated a third, and called for the elimination of all land-based missile systems with multiple warheads—a suggestion that subsequently was incorporated in the START II treaty. This unusual initiative was undertaken in response to the attempted coup that had been staged against the Soviet leader Mikhail Gorbachev the previous month. As intended, it stimulated a series of corresponding measures in the Soviet forces just as the Soviet Union itself was being dissolved. Bush clearly was concerned about the integrity of control within the Soviet force, and the ready political acceptance of his sudden and unprecedented actions within the United States as a whole indicated that his judgment was widely shared. Unilateral measures of that sort would have inspired vehement opposition before the coup attempt. Political assent was based on the fact that the initiative, even with subsequent elaborations, did not fundamentally alter the basic operational pattern of deterrent forces. The long-range missile forces on both sides have remained continuously poised for rapid operations, and both sides remain committed to generating yet larger forces at a higher level of readiness in response to circumstances considered to be threatening.

In order to alter decisively the ingrained timing of deterrent operations, the de-alerting process would have to be both comprehensive and transparent. It would have to apply to all fabricated weapons and to all of the delivery systems capable of carrying them. It would have to provide for reliable verification. And, most important of all, the restrictions would have to be maintained not only under routine circumstances but also under the pressures of crisis engagement right up to the point that a commitment was made to use nuclear weapons. De-alerting of nuclear forces in their routine configuration is symbolically important because it projects more benign intention and offers additional protection against operational accidents. However, it does not address the more serious problem of an inadvertent engagement.

There are many technical methods that might, in principle, be used to embody the requirements of a comprehensively de-alerted operational posture. The spectrum of possibility runs from physically decisive measures, such as the separation of weapons and delivery vehicles or the removal of critical components that cannot be replaced quickly, to operationally more convenient measures, such as embedding warning mechanisms and time delays in the various locking devices used to prevent the unauthorized or unintended operation of weapons and delivery systems. It is not difficult to devise effective ways of disabling deployed weapons systems in a manner that imposes a predictable time requirement for bringing them to immediately responsive status. For example, in-flight guidance batteries could be removed from ballistic missile systems, as could the explosive charges necessary to blow the heavy protective lid off missile silos. It normally would take several hours to reverse these measures for each weapon deployed and, depending on the number of people involved, up to several days to reverse them for an entire force.[40] It is more difficult to impose these delays in a manner that is verifiable. Cooperative methods presumably would have to be used to do so, particularly since the provisions of verification would have to reflect the interests of all states affected by deterrent operations, not merely the two principal protagonists.[41] Nonetheless, the difficulty is largely a matter of political attitude. It is technically feasible to attach tagging devices to deployed weapons that would determine or even control their operational status. Such devices can be designed to enable remote interrogation and to preclude their removal without generating a warning signal. Systematic application of those devices would enable reliable verification.

The need to provide adequate protection for a de-alerted force could be claimed as a prospective benefit rather than a necessary precondition. If adaptive targeting practices and comprehensive de-alerting provisions were implemented jointly by Russian and U.S. nuclear forces and if verification arrangements were applied to both, the resulting situation would provide much better protection against preemptive attack than the alert posture provides. The arrangement would sharply restrict the element of surprise and would allow greater reliance on methods of dispersal planned in conjunction with the time controls imposed on the generation of an immediately ready attack capability. Most notably with time controls imposed on the operation of all delivery systems, the command systems could perform their functions under much less duress, which would mitigate much of their vulnerability. There inevitably would be speculation and some degree of practical worry about systematic subversion of the arrangement to screen the preparation of a surprise attack, but any competent design would render the possibility of decisively effective surprise a great deal more remote than it currently is. Russia would have substantially greater reason than the United States to worry about the potential threat of conventional tactical air forces to their nuclear weapons deployments, but that problem would be much more tractable if it were disassociated from the much more pressing threat of nuclear operations. Comprehensive restraints on the scope and timing of nuclear force operations would render the pattern of deployment less vulnerable than it currently is or historically has been.

Practical Approximation

It would take a considerable amount of time and effort for the American and Russian command systems to work out the exact provisions for adaptive targeting and comprehensive de-alerting in the robust detail that implementation would require. A number of important trade-offs would have to be balanced in the process. The decisiveness of alert restrictions would need to be weighed, for example, against the ease of responding to mission requirements. The time, procedures, and technical requirements for bringing deployed weapons to a state of immediate availability would have to be determined precisely with both considerations in mind. Similarly, the assurance of verification would have to be balanced against the legitimate interests of internal security. It would have to be demonstrated that the information used to prove that deterrent capacities have not been activated would not prevent them from being activated if the forces are legitimately needed or subject them to a risk of preemptive attack. In working out these balances in appropriate detail, the conception of deterrence itself would have to be weighed against the objective of reassurance.

There is no reason to believe that any of the necessary specifications would be intractable. In fact the technical difficulties are not likely to be as great as those encountered and mastered in establishing the existing alert postures. It is unlikely that, in the absence of some motivating disaster, either Russia or the United States would attempt to transform the prevailing operational pattern in a single comprehensive exercise explicitly dedicated to that purpose. Under normal circumstances, neither political system could be expected to muster the clarity of intent, the degree of consensus, or the concentration of executive authority that would be necessary. If an inherently safer configuration of deterrent forces is to be achieved, it undoubtedly will have to be done in a series of gradual stages, and the underlying purpose is more likely to be acknowledged at the advanced stages of such a process than at the beginning.

Whether or not it proves to be the leading edge of such a process, the basic elements of a gradual adjustment have begun to enter public discussion in the manner that might be expected of a major reform in its early stages. Several prominent reports have been issued in recent years outlining a program of progressive restraint on nuclear weapons operations.[42] The idea is to pursue a combination of measures that would not only reduce the level of nuclear weapons deployment but also limit their scope of application and diminish the inclination for massive operations rapidly enacted. Such measures would include:

— A declaratory commitment never to initiate the use of a nuclear weapon and therefore to undertake retaliation only in response to a nuclear attack,

— Further reductions in the deployment of nuclear weapons delivery systems to constrain the total amount of firepower dedicated to deterrent missions,

— Corresponding reductions in nuclear weapons inventories accompanied by direct verified controls on those inventories,

— Partial alert restrictions to reduce the number of weapons normally held immediately available to levels below what an effective preemptive attack would require, and

— Reaffirmation of restrictions on ballistic missile defenses sufficient to assure that the reduced and operationally restricted deployments could perform legitimate deterrent missions.

These measures would not transform the established practice of active deterrence, but they would mitigate the danger of an inadvertent engagement between the two major forces and would bolster the international arrangements for preventing proliferation. The threat of proliferation is acknowledged more readily at this point than is the possibility of inadvertent war, but the two issues ultimately are connected and require similar means of restraint.

The declaratory commitment, generally known as a no-first-use declaration, is a categorical item on this reform agenda that is directed to the world as a whole with the problem of proliferation primarily in mind. It would require both Russia and the United States to accept a more restricted deterrent policy than either has been willing to proclaim. By itself it would not offer decisive reassurance, since a doctrinal declaration could be revised instantaneously in the course of a military confrontation. It nonetheless would align Russia and the United States with the international standard of legitimacy widely considered to be the only viable foundation for preventing the potentially extensive proliferation of nuclear weapons operations over the longer term. The nuclear nonproliferation treaty (NPT) codifies the agreement of 182 of its 187 signatories not to acquire nuclear weapons, many of which are technically capable of doing so.[43] The treaty was given indefinite duration by unanimous consent on May 11, 1995.[44] It also was subjected to formal review every five years for the purpose of determining whether progress in restraining the nuclear weapons deployments of the five states allowed to maintain them is sufficient to justify their renunciation by all the other parties. The NPT explicitly protects the signatories that do not possess nuclear weapons from being subjected to a threat of their use by those that do and by extension sets a presumption against any legitimate initial use of the weapons. Of all the parties to the treaty, the United States is the most capable of upholding this presumption. Its national territory is not subjected to any proximate threat, and its conventional military forces clearly are superior to those of any other country. In the inevitable logic of equity, if the United States does not honor the standard, then no one else can be expected to do so either. It is quietly conceded that Russia has more of a problem than the United States. Even so, Russia, for all its burdens, has less reason to evoke nuclear weapons for general security proposes than many of the other parties to the treaty have. A no-first-use declaration is almost certainly a necessary element of credible restraint as far as the international community is concerned.

Otherwise the basic elements of the reform agenda can be developed in convenient increments designed to mitigate the practical problems involved in establishing an equitable configuration of American and Russian forces. Both of the major establishments will need to be eased beyond the uncertain but important threshold at which constraints on deployment would begin to restrict the magnitude of threatened damage that would underwrite the deterrent effect. The target of a 2,000-warhead level of deployment that was announced at the Helsinki summit in 1997 approaches the point at which this becomes a significant consideration. Below that level, the respective forces would have to make more meaningful choices regarding the number and type of targets used to embody the deterrent effect and would have to revise their traditional commitment to maximal retaliation. By introducing alert restrictions along with force ceilings, the gradual reform program would allow a sharply restricted but immediately available deterrent force to be supplemented by a process of mobilization in response to any circumstance that seems to require a larger deterrent. That feature clearly would compromise the interest of operational safety by enabling and probably encouraging full-scale mobilization under crisis conditions, but it would begin to accommodate the deployed forces to a more restricted standard.

The introduction of agreed alert restrictions as a method of control also would help to address the need to establish equitable force ceilings. Quite apart from the question of what deterrence actually requires, Russia faces a serious question of what is reasonably affordable. In the process of redirecting resources within its developing market economy, the Russian Federation has not maintained the rates of investment that would be necessary to sustain the nuclear weapons delivery systems it inherited at the ceiling levels defined in the arms control agreements. Although the exact details are difficult to determine from the public record, available information on rates of production indicates that Russia will not be able to replace existing weapons systems at the end of their normal service life, and it is questionable whether sufficient maintenance is being done to extend their duration of service. The principal new delivery system that has entered into operational service under the Russian Federation has been the single-warhead ICBM (intercontinental ballistic missile) with solid propellant, designated the SS-27 by NATO and the Topol M by Russia. That missile is designed both for mobile and for silo-based operations. It reportedly is being produced at the rate of ten per year at the same production facility in Votkinsk that produced its predecessor, the SS-25.[45] That is far too low a rate of production to sustain the levels envisaged under the START II and the projected START III treaties, and the rates of refurbishment and new production for the submarine-based force are even lower. The virtual collapse of Soviet-era strategic system development and production activities indicates that by 2010 the number of nuclear weapons that Russia will be able to operate at intercontinental range on reasonably short notice—within a week or so—is not likely to exceed 1,000 and might be as low as 500. Deployments at that level would still provide a powerful deterrent reasonably judged to be adequate but would not meet the maximum standards that traditionally have prevailed. Nor would they match the force levels that the United States is planning to maintain and can readily afford. In the initial stages of a gradual reform effort, it would be easier to equalize the number of nuclear weapons that Russia and the United States maintain on alert status than it would be to bring the total weapons inventories, duly verified, to the levels that Russia can reasonably sustain.

Under these circumstances it is plausible to imagine a first-stage reform in which American and Russian forces are confined to retaliatory operational doctrines and their active deployments are restricted to 1,000 nuclear weapons launcher positions, no more than 500 of which could be brought to immediately available alert status within a period of twenty-four hours and none of which would be routinely maintained in that status. The deployment restrictions would be based on delivery system counting rules, but they would be comprehensive, including all systems configured to carry nuclear weapons. The practice of counting deployed weapons by remote observation would be supplemented by collaborative arrangements for determining their status of availability. Those weapons that provide the most advanced capability for preemptive attack would be excluded from active deployment status—specifically, the MX/Peacekeeper missile and the Trident II D5/Mk5 missile with the 475-kiloton W88 warhead on the American side and all the variations of the SS-18 missile system on the Russian side. Otherwise the forces could be configured to suit the operational preferences of each country. Table 2-5 summarizes the configurations that each country might select in order to comply with the restrictions, although in the Russian case the table assumes a doubling of the demonstrated rate of production of the SS-27 system. These options would comply with the recommended force size advanced in the various reports urging progressive restraint.[46]

Such an outcome is near the limit of what would likely be considered reasonable for a bilateral agreement between Russia and the United States not involving the other actively deployed nuclear forces. It probably would have to be accompanied by a reliable understanding that the other forces would not be increased beyond their prevailing levels. Since it would preserve a significant numerical advantage for the two principal establishments, however, it presumably could be achieved without undertaking the difficult multilateral negotiation necessary to set a specifically agreed configuration for all of the deployed forces. Similarly the illustrative outcome is nearly the limit of what can be expected without elaborating the existing restrictions on defensive system deployments or introducing provi-

Table 2-5. *Hypothetical Deployments in Russia and the United States, 2010*

Country and launcher system	*Number deployed*	*Warhead positions*
Russia		
SS-25 (RT-2PM Topol)	300	300
SS-27 (RT-2PM2 Topol M)	250	250
SS-N-23 (R-29RM) on seven Delta IV submarines with sixteen tubes each	112	448
United States		
Minuteman III	500	500
Trident II on seven submarines with twelve tubes each	84	336
B-2 bombers	10	160

Source: Author's estimates.

sions for direct control of nuclear weapons themselves, as distinct from their more readily observed delivery systems. For those reasons it provides a natural benchmark for a partial, first-stage reform of active deterrent practices.

If it were achieved, this outcome would force more restrictive targeting policies, but it still would enable extremely destructive retaliation plans to be formulated and would not compel a switch to adaptive targeting practices. Similarly, it would relieve but not entirely eliminate the capacity for preemption that has driven rapid reaction policies and thereby created the potential for a catastrophic breakdown. With the most advanced hard-target weapons removed from service and overall force loadings adjusted toward single-weapon configurations, comprehensive attack on the opposing delivery system would be less feasible and the trade-offs with other target categories would be more significant. Nonetheless, the 500 rapidly deliverable warheads on each side still would pose a major threat to the opposing command system, and at these lower force levels the potential contribution of conventional forces to preemptive attack would be more relevant. Partial reform stops short of what decisive standards of safety would require, but it does provide practical measures for alleviating the severe managerial pressures that have been imposed on the Russian force. The unavoidable implications of those pressures can be expected to drive the American and Russian governments into some variant of a first-stage reform effort regardless of whether they explicitly adopt the idea of progressive restraint.

Subsequent Stages and Ultimate Outcomes

Beyond that reasonably evident first stage, however, the pursuit of progressive restraint becomes increasingly more demanding and the outcome more uncertain. To the extent that additional reductions in deployment and tighter operational restrictions are seriously contemplated, fundamental problems of security conception and of political attitude are likely to be encountered.

For those who consider the preservation of deterrence to be the primary basis of security—clearly the prevailing opinion both in Russia and in the United States—very small and very restricted force deployments are bound to be seen as hazardous. Not only would such a pattern diminish the magnitude of threat on which the deterrent effect is normally judged to depend, it also would render the balance of forces more sensitive to rapid or undetected violations. The thought that one side might acquire 100 new nuclear weapons or might apply extremely precise conventional force capabilities is more unsettling if the allowed level of deployment of deterrent forces is a few hundred weapons than if it is many thousands. It is generally assumed, therefore, that the collateral regulations and measures of verification required to support a smaller and operationally more restricted pattern of deployment would have to be commensurately more elaborate and presumably more intrusive. But that assumption produces an apparent paradox. A sharply restricted deterrent posture designed to be operationally safer and politically more accommodating must be accompanied by collaborative provisions that, in effect, formalize a greater degree of suspicion.

Strategic analysts seasoned in the logic of confrontation might absorb that twist without major difficulty; but at least some members of the affected citizenry—those inclined to apply the broader logic of human relationships—are likely to see something wrong with the picture. If intricate collaboration is possible, then more refined principles of security also should be possible. Deterrence, after all, is among the more primitive forms of interaction. When accommodating reason is not effective, one sticks a gun in an adversary's face, but one does not attempt to conduct normal business that way. If reasonable collaboration can be arranged, then there is no need to brandish the gun, and it generally is considered poor form to do so. From this perspective, it appears doubtful that the practice of deterrence could be civilized to a highly refined standard without calling the practice itself into question, a point that has been made in recent years by many prominent veterans of the practice. The most forceful of these, General Lee Butler, retired commander of U.S. strategic forces, dared to suggest in 1996 that the practice of deterrence has always been far more of a peril than a benefit. On the basis of as much direct operational experience as any individual has ever had, General Butler expressed his personal conviction that the overriding security interests of the United States and of the world as a whole required deterrent force operations to be terminated entirely and nuclear weapons deployments to be eliminated completely.[47] That outcome, of course, would provide the ultimate guarantee of safety, if it could be achieved and preserved.

As Butler subsequently acknowledged in helping to formulate the program of progressive restraint on nuclear weapons operations advanced by the National Academy of Sciences, it would be extremely difficult for any large democracy to undergo a transformation as radical as his 1996 statement outlined.[48] The termination of deterrence and the elimination of nuclear weapons would require a much more dramatic revision of perspective than governments dependent on consensus usually are capable of undertaking. In the United States, at the moment, official policy nominally espouses the goal of ultimate elimination, as required by Article 6 of the nonproliferation treaty, but it does so with an overriding presumption that the goal will not be feasible anytime soon. A solid majority appears determined to preserve a robust deterrent force indefinitely. A substantial segment of that majority believes that something akin to a change in human nature would have to occur and that most of the contentiousness would have to disappear from international relationships before it would be desirable to relinquish reliance on active deterrent operations. This bedrock opinion, reciprocated even more intently in Russia, is a significant obstacle to the more advanced stages of a progressive reform effort.

The difficulty is compounded by the fact that a competing conception of radical reform is advanced in the United States by an intense minority capable of exercising influence disproportionate to its numbers. That conception begins with the observation that a security arrangement based on defensive capability rather than countervailing offensive threat would be morally and strategically superior to the traditional practice of deterrence and would be inherently safer as well. It proceeds with the conviction that with sufficient dedication the technical requirements of such an arrangement can be achieved by methods that do not depend on the collaboration of potential opponents. The image is of an eventual configuration of forces that could destroy attacking weapons after they have been launched but before they have reached their targets, thereby recreating the physical barrier against assault that military forces once were able to provide or at any rate to promise with some credibility. That is the image that President Ronald Reagan explicitly evoked in a widely noted speech in 1983 initiating a program to develop direct defenses against ballistic missiles.[49] The advocates have since become more circumspect in their claims as the resulting development effort documented the technical difficulties involved, but the idea of dominant defenses has remained the principal commitment of an unusually dedicated faction in the American political system.

As far as the underlying technology and logic of strategic interaction is concerned, the conception of a security policy primarily based on defensive capability could be assimilated into a program of progressive restraint on existing deterrent operations. As a practical matter, any realistic defensive arrangement would have to be supported by comprehensive restrictions on the number of offensive systems deployed, on their technical elaboration, and on their operational practices. One can reasonably judge in advance of any technical development effort or any detailed assessment that if there are too many apparently threatening objects to be dealt with over too broad an area and if they can engage in unlimited subterfuge and direct sabotage, then no defensive system of whatever sophistication can be expected to resist penetration to the virtually perfect standard that reliable protection against nuclear weapons requires. However, if drastic restrictions were imposed on offensive operations, then it would be possible to shift the basis of security from a countervailing offensive threat to an effective defensive reaction. That clearly would have to be accomplished on an agreed and simultaneous schedule for all actively deployed forces. Otherwise, a force still committed to offensive retaliation would experience a significantly increased incentive to react rapidly under crisis conditions as its potential opponents shift emphasis.[50] And if the transition is to be agreed, it would have to be equitable. Nonetheless, under those conditions agreed defensive deployments could be considered at the advanced stages of offensive limitation as a hedge against small violations.

In political terms, these two conceptions are not compatible. The principal advocates of a defensive system in the United States have not accepted the limiting conditions associated with the provisions of progressive restraint. They have been generally skeptical of offensive force limitations on grounds that any international agreement is unreliable, and they have been assertively hostile to the 1972 antiballistic missile (ABM) treaty, the document that provides the legal basis for international regulation of ballistic missile defense. They have rejected the central procedural rule established in the treaty—the provision that any strategically significant deployment of the defensive system must be agreed mutually among the treaty signatories—and have insisted on the right to undertake a unilateral national program.[51] That stance has been interpreted in Russia as a disingenuous attempt to promote decisive strategic superiority—a combination of offensive and defensive capability that might enable the United States to initiate a disarming attack and then defeat the ragged retaliation that might follow. Since the limitation of offensive forces is a requirement for effective performance of any defensive system yet conceived, the Russian suspicions are technically plausible enough to be politically compelling.

Moreover, Russia clearly is in no position to match the extensive development effort and deployment program that a defensively based strategic posture would require. To have any meaningful capability at all, a large integrated network of sensors and interceptors would have to be created that is capable of reacting not only to the readily observable and predictable trajectories of ballistic missiles but also to the stealthy maneuvers of aircraft and cruise missiles. Minimal investments would run in the range of hundreds of billions of dollars. The entire budget for all of the Russian government's activities has not exceeded the equivalent of $40 billion for any year of the federation's existence, and by 1999 total cash tax receipts were running less than $10 billion for the year. As long as any significant offensive deployments remain, Russia simply cannot afford the effort to negate them. If offensive forces could be virtually eliminated, then the somewhat more modest effort required to counteract residual errors is not likely to be an investment priority.

Given this diversity of perspective and the intensity of the opinions involved, the conceptual harmonization necessary to design an ultimate outcome is beyond the immediate capacity of practical politics. This means that the more advanced stages of progressive restraint, if they are to occur, are likely to be driven by the pressures of observable circumstances—not the largely hidden dangers of potential crisis interactions, but rather the matters relating to routine operations. It also means that the provisions most likely to be developed are those that cut across the underlying divisions of opinion. At least two such provisions might play a leading role in this situation: the comprehensive accounting of fissionable material and the integration of surveillance activities.

Comprehensive Accounting

Since nuclear weapons have been considered the citadel of national security by those countries that have developed them, the associated information and materials have been the most zealously guarded of all commodities. The core functions of managing these commodities—operation of the systems for accounting and for physical protection that keep track of fabricated weapons and of the fissionable material that provides their explosive power—are performed by specialized organizations that are highly protected from outside scrutiny. The overriding purpose of these organizations has been to provide the weapons and material for national use while denying access to anyone not authorized to have it. There have been public declarations about the size of the arsenals and some limited experimentation by Russia, the United States, and Australia in the joint monitoring of fissionable material. There has been no international arrangement, however, for determining the total world inventories of fabricated weapons or weapons-grade fissionable material. Combining published national estimates of these inventories cannot establish the number of available weapons any more accurately than a range of about 5,000—an uncertainty band twice as large as the agreed deployment ceilings for Russian and U.S. forces projected at the 1996 Helsinki summit.

It is accepted that the respective national accounting systems know their own holdings much more exactly, but it is far from evident just how exactly that is, particularly in the Russian case. The control system that Russia inherited from the Soviet Union appears to have placed more emphasis on physical security than exact accounting—that is, controlling the areas where weapons and materials were held as distinct from determining exactly how much material was held there. Even the United States, which aspires to exact accounting, has admitted that its records are ambiguous about the fate of some 2,750 kilograms of plutonium produced over the history of its national weapons program—enough to fabricate more than 500 weapons.[52] Since organizations that are protected from close scrutiny and from the pressures of commercial market competition virtually always develop unfortunate habits, it is prudent to assume that neither the American nor the Russian control systems perform the core functions of accounting and physical custody to a standard that is beyond improvement. It is especially prudent to assume this in the case of the generally beleaguered Russian system.

These circumstances already have commanded attention. The image of "loose nukes" escaping managerial control has entered the professional literature, the daily press, and the popular culture even without an actual incident to stimulate it. The intuitive sense of Russian vulnerability was strong enough in 1991 to stimulate special legislation in the United States providing authorization to assist in the repatriation and deactivation of nuclear weapons that Russia acquired from the Soviet arsenal. Under the resulting Nunn-Lugar program, named for the co-sponsors of the legislation, the United States spent $1.5 billion through June 1999 providing equipment and services designed to bolster managerial surveillance and physical security for a limited portion of the Russian arsenal.[53] So far, that effort has only affected the margins of the business. It has been directed to weapons being removed from active service and to excess material largely in reserve status. It has not been extended to the management of active forces, a fact that is hardly surprising since those forces are still engaged in operational confrontation. An initiative to broaden collaboration was announced at a summit conference in September 1994, where the American and Russian presidents agreed in principle to exchange detailed information on their total weapons stockpiles, but subsequent efforts to negotiate the enabling agreement for cooperation required under U.S. law stalled on the Russian side, and the exchange has not occurred.[54] Overall the need for better management has been admitted, and the inclination for collaboration has been tentatively demonstrated, but systematic provisions have not yet been developed.

Despite the initial limitations of this initiative, there is good reason to believe that it provides the most likely spearhead for advanced stages of the progressive restraint idea. The inexorable process of deterioration occurring within the Russian military establishment as a result of systematic underfinancing is serious enough to affect all of its activities, including those of highest priority. Of all those that are affected, the United States is bound to care most about the integrity of the Russian nuclear materials management system, a matter acknowledged to be of vital importance across the entire spectrum of opinion regarding deterrent force operations. The United States is also likely to experience a change in perspective regarding materials management as a result of its direct involvement. Marginal as they have been, the projects conducted under the Nunn-Lugar program have created a continuous process of engagement that naturally produces a type of understanding much more refined than the one that results from remote observation and adversarial bargaining. Already the relationships among the scientists from the respective weapons laboratories who are engaged in the collaborative monitoring of weapons movements and fissionable materials storage are more constructive than those that occur on other channels of interaction, and the consequences of that can be expected to be cumulative. The situation in Russia can be counted on to document the defects of nuclear materials management, and it is unlikely that the implications will be confined to Russia. As the United States seeks to provide effective assistance, its own practices will not be exempt from scrutiny and are not likely to remain completely unaltered. This is one set of problems that can discipline even the most entrenched orthodoxy.

It is a reasonable projection, therefore, although certainly not a guarantee, that the mutual involvement of Russia and the United States with the subject of nuclear materials management eventually will generate a serious effort to set comprehensive standards for accounting and physical security and to vest some international entity with the capacity to monitor and reinforce them. At a minimum such an arrangement would attempt to create an accounting system that could determine the number of nuclear weapons in existence down to the single unit—a determination that would have to encompass all fissionable materials that can be used in weapons, including the large amounts of plutonium contained in spent reactor fuel held at thousands of sites throughout the world. Although that is clearly a demanding objective, it would be difficult for a credible effort to stop short of that aspiration. With the unqualified cooperation of all countries that possess relevant nuclear materials, currently forty-four in all, monitoring technology could be applied that would achieve the accounting standard for existing stocks and would upgrade physical security practices as well. There would be inevitable concern about the possibilities for deliberate evasion; but, if supplementary rules were adopted allowing environmental sampling to be conducted in instances of suspected evasion, the practical scope for undetected production of new materials would be extremely limited. Uncertainties associated with the production of fissionable materials for the existing national stockpiles might well take some time to transcend, but once initiated a comprehensive monitoring and accounting system would become progressively more reliable and the residual uncertainties progressively less significant.

Recent progress in relevant technologies—sensors, communication links, tamper-resistant designs, encryption techniques, controlled access databases, and such matters—would enable such a system to be created and would provide for substantial improvement in the current national management systems as that is accomplished. Up to this point the stocks of fabricated weapons and fissionable materials have not been systematically provided with labels that record their identity, dispositional history, and current status in a manner that cannot be altered without detection and can be checked from remote locations. But something like that would be done in a comprehensive, state-of-the-art managerial system. With appropriate design, the system could protect the legitimate prerogatives of national governments and guarantee duly specified international access. An important part of the effort involved in creating the system would be concerned with defining these boundaries of authority. Those definitions then would have to be embedded not merely in the implementing technology but also in the legal operating rules—rules that basically would determine who gets what part of the information that is generated and how that information is to be used. Aggregate numbers of weapons and amounts of materials presumably would be recorded internationally and reported in summary format. Distributional details would be held by national governments under standard security classification. The integrated system would assure consistency between aggregate and unit information while preserving the rules of access. Since an arrangement of this sort has not yet been prominently visualized, very little of the effort required to design it has been undertaken, but again, there is no reason to believe that doing so would be intrinsically impossible.

This conception unquestionably belongs to the more advanced stages of a reform program requiring more intimate collaboration than so far has been considered realistic in political terms. Such an arrangement is strongly encouraged, however, by the relentless pressures being imposed on the Russian system and is enabled by available technology not yet applied. Moreover, accurate, comprehensive accounting is virtually certain to be a necessary gateway to any of the other advanced stages of restraint. An international accounting system is likely to be a precondition for setting offensive force deployments at the low levels that Russia might reasonably be able to sustain and is certain to be a precondition for any serious attempt to eliminate active deployments. It also is likely to be recognized as increasingly necessary protection against the theft of weapons or materials by the highly dissident organizations that are being generated in the new international environment and are operating like everyone else on a global scale. More broadly, the accurate accounting and continuous monitoring of what is acknowledged to be the most dangerous of all the materials that human societies use are likely to lead to the arrangements that will eventually have to be applied to many other materials and commodities, not only for reasons of security but also for environmental sensitivity. Unless it is transposed into some other form, plutonium in particular will be dangerous for exceedingly long periods of time—tens of thousands of years.[55] The current national management systems cannot claim to exercise control over that time span, nor has a method of disposition been determined that would eliminate the need for active management. If, as the proverb holds, necessity is truly the mother of invention, then the accurate monitoring of dangerous materials is one of the major innovations that the overall process of transformation can be expected to produce.

Collaborative Surveillance

In addition the collaborative monitoring of fissionable materials might eventually be extended to the monitoring of force operations. Once the first problem is admitted, the second is easier to appreciate.

By their very nature, active deterrent forces poised for rapid reaction to impending attack make the acquisition of timely and reliable information about the disposition of the opposing force nearly as vital as the wielding of imposing firepower against it. In recognition of that fact, during the cold war the two principal antagonists—the United States and the Soviet Union—directed a great deal of effort to monitoring each other by remote observation, and the magnitude of that effort distinguished them from the other states with nuclear weapons as much as did the scale of their weapons deployment. The intelligence services developed for that purpose and the imaging and electronic intercept technologies on which they depended were regarded as critical national assets to be protected as zealously as the weapons themselves. There was, however, an obvious and significant difference between weapons and information as national security commodities. Weapons are created by applying physical laws that do not alter themselves in order to thwart the purpose at hand. Information is necessarily acquired from an opponent whose inclination and capacity to resist strongly affect the results achieved. It is not possible, of course, to assess the results that were achieved in the manner that, in principle at least, one can count weapons inventories and estimate their destructive potential. The details are heavily protected by security classification, and, even if they were all to be revealed, their meaning doubtless would be subject to widely varying interpretation. The main outlines of the situation nonetheless are reasonably apparent. The national intelligence services have been able to determine the number of deployed weapons quite accurately without depending much on arranged cooperation.[56] The mobile operations of weapons launchers—submarines on submerged patrol, aircraft in flight, and rail or road mobile missiles engaged in field maneuvers—have been able to conceal their exact location for significant amounts of time, but not their existence. Major departures from the pattern of routine operations usually are detected, but that does not preclude the possibility that significant operations of modest size might be concealed. The United States, for example, did not detect the deployment of Soviet offensive missiles to Cuba in 1962 until the advanced stages of that operation, and although the capacity for remote observation has become more sophisticated in the meantime, so also has the capacity for concealment. In general the national intelligence services have been dependent on remote observation for the information required to manage their deterrent force operations. It is fairly evident that whatever they achieve by the fabled methods of spying does not allow either of them to read the internal decision processes of the other with anything like the fidelity and confidence they would require to determine their own operational decisions. The bottom line is that they each know with confidence the size and basic capability of the force that is arrayed against them and have learned to recognize its routine operational patterns. They both would be prone to substantial uncertainty and serious confusion, however, if confronted with a circumstance in which the opponent's operations departed from established routine.

The implications of that base circumstance are a daily concern for both of the major forces, but the burdens do not fall evenly on them. Russia is necessarily much more sensitive to exact operational conditions since the potential for the United States to initiate an effective attack is substantially greater. To compound that sensitivity, Russian territory is also much more vulnerable to offensive penetration and its surveillance capability is much more limited, so much more in fact that the overall integrity of the incomplete system inherited from the Soviet Union could be questioned. Whatever priority Russia might give to improving this capability, its investment assets are limited so severely that it is extremely doubtful a full-scope national surveillance system with advanced capability could be developed anytime soon. Even if it could be acquired, the resulting system could not be expected to remove or even diminish the operational burdens. Unless assisted by cooperative methods, Russian national surveillance of force operations—in particular the observation of missiles and aircraft in flight—has very little chance of keeping up with the many evasive and preemptive techniques that the more advanced offensive systems are capable of applying. That is a potential problem for the United States as well, but it is an immediate and severe issue for Russia.

Unless the problems are dramatized by some sensational event, routine operational surveillance seems unlikely to become an immediate public concern. Nonetheless, appreciation of the situation within the respective military establishments might well be sufficient to provide some impetus to the more advanced stages of progressive restraint. Both sides have long recognized the desirability of coordinated reaction to potentially ambiguous events. Both were reminded of that concern in 1995 when a research rocket launched by Norway triggered the initial stages of an emergency reaction in the Russian nuclear forces before it was identified correctly. In that case effective implementation of the rules of prior notification presumably would have preempted the confusion. Russia had been informed in advance of the intended launch, but the information had not been recorded at the relevant nodal point of the surveillance system. In other instances, such as the misconstrued attack by Soviet air defense forces on a Korean Airlines passenger jet on September 1, 1983, some immediate coordination would be required. For reasons that remain obscure, the Korean aircraft was flying outside the bounds of its assigned route, thus contradicting what prior notice indicated it should be doing.[57] In instances of this sort, it clearly would be useful for the surveillance systems to be able to exchange immediate information, including tracking data. That much is readily recognized. Extending the thought to imagine not merely protocols for emergency consultation but systematic integration of all operational surveillance still would be considered venturesome, but there has been some official exploration of broad collaboration. Russia, for example, has participated to some extent in the negotiations to extend NATO's air traffic control system into central Europe, and the possibility of its being included in the system has been contemplated. As a practical matter, unless Russia is included, not just tangentially but systematically and not only for air traffic control but for missile launches as well, it is unlikely to be able to sustain the capacity for surveillance across all of its territory that would be considered a basic requirement for responsible management of deterrent force operations.

Systematic development of this theme poses fundamental questions that belong to the advanced stages of an effort to restrain deterrent force operations. It has been demonstrated that data from widely dispersed radar installations can be combined instantaneously to provide much more accurate tracking of flying objects, a technique that is considered to be a key to the design of advanced ballistic missile defense systems. That has opened up the possibility of a globally integrated surveillance system capable of much higher standards of performance than have been possible historically. That in turn raises the issue of who is to benefit from the development of this potential and for what purpose. The standard answer is that the United States and its allies are to benefit for the purpose of enhancing deterrence. As a practical matter, this grouping of countries has considerable scope for imposing that answer. For the moment and in all probability for several decades to come, they are the only ones with the technology and the financial resources necessary to undertake the effort. The reformist answer is that advanced global surveillance will have to be of global benefit to be globally acceptable and that safety necessarily will be the central purpose. The countries currently outside the U.S. alliance system cannot aspire to create a competitive global surveillance capability anytime soon, but they certainly can contest the legitimacy of the U.S. effort, and if sufficiently determined, they could do a great deal to impede its development. The critical point of leverage is provided by assets in space, which are vital to surveillance activities and also vulnerable to relatively crude forms of attack. To the extent that global surveillance becomes precisely, continuously, and comprehensively accurate, it also becomes extremely intrusive. At some point on the spectrum of development not far from what has been accomplished already, the degree of intrusiveness will introduce the new forms of military interaction that will generate new principles of security. The implications extend well beyond the management of nuclear forces, but the process of adjustment will have to involve those forces and probably will be driven in part by the problem of assuring adequate operational vision for the Russian establishment.

At their summit meeting in Moscow in September 1998, President Clinton and President Yeltsin took a tentative step toward direct collaboration on missile surveillance. They announced an agreement in principle to establish a joint center that would share information on missile launches. The purpose of such an exercise is to enable the United States to devote some of its superior surveillance capability to the mutually vital objective of reassuring Russia at every moment that its nuclear forces are not under attack. The details were not yet worked out at the time the agreement was announced, and they are very demanding. In order to provide reassurance that Russia would be willing to rely on at a moment of serious stress, the United States would have to integrate Russia deeply into its surveillance operations and would have to take down many of the barriers of extreme secrecy constructed in support of direct confrontation. An effort to preserve those barriers would undermine the objective of reassurance and could do more harm than good under crisis pressures. The two presidents advanced this agreement at a moment when their personal authority was in serious question within their respective political systems, and it remains a serious question whether it can be implemented to the very demanding standard that would be required to have a constructive effect. Like the similar agreement in 1994 to share information on weapons stockpiles, the intended effort may not be able to overcome the entrenched habits of confrontation, but like that earlier agreement, its mere existence documents official recognition of the need to do so. The cold war will not be over until the practice of deterrence is revised much more substantially than it has been. That revision would be a vital interest under any circumstance. The internal convulsion in Russia and the general process of globalization make it especially critical.

CHAPTER THREE

Assuring Conventional Missions

The justification of military forces has traditionally been based on the assertion and the protection of national sovereignty. Military forces are understood to be a necessary instrument for constructing a viable state and a companion to consensus for establishing constitutional authority and preserving basic civil order within a defined territory. They are also the principal means of defending that territory against hostile incursion and of protecting national interest generally. In performing these functions they embody the sense of identity and evoke the political emotions that are critical to social coherence. In recognition of their significance for the entire scheme of human organization, the right to assert sovereign jurisdiction and to defend it by force has long been considered the central principle of international security. It was embedded in the treaty of Westphalia in 1648, generally considered to be the founding document of the nation-state system. It was reiterated in the United Nations Charter in 1945.

From the outset, this formula for the justification of security has encountered major difficulty in the actual practice of it for obvious and well-rehearsed reasons. National sovereignty is not an idea that yields a complete or stable determination of legitimate authority. Conflicting conceptions of political identity have generated many battles over sovereign jurisdiction.

Conflicting conceptions of interest have extended well beyond questions of territorial control. The various states entangled in disputes over sovereign prerogatives, moreover, have differed substantially in their capacity to support military forces. Collisions of asserted interest and imbalance in capability have been serious enough to generate a scale of warfare that even the largest and most capable of states could not settle by exclusive reliance on national assets.

In the major instances of conflict between sovereign states during the twentieth century—the formative episodes for contemporary military establishments—the contending forces were organized and operated through national command channels. They also were involved in elaborate coalitions on which their capability depended. That certainly was true for the allied forces that prevailed in the two world wars, especially for the U.S. forces that emerged as the strongest of the national military establishments. The allied operations in which the United States was involved were conducted primarily through other sovereign jurisdictions in response to conceptions of interest that extended far beyond territorial defense of the United States itself. Sovereign states have not been as independent or as self-determined as they would wish or as their justifying principles would require. National security has proved to be a collaborative enterprise.

In an effort to deal with this uncomfortable reality while preserving the primacy of national sovereignty, the UN Charter espouses the principle of collective security. Under that principle, all legitimate states are accorded the rights of self-determination and territorial integrity, and all are obliged to defend those rights for all other states, actively if necessary. This was intended to be a universal principle: all states would conduct their own territorial defense but would be able to command assistance from any other state if attacked. It was quickly superseded, however, by the formation of antagonistic alliances during the cold war period. By their very nature, the alliances extended preferential protection to their members, threatened their designated opponents, and discriminated against any state that did not fit either category. They were justified as the voluntary association of similar national interests, and they were intended to create coalitions of capability large enough to meet the requirements of national security.

It originally appeared that the unique destructiveness of nuclear weapons might shatter this traditional conception by rendering territorial defense a hopeless objective and by making the protection of all interests dependent on global deterrent operations. Reflecting that thought, the phrase *conventional forces* emerged to refer to the entire array of weapons and military operations that were not based on nuclear explosives and therefore were conducted on a scale of destructive energy six orders of magnitude less than what nuclear weapons could provide. Since conventional forces could not threaten industrial infrastructure or opposing military establishments with anything like the same efficiency or operate at intercontinental range with anything like the same speed as nuclear weapons, it initially appeared that they would be substantially replaced by more powerful nuclear arsenals. As the intrinsic constraints on warfare at massive levels of destruction came to be acknowledged, however, the deployment of nuclear weapons stimulated rather than retarded corresponding investment in conventional capability. Global deterrent operations were accompanied by major concentrations of conventional forces in the principal areas of confrontation between opposing alliances—most notably in central Europe and on the Korean peninsula. Their purpose was to defend against the large combined-arms assaults that had been demonstrated in World War II under the assumption that such attacks might be undertaken with very little effective warning and might be sustained despite the superior firepower of nuclear weapons.

Extensive investments were made to enable conventional forces to initiate operations over an entire theater of engagement within a few weeks and to sustain intensive combat from their munitions stockpiles over a period of six months or more—the duration judged to be required to redirect national economies to full-scale war production. From 1950, when investment in immediately available military capability began in earnest, to 1990, when confrontation between major alliances effectively ended, the United States spent $13.63 trillion in constant 1999 dollars preparing its military establishment to conduct immediate operations, an average of $332.4 billion a year. More than 80 percent of the amount was directed to conventional forces. Of the total worldwide military expenditures from 1963 to 1990, estimated to be over $34 trillion in constant 1999 dollars, more than 80 percent was devoted to conventional forces.[1] The working presumption was that the deterrent power of nuclear weapons did not preclude major episodes of conventional warfare and that the threat of war was imminent enough to require continuous preparation. Conventional defense became a supplementary principle of the cold war, as deeply entrenched and as actively practiced as the concept of deterrent retaliation.

Moreover, within the U.S. military establishment, whose capabilities now set the international standard, the commitment to conventional defense not only has survived dissolution of the cold war confrontation but also has become stronger in the aftermath. Under current policy U.S. forces are designed to fight in two major conventional conflicts, notionally associated with Iraq and North Korea, under the assumption that these conflicts might occur rapidly and nearly simultaneously, thus requiring substantially separate commitments of immediately available assets. The number of conventional force units maintained for this purpose has been reduced to levels 30 percent lower than the 1990 base force, but improvements in their equipment and operational practices and the effective disappearance of the conventional force establishment operated by the Soviet Union have more than compensated for the decline in deployed units. The greater capacity of these forces relative to the potential opposition has been translated into a higher standard of expectation. At the height of the cold war, U.S. and allied conventional forces at the principal point of engagement in Europe were not officially expected to prevail in the conventional phase of battle, only to hold out against a Soviet assault for a few days until the overwhelming firepower and sobering deterrent effect of nuclear weapons could be brought to bear. Under the revised expectation, U.S. and allied forces, having ceded territory to the opponent's initial assault, now are expected to win back that territory decisively with conventional operations alone and to do so rapidly while suffering low levels of casualties.[2]

This upgrading of the standard of performance for conventional forces consolidates what is perceived to be a major historical accomplishment. The cold war period was bracketed by two episodes that bore some semblance to the World War II pattern. In Korea in 1950 and the Persian Gulf in 1991, initially successful attempts to seize territory by force were followed by liberating counterattacks organized and led by the United States. Those episodes demonstrated that the traditional form of aggression could occur in the presence of nuclear weapons and that the response would be confined to conventional means. But neither of these conflicts developed into broad-area engagements, nor did any of the others that occurred during the intervening time. Warfare has not been attempted on a continental scale for more than half a century, and the considerable violence that has occurred is well short of the potential that even conventional weapons alone could inflict. Strictly speaking, that fact could be credited to the extended deterrent effects of nuclear operations, to the direct resistance of conventional force deployments, or to the possibility that the major contending establishments were not inclined to engage in major aggressive ventures. But prevailing political judgment does not quarrel with the results achieved and does not question its determinants too closely.

That does not mean, however, that the configuration of conventional forces derived from the experience of World War II and developed over the course of the cold war has been exempted indefinitely from the transforming effects of globalization. Quite the contrary, the context in which these forces operate is changing so dramatically that it seems evident that their central features eventually will be subject to substantial revision—from the conception of threat that has provided their organizing focus, to the mission commitments derived from it, to the operational principles applied, and to the deployment patterns that result. Since no military establishment is in a position to undertake the continental-scale aggression characteristic of World War II and since practical incentives appear to be tilted heavily against such an exercise, issues of efficiency and equity can be expected to overtake the preparations for that type of contingency. Since the more pressing threat appears to be arising from small-scale assault and spontaneous civil violence, it is reasonable to expect that conventional operations ultimately will have to adjust a great deal more than they have. In sheer magnitude, those adjustments would not have as much consequence for the state of international security as the process of progressive restraint on nuclear weapons, but they would have a more pervasive effect. Conventional forces inflict most of the violence that occurs. Their disposition sets the context of most security relationships.

The Balance of Capability

The drastic difference in explosive energy provided by nuclear and conventional weapons has fundamental implications both for the character of military operations and for the process of judgment underlying security policy. Nuclear weapons can reliably produce massive effects with comparatively simple and predictable operations. Although a great deal of coordinated effort is required to fabricate a nuclear weapon and to fit it on a ballistic missile launcher, most of that effort occurs in the process of development, and most of the uncertainty can be eliminated by testing. In contemplating the authorized use of a mature nuclear weapon system, the consequence can be known without much question and does not depend heavily on variable details of immediate context or human performance. The explosive power of the weapon overwhelms most of the situational uncertainty entailed in its use, and a convincing image of an initiated mission can be formed on the basis of a few physical parameters—the number and yield of the warheads involved and the statistical reliability and accuracy associated with their delivery systems.

By contrast conventional forces using lesser scales of explosive power must achieve the concentration and repetitive use of many different weapons to have any extensive effect. The results therefore depend on the many things that affect the detailed performance of individuals and organizations, and those results can vary over a wide range. There is no agreed way even to list all the parameters that might have a decisive effect on a conventional battle, let alone to calculate their combined consequence. The outcome of any conventional battle will have something to do with the size, relative number, and quality of the weapons involved, but skill, will, maneuver, supply, timing, weather, terrain, position, and many intricate details of interaction can override the gross effects of firepower, as has been demonstrated repeatedly in legendary examples. If nuclear weapons operations, in their initial phase at least, can be considered an exercise in applied science, conventional operations are more like a performing art.

This simple distinction reveals the difficulty that confronts military planners as they determine the size and composition of the conventional forces they deploy, as they assess the mission capabilities of those forces, and as they prepare for actual operations. Virtually all of the people who make these decisions are at least subliminally aware of the battle of Agincourt in 1415—immortalized in Shakespeare's *Henry V*—where a band of English soldiers slaughtered a French force that was substantially superior in numbers and equipment and was fighting on its own territory. They are also acutely aware that Germany's stunning assaults on France in 1940 and on the Soviet Union in 1941 were based on tactical surprise and a superior concept of operations, not on aggregate firepower advantages. The refinements of performance are too elusive to be an adequate basis for security policy, however, and military planners do base their judgments on comparisons of firepower even as they admit the uncertainties involved. The conventional force assessments made within the major military establishments are informed by counts of weapons and organized units. Weighted scoring systems are used to devise a comparable metric for the combat potential of observed deployments. Battles are simulated by analytic models that calculate the attrition expected to result from an engagement of forces with the specified firepower potential. The operational commanders, charged with translating raw potential into actual performance, are quite attentive to these quantitative comparisons and have derived some basic presumptions about them from the record of conventional battles. It is presumed, for example, that a substantial firepower advantage—a factor of three or more—must be brought to bear at the point of attack in order to dislodge a defending opponent from an entrenched position. It is presumed as well that a military unit will not fight effectively once it has lost half of its people and equipment. A commander operating outside the bounds of these presumptions might be worshiped if the outcome was favorable but would be vilified if it was not. Very few would choose to run the risk, and those who did would be driven more likely by desperation than by perceived opportunity.

The balance of conventional capability that emerged from the military planning systems using these methods is presented in table 3-1. The table shows the active deployments of the respective alliance systems in 1982, an advanced stage of the cold war when both sides had more or less completed the process of investing in conventional forces that accompanied the deployment of nuclear weapons. The comparisons indicate a firepower advantage on the Soviet side that created a strong sense of vulnerability among the members of NATO (North Atlantic Treaty Organization) but would hardly be considered decisive under a truly dispassionate assessment. As can be appreciated better in retrospect, the allied forces in the Central European countries probably would have been a net burden to the Soviet Union's national forces, particularly in an engagement of conventional forces initiated by the Soviets. But the Soviets felt compelled to initiate any engagement that occurred. Without exploiting the advantages of surprise and without conducting an operation that could be concluded swiftly, the Soviet Union had very little chance of prevailing against the superior economic potential of the western alliance, particularly since its conventional forces could not reach its major redoubt in the United States.

Neither side could be entirely comfortable with its cold war position, and the context of political antagonism created some real danger. Had the Soviet Union ever concluded, for whatever reason, that a major war was being unavoidably thrust on them—as had occurred in 1941—then its military leaders might well have attempted an assault on Western Europe in order to avoid the massive trauma experienced in World War II. But the greater inertia and much slower timing of conventional operations made their interaction less volatile than that of nuclear forces, and the overall balance of discomfort was reasonably equitable. NATO with its greater potential had the lesser immediate capability and had not configured its

Table 3-1. *NATO and Warsaw Pact Nonnuclear Forces in Europe, 1982*

Type of force	*NATO*	*Warsaw Pact*
Military manpower (millions)	3	4
Ground forces		
Total organized divisions	84	173
Divisions immediately available in peacetime	45	78
Divisions standardized for capability	45	51
Main battle tanks	13,000	42,500
Antitank guided weapon launchers (crew served or mounted)	8,100	24,300
Artillery and mortars (tubes 100 millimeters and above, including rocket launchers)	10,750	31,500
Armored personnel carriers and infantry-fighting vehicles	30,000	78,800
Aircraft		
Helicopters		
Attack	400	700
Transport or support	1,400	300
Combat aircraft		
Fighter-bomber and ground attack	1,950	1,920
Interceptors	740	4,370
Bombers	...	350
Reconnaissance	285	600
Naval forces		
Aircraft carriers	7	...
Kiev-class ships	...	2
Helicopter carriers	2	2
Cruisers	15	21
Destroyers and frigates	274	182
Amphibious ships (ocean-going)	41	16
Mine warfare ships	257	360
Long-range attack submarines	60	149
Sea-based tactical and support aircraft (including helicopters)	712	146
Land-based and tactical support aircraft	180	719
Land-based antisubmarine warfare aircraft and helicopters	450	179

Source: William W. Kaufmann, "Nonnuclear Deterrence," in John D. Steinbruner and Leon V. Sigal, eds., *Alliance Security: NATO and the No-First-Use Question* (Brookings, 1983), p. 46. For divisions standardized for capability, William P. Mako, *U.S. Ground Forces and the Defense of Central Europe* (Brookings, 1983), p. 108. For divisions immediately available in peacetime, International Institute for Strategic Studies, *The Military Balance, 1982–1983* (London: IISS, 1983), p. 132.

... Not applicable.

conventional forces for a rapidly initiated forward assault. The Soviet Union could hardly risk a surprise attack, particularly since nuclear weapons were deeply engaged in the situation. The 1982 deployment of conventional forces could be considered a crude and uncertain, but viable, balance of power.

The situation fifteen years later was entirely different. As summarized in table 3-2, the deployment of gross conventional forces appeared to be roughly comparable among the major countries as of 1997, but the circumstances of affiliation, investment, and overall capability were not remotely so. The alliance arrangements of the United States were intact. They had been reaffirmed both in Europe and in Asia and were expanding in Europe. Enabled by these arrangements to conduct conventional operations at global range, the United States had sustained investment in the necessary support services—logistics, communications, and surveillance—that no other military establishment had matched. It also had sustained unmatched investment in upgrading the quality of its conventional forces, most notably in the application of information technology to make conventional munitions more precise but also in the training of personnel and the operational exercises required to integrate those advanced capabilities into combat operations. From 1982 through 1998, the United States invested $1.75 trillion in 1999 dollars in enduring improvements to its conventional forces, as distinct from immediate operations, and continues to do so at an annual rate of around $90 billion.[3] As reflected in table 3-2, that figure exceeds the total of all of its allies. The combined investment of the United States and its allies eclipses that of the other major national establishments. There is no opposing alliance.

The resulting deployment of conventional forces in the aftermath of the cold war is not a balance between plausibly competitive opponents, but rather an overriding superiority established by the U.S. alliance system. The advantage is arguably the most substantial that history has ever seen. The level of conventional capability is certainly the most advanced that has ever been maintained routinely in peacetime.

The established advantage, moreover, can be expected to endure for more than the fifteen-year period over which it emerged. None of the military establishments outside the U.S. alliance system are in a position to emulate either the rates of investment or the scope of effort, and none are attempting to do so. They do not have full access to the technical base that supports the effort and could not quickly and independently reproduce it. It is not simply a matter of building individual weapons that move faster over longer distances and fire with more deadly effect. Advanced conventional force capability has a great deal to do with the gathering, absorption, and effective application of detailed information and with the mastering of all the operational functions involved. It also has to do with collaboration across sovereign jurisdictions. With the United States sustaining a comprehensive investment program and with all the industrial

Table 3-2. *Force Comparisons of Selected Countries, 1996*

Force component	*United States*	*NATO (without the United States), Japan, and South Korea*	*Russia*	*China*	*Iraq*	*North Korea*
Military personnel (thousands)	1,482	3,491	1,270	2,930	382	1,054
National defense outlays in 1996 (billions of U.S. dollars)						
Total	266.3	222.7	40.0	40.0	2.7	2.4
Investment only	91.3	64.5	15.6	14.9	0.8	0.8
Nuclear weapons						
On long-range launchers	8,106	544	8,586	7	0	0
Total inventory	9,255	710	11,900	400	0	0
Army brigades						
Number	36	297	144	264	81	112
Annual investment per brigade (millions of U.S. dollars)	435.9	50.3	23.2	26.4	6.4	4.6
Relative investments (percent)	100.0	11.5	5.3	6.1	1.5	1.1
Navy ships and submarines						
Major combatants	218	471	299	105	...	28
Annual investment per vessel (millions of U.S. dollars)	164.8	50.3	11.4	24	...	2.9
Relative investments (percent)	100.0	7	6.9	15.1	...	1.8
Air force aircraft						
Combat aircraft	1,531	4,375	1,775	4,960	320	611
Annual investment per aircraft (millions of U.S. dollars)	25.9	4.1	4.7	1.1	0.4	0.1
Relative investments (percent)	100.0	15.8	18.2	4.3	1.4	0.4
Lift capacity						
Inter-theater aircraft	364	...	595	...	...	...
Millions of ton-miles a day	51	...	28	...	...	...
Intra-theater aircraft	388	146	222	...	...	...
Millions of ton-miles a day	11	4	2	...	...	...

Source: John D. Steinbruner and William W. Kaufmann, "International Security Reconsidered," in Robert D. Reischauer, ed., *Setting National Priorities: Budget Choices for the Next Century* (Brookings, 1997), p. 158.
... Not applicable.

democracies involved in operational collaboration that has developed over a five-decade period, there is no scope for an opposing alliance with comparable potential unless there is a decisive fissure in the American system.

This enduring advantage does not confer unlimited power or even the ability to impose the type of direct physical control implied by the word *hegemony*. The United States alone would not be able to seize and hold the territory of another state of any significant size. Its available conventional forces are large and capable, but not that large and not that capable. Its global operations, moreover, are critically dependent on the collaboration of allies willing to provide access to installations on their sovereign territory and therefore are constrained to remain within the bounds of purposes that are broadly accepted as legitimate. But the advantage does confer the capacity to defeat any major form of conventional aggression. No state outside the dominant alliance—or within it, for that matter—could seize and hold the territory of another if the United States chose to resist. Moreover, the advantage confers effective initiative on virtually all other security matters. Since the United States can control the projection of power beyond anyone's national territory, it necessarily plays at least a permissive role and usually an active role in any international security operation. As a result, any state outside the U.S. alliance system has a lower standard of assured protection and is more vulnerable to intimidation than the states within it. Any purpose that the dominant alliance decides is legitimate and important can be supported by superior force.

Mission Implications

The implications of this situation are not uniformly global, however. When it comes down to practical details, the balance of conventional forces differs substantially depending on the specific mission to be performed at a specific location. Although conventional military units often are referred to as general purpose forces because they can undertake many different missions, they are not prepared to do just anything that might involve the application of force, particularly not anything major. As with any performing art, a great deal of training, choreography, and rehearsal goes into any exercise, and the effective integration of activity is necessarily done with reference to some designated script. Military establishments can be remarkably adaptive in response to specific circumstances, but they are not adept at open-ended improvisation. Most of their preparations are done with a particular contingency in mind.

During the cold war surge of investment, the contingency that dominated conventional force preparations was a combined-arms operation designed to occupy a significant amount of territory and to hold it against counterassault. Combined arms meant that ground, air, and naval operations were to be coordinated to produce a single strategic result. Having learned the horrors of static trench warfare in World War I and the effectiveness of blitzkrieg operations in World War II, the major establishments designed offensive operations even as they espoused defensive purposes. They did this under the assumption that such an operation would have to be undertaken on short notice in response to circumstances that could be neither controlled nor predicted much in advance. The necessary forces therefore had to be equipped, trained, and continuously poised for their assignment. Much of the expense and the focusing of effort at specific locations was driven by the perception that a major contingency could arise quickly without effective warning.

In the cold war configuration of conventional forces, the Soviet Union was considered a plausible initiator of a large offensive operation even by those who did not credit them with any major imperial zeal. The combination of geographic exposure and inferior economic assets gave them an incentive to attack once they judged that a major war could not be avoided, and that judgment anchored the confrontation of forces that developed in Europe.[4] With the dissolution of the Soviet Union and its alliance system, that confrontation has been eliminated in Europe, and prevailing military planning no longer presumes that a large-scale ground offensive could develop there on short notice. The members of NATO have the exclusive potential to conduct a major offensive but have not even provisionally formulated the intention or prepared the operation. Whatever qualms Russia may have about that, it does not have the capacity to prepare an offensive operation of its own. By default standard planning contingencies have been redirected to the Persian Gulf and the Korean peninsula—the only two locations where military planners can seriously imagine a rapidly developing engagement and where they continuously maintain specific operational preparations. These are the contingencies currently used for judging the global balance of conventional force capability.

Despite the uncertainties that surround ultimate performance, there is very little doubt about either of these situations. Unless the capacities of the U.S. alliance system are withheld or seriously mismanaged, there is no realistic scope for either Iraq or North Korea to undertake even a temporarily successful ground offensive even if they should contrive to coordinate their efforts to do so. In presenting their requests for the allocation of resources necessary to sustain U.S. forces, American military planners express concern about their capacity to handle the two contingencies simultaneously, and that concern is undoubtedly sincere within the assumptions that are applied. As reflected in table 3-2, the gross comparisons of available units do not suggest absolutely decisive capability of U.S. forces alone in a simultaneous contingency, particularly if the initial assault is conceded to the opposition and U.S. forces are given the mission of liberating occupied territory with help only from the local allies. When qualitative differences are considered, however, and when the standard analytic assessments are made, it is evident that the United States does have the basic capability to prevail in both contingencies even under the highly prejudicial set of assumptions used to justify military expenditures.[5] Both the cumulative and the continuing disparity in investment are so large that the operational consequences are unmistakable. Neither Iraq nor North Korea could stage a combined-arms operation. Their tactical air and naval assets are so overmatched that they could not play a major role. Neither country has anything like the capacity of the United States to track battlefield movements and to concentrate firepower in reaction to emerging situations. If the advantages of the United States were applied effectively in either situation or in both, they could decisively stop a ground offensive, and they could, if they so chose, conduct one of their own. As far as military capability is concerned, the most likely outcome in the posited contingency is that Iraq and North Korea both would be occupied in a counterassault.

The more fundamental fact, moreover, is that the assumptions advanced for justifying the level of conventional force deployment and the rate of investment are not responsible guidelines for managing the contingencies posed. In particular there is no operational excuse for the tardy reactions imagined in budget deliberations. In terms of the amount of effort that has to be expended and the number of casualties incurred, it is far more efficient to stop an offensive operation at the outset than to roll it back once it has seized a victim's territory. For the contingencies that are placed at the center of operational planning, that is the appropriate expectation, and it also is the direction in which conventional force operations clearly are evolving. As a priority of its investment program, the United States has developed the ability to maintain what has been termed situational awareness—basically the capability to monitor the details of military deployment both in an immediate battle area and over a broad area of engagement.[6] Naturally enough, that capability is being applied preferentially in the two contingency areas, making it very difficult indeed for Iraq or North Korea to prepare an offensive operation without being detected. And once such activities are detected, they can be effectively threatened or, if necessary, attacked, using tactical air assets that can be mobilized within a few days. The fact that an offensive occurred without preemptive reaction once in each instance is not reason to assume at the operational level that it will happen again. Rather it is reason to assure that it will not happen again, and that determination has been demonstrated pointedly in the Iraqi case.

In the third week of September 1994, Iraq began moving two of its more capable ground force divisions from base areas near Baghdad and Mosul in northern Iraq down to positions near the southern border from where they might be used to spearhead another assault on Kuwait. Added to the six divisions of lesser stature that were already stationed in the area, they created a combined force of 80,000 troops. The United States detected this movement and immediately conducted a countervailing reinforcement in an operation suggestively named Vigilant Warrior. A combat headquarters unit was sent to the region for the first time since the Gulf war in 1991, and some 36,000 combat troops were alerted for redeployment to supplement the 20,000 already in the area. By the end of October, 28,000 of these troops had arrived, including two mechanized infantry brigades, 200 additional aircraft, and twenty warships. Already on October 10, Iraq sent a letter to the UN Security Council announcing its intention to withdraw the two divisions in question, but at the time it had not yet done so. Not willing to accept a statement of intention, the United States initiated a Security Council resolution, unanimously approved on October 15, demanding that the Iraqi forces withdraw to their previous positions. And on October 20 both the United States and Great Britain delivered separate diplomatic démarches to Iraq making it apparent that the reinforcing forces would be attacked if they were not withdrawn. Despite its reputation for belligerent intransigence in defense of sovereign prerogatives, Iraq quickly complied with the demand. In the denouement of the event, the United States made it apparent that Iraqi ground force reinforcements would never again be tolerated south of the thirty-second parallel. That rule supplemented the prohibition of Iraqi tactical air operations in the area, which had been maintained since the Gulf war and enforced by means of daily combat air patrols conducted by the United States, Britain, and France. The settlement did not contest the continued presence of the six less-capable Iraqi divisions, however, conceding the legitimacy of their internal security functions.

The incident reflects the leading edge of operational practice for standard contingencies and is likely to be an enduring precedent. With an overriding advantage at its disposal, with the ability to monitor the movements of major conventional force units, and with the ability to mobilize tactical air assets very rapidly, the U.S. alliance has the capacity to interdict the operational preparations necessary to stage a major ground offensive at the designated locations and can be expected to do so. In Korea that commitment would be more demanding than in Iraq because North Korean forces have been concentrated along the fortified armistice line since 1953. The indication of preparations for a large-scale offensive would not be as obvious as the movement of divisions over several hundred kilometers in Iraq. But much better defensive fortifications are in place in Korea, in effect forcing any effort that is meant to seize territory to a level of preparation that would be visible. With virtually no capability to deny access to its air space, North Korean efforts to prepare an offensive would be vulnerable to the type of preemptive intimidation used against Iraq in 1994, and that is quite likely to be the operational practice if the situation should arise.

Although not yet explicitly stated as such, the prohibition on advanced preparations for a major ground offensive is an incipient rule for the designated contingencies, and it provides reasonably good assurance that the pessimistic scenarios used in the United States for force planning will not in fact occur—not, at any rate, in full form. The degree of assurance is less well established in other disputed areas that have not been the focus of operational preparations, but there is nonetheless a meaningful global effect. No major ground offensive would be immune from preemptive interference wherever it might be contemplated. With residual uncertainties admitted and assuming that the established practice of vigilance continues, the classic problem of cross-border aggression has been handled tolerably well. That is indeed a major historical accomplishment, a benefit of the globalization process.

It is not, of course, a complete security outcome. If the dominant alliance can use its assets effectively to prevent any major exercise to seize territory by force and does not itself pose an imminent threat to initiate such an exercise, the question of forceful intimidation not connected with an immediately threatened ground offensive is much more open. The very assets that allow large-scale offensive operations to be prevented also enable small-scale offensive operations to be conducted. The ability to locate specific targets in space and time and to attack them very precisely over very long range is making the illegitimate occupation of territory increasingly difficult. It also is making remote bombardment increasingly possible and increasingly effective in principle. Small-scale conventional operations directed against airports, loading docks, power grids, phone systems, petroleum pipelines, space assets, and such things are not a means of conquest, but they can be monumentally disruptive, especially to societies increasingly dependent on globally integrated economic activity or to a military establishment conducting global operations. The world has not yet seen much of this form of warfare, but it also has not yet fully absorbed the technology or fully reacted to the strategic circumstances that could be expected to inspire it.

In fact, as the operational leader of the dominant alliance and principal entrepreneur of the relevant technology, the United States has unintentionally created the conditions that might well stimulate the systematic development of small-scale conventional operations by other military establishments. The United States itself cannot be subjected to the threat of a combined-arms ground offensive. Nor can its capabilities to conduct major combined-arms operations in contingency areas be realistically matched. Screened by geographic isolation and by military superiority from any commensurate retribution, the United States has demonstrated a willingness to initiate military attack for reasons that are not confined to the prevention of classic aggression and are not subjected to the deliberations of the UN Security Council. The most notable instance again involves Iraq. On June 26, 1993, two U.S. naval vessels launched a combined total of twenty-three conventionally armed cruise missiles against the headquarters building of the Iraqi Intelligence Service located in a protected compound in a residential area of Baghdad. The attack caused considerable damage to the building and some loss of life, including killing people in the surrounding area when at least one of the missiles missed the compound. The reason for the attack was an alleged assassination plot against former President Bush during his visit to Kuwait the previous April. A car bomb had been found in Kuwait in the possession of an individual who confessed that he had intended to use it against the former president and who said that he had been commissioned to do so by the Iraqi Intelligence Service. Details of the construction of the bomb were said to support that contention. The indictment, which was denied by Iraq, was not subjected to anything resembling the due legal process that would have to have been applied within the United States, but no significant objection to the action was raised either within the American political system or at the UN Security Council. The incident was accepted as a legitimate defense of national interest. It established a precedent.

In August 1998, the precedent was extended to cover terrorist activities not considered to have been undertaken directly by any state but nonetheless tolerated on their territory. On August 7, the U.S. embassies in Nairobi,

Kenya, and Dar es Salaam, Tanzania, were simultaneously bombed, causing more than 200 deaths, hundreds of gruesome casualties, and extensive physical damage. Although no credited statement of responsibility was issued, within a week anonymous U.S. officials named Saudi Arabian national, Osama bin Laden, as the lead suspect, based on his alleged connections with several suspects who had been arrested and on other evidence not revealed.[7] On August 20, the United States conducted cruise missile attacks on an area in Afghanistan alleged to be a training base used by bin Laden and on a pharmaceutical manufacturing plant in the Sudan alleged to have produced at his behest a precursor chemical used exclusively for the manufacture of the chemical weapons agent VX.[8] There was apparently no consultation with the Afghan or Sudanese governments prior to the attacks and no formal process for vetting information and applying legal standards beyond the secret deliberations of a few high officials of the American government. With the bombing incidents a good deal more appalling than a foiled assassination plot, however, and with the Afghan and Sudanese governments nearly as isolated in political terms as Iraq, no major objections were raised to the American operation, even after it became apparent that whatever else it might have done the pharmaceutical plant was producing legitimate medicines, in part under UN contract.

For countries that have not been given the protection of a formal alliance and especially for those that might be entangled in some dispute with the United States, these incidents constitute an implied threat. The right of retribution successfully asserted might be applied to many types of grievance, and the scope of application cannot be readily confined, at least not equitably. The United States historically has been implicated in alleged assassination plots against Cuba's Fidel Castro and clearly would not allow the Iraqi precedent to be applied to itself. At any rate, assassination plots are too easy to fabricate and circumstantial blame for anonymous violence too easy to assign for those to be a practical rule outside of a regulating process. Those without the legal or political basis for controlling acts of retribution have an incentive to seek some countervailing leverage, and small-scale conventional operations designed to produce high-leverage disruption are a promising means of acquiring it. They offer a potential means of either emulating or fending off the unilateral actions of a superior military establishment in a manner that does not involve the operational dangers and the intense political pressures associated with weapons of mass destruction. They have the considerable advantage that they do not cross the major barriers of legitimacy. They are being enabled by the general onslaught of technology that is being advertised within the U.S. military establishment as a revolution in progress. As an available reaction to an otherwise intractable disadvantage, the assertive development of these operations is one of the more predictable consequences that can be expected to emerge from that process.

Technical Revolution

The image of an impending revolution was initially advanced, at least most prominently so, by Marshal Nikolai V. Ogarkov of the Soviet Union in a series of papers published in the late 1970s and early 1980s when he was chief of the General Staff.[9] He had noticed the beginning of U.S. investment in advanced conventional munitions, and he forcefully warned of the potential consequences. He was concerned specifically that the capacity for comprehensive reconnaissance combined with the accurate delivery of conventional weapons over long range would generate a dire preemptive threat to the existing configuration of Soviet forces, both conventional and nuclear. His formulation of a "military technical revolution" was subsequently amplified by American intelligence analysts and expanded to encompass all of the emerging technologies that might have military application and all of the conceptual and operational changes that might be involved in working out those applications. Under the American elaboration, the notion of a revolution in military affairs, or RMA in the currently fashionable bureaucratic acronym, was advanced as a much broader process than merely a response to technology. Nonetheless most of the discussion devoted to the subject has been concerned with imagining how new technologies might alter the ways in which battles are waged and wars are won. And the central preoccupation has been that of determining how a national military establishment might use this technology to secure and sustain a decisive advantage over its potential adversaries in performing standard military missions. As with the advent of nuclear weapons, the dominant instinct has been to assimilate new technologies to traditional patterns of international relations.

The technologies in question involve a wide variety of basic and applied areas of science, including not only those that contribute in some way to the use of information but also those that are producing dramatic progress in the understanding of biological processes and the construction of physical materials. Official planning documents identify six priority topics—biomimetics, nanoscience, smart structures, mobile wireless communications, intelligent systems, and compact power sources.[10] A major intent is the development of small and durable devices that can absorb information, can autonomously perform interpretative functions associated with the basic military process of identification and attack, and can be integrated into networks performing these functions over a broad area of interest. In operational terms, this is meant to provide the ability to discern both the overall pattern and the intricate detail of an opposing military deployment, to extract the combat implications quickly, and to react both efficiently and decisively. It is conceded that these basic aspirations are still in an early phase of realization, but the more enthusiastic proponents of RMA have explored the outer boundaries of what might be accomplished. It has been imagined, for example, that battles might be waged primarily by autonomous machines, with the outcome being accepted as decisive by their human masters, that nonlethal means of incapacitation might be substituted for lethal explosives to render warfare more benign, that reliable physical means might be devised to exercise direct positive control over the thoughts and attitudes of opponents, making even benign warfare unnecessary, and that information might become the principal means of attack rather than merely the facilitator of physical destruction.[11] These and other lines of speculation so far have been received by operational planners with considerable skepticism but attentive interest. They reflect a widely shared sense that military operations currently labeled conventional might evolve in ways not as yet visualized.

As the far reaches of imagination are being explored, however, a leading conception of the revolution has emerged in the practical world of operational planners. It involves the application of information technology in the manner that Ogarkov anticipated, and it was set by the Persian Gulf war with an authority that only combat experience can establish. The counteroffensive that liberated Kuwait was unprecedentedly effective. As of January 17 when the campaign began, more than forty-two Iraqi divisions were installed in fortified positions designed to contest both the sea and the ground approaches to the capital area.[12] In a combined-arms operation featuring superior visualization of the battlefield and the use of precision munitions, all of those forces were either overrun or driven back into Iraq. The campaign lasted only forty-three days and inflicted fewer than 200 combat deaths on the attacking force—much faster and at far lower cost than anticipated by the standard analytic models of conventional warfare based on historical experience.[13] In the detailed assessments that followed, it was apparent that the advanced technologies used had been mastered only incompletely and that Iraq's forces had offered only minimal resistance, but it was generally accepted that the basic character of the revolution had been demonstrated.[14]

In the aftermath of the Gulf war, U.S. military forces have been intent to develop the full capability they had provisionally displayed against nominal opposition.[15] They want to be able to make a large area of contention preferentially transparent. The area in question might be a classic battlefield occupied largely by antagonistic armies, or it might be an urban society embroiled in internal conflict, or it might be some combination of both. The idea is to saturate the area with a variety of sensors that in the aggregate are able to map it with a fine degree of resolution and to track relevant movements as they occur. The information gathered would be rapidly communicated, integrated, and interpreted. The results would be made instantaneously available to the various echelons of military command whose assets could then be coordinated rapidly to perform whatever specific missions the situation requires. Any opposing asset of concern, whether large or small, stationary or in motion, could be attacked at any time by any of the coordinated weapons suitable for the purpose. At the same time the corresponding vision and capacity for coordination would be denied to the opposing force. The official planning documents project an intention "to dominate an opponent across the range of military operations."[16] "Full-spectrum dominance" is said to be the key characteristic sought for American forces of the twenty-first century, and that characteristic is to be based on "dominant battlespace awareness."[17]

Two episodes that occurred during the Gulf war revealed the state of this art as of 1991. On the evening of January 29, 1991, with the coalition's air war against Iraq in its twelfth day and the beginning of the ground counteroffensive still three weeks away, elements of three Iraqi divisions in Kuwait attempted a preemptive attack against the observation posts and relatively small mechanized infantry and armored cavalry units that were guarding the border of Saudi Arabia to the north and west of the town of Ra's al Khafji. Two U.S. marine divisions that were still preparing for the coalition's impending ground offensive were located some 60 kilometers south of that border area at the time, and a major supply base being constructed north of their position was highly vulnerable to the Iraqi operation. The Iraqi attack was not anticipated, indicating that a multiple-division force already in the area could be maneuvered into position for attack without its intent being inferred from observation of its initial positioning movements. Tank columns associated with the assault were detected, however, by an experimental surveillance aircraft then known as the Joint Surveillance Target Attack Radar System (JSTARS), two of which had been diverted from development trials in Europe. The tactical information was used to direct a withering air attack on the columns before they could engage the coalition's border units, thereby enabling those units to repel the Iraqi assault without requiring major reinforcement. That result probably had a significant effect on the coalition's subsequent offensive.[18] It seems evident in retrospect that Iraq intended the assault on Khafji to be a major preemptive effort rather than the brief skirmish it turned out to be, and it did have the potential for making the coalition's offensive in Kuwait much more difficult than it actually was.

During the course of that offensive, however, artillery units stationed in Iraq succeeded in launching some eighty ballistic missiles armed with conventional warheads against urban areas and major military bases in Israel and Saudi Arabia, one of which caused more than one-third of the combat casualties that American forces suffered in the entire war. There was a widespread perception that this action might split the international coalition by provoking an Israeli military reaction, and in order to prevent that, U.S. forces made an extensive effort to locate and destroy the mobile launchers being used to fire the missiles. Of the combat sorties flown by the most advanced tactical aircraft, 20 percent were dedicated to that effort, but they did not destroy a single Iraqi missile launcher.[19] The contrasting experience demonstrated that the actions of ground maneuver units could be detected and defeated, but that the smaller, more rapid, and more readily concealed operations of a mobile missile launcher could not be.

There has been continuous technical progress since the Gulf war, enabling better resolution and more rapid reaction. JSTARS, the surveillance aircraft that detected the Iraqi assault, has completed its development phase and is in active deployment. Five of the aircraft were in service with U.S. forces as of 1998, and they are being acquired by major allies as well. Various programs to improve coordinated reaction also are more advanced. Prudent military commanders throughout the world are required to presume that ground unit maneuvers of any significant size can be detected immediately and under most circumstances could be subjected to air interdiction before they have time to accomplish any meaningful objective. They also are entitled to presume, however, until it is demonstrated to the contrary, that the mobile missile launcher problem has not yet been solved and that the practical limits of situational resolution and operational reaction are an open question. A single-stage ballistic missile capable of firing to a range of 600–900 kilometers might weigh some 13,000–15,000 kilograms and might be carried on a mobile launch apparatus comparable in size and perhaps in appearance to a large commercial truck and capable of traveling over road surfaces at normal traffic speeds. From presurveyed launch sites or with assistance from navigational satellites, it might be able to conduct launch operations and depart the launch site within a few minutes. According to the U.S. government, within ten minutes after launch, an Iraqi mobile Scud launcher could be anywhere within 8 kilometers of the launch site.[20] This implies a detection and completed reaction time of a few minutes to ten minutes over an area that might be as large as 256 square kilometers, if the launcher rather than the missile itself is the target.[21] If the objective is to destroy the missile before it can be fired, the time might be less than thirty minutes.[22] As far as the raw capacity to gather, process, and transmit information is concerned, it is possible to project an eventual capability of that sort for a previously identified contingency area, but it still would have to be considered a distant prospect.

When all the many things that might affect hide-and-seek interactions between operational forces are taken into account, assuming sufficient knowledge to take them into account, it is far from clear that the problem can ever be solved decisively in practical terms. Moreover, yet more demanding problems can be imagined. Cruise missiles, for example, are smaller and more readily concealed than ballistic missiles and can pose yet more difficult requirements for detection and reaction. For all the uncertainties involved in assessing the consequences of rapidly advancing technology, it is apparent that realistic operational capability will remain within the bounds demonstrated in the Gulf war for a period of time long enough to shape the pattern of conventional force development.

And therein lies the incentive for the development of small-scale operations. At the level of ground unit maneuvers, the capacity to detect and react has been established and could be extended to any major tactical air or surface naval operation. For U.S. forces at least, that capacity will become progressively stronger over time. Unless it could be negated through some critical nodal failure or overwhelmed in a preemptive attack, there is very little scope for large-scale offensive operations, and that scope is continuously declining. Neither possibility for overturning this situation is promising enough to provide an attractive strategy to a potential adversary. At the level of small-scale operations, however, the burden shifts, and the scope for initiative increases. Assuring detection and timely reaction at fine degrees of resolution over broad areas is massively difficult, and eluding detection is correspondingly more feasible. At smaller scale there is reasonable prospect for an adversary of whatever size to develop a responsive capability without having to match the investment undertaken by the United States. The requirements are not trivial, and there are significant constraints. A fair grasp of detection capability would be necessary in order to elude it with confidence. The various technologies involved in precision navigation over long range would have to be mastered. Operational implementation would have to be directed to fixed targets rather than mobile ones if the greater ease of effort is to be preserved. But the basic ingredients for a countervailing strategy based on small-scale retribution appear to be available, and it is unlikely that the technical advantages of the United States can be made decisive enough to preclude that option.

The strength of the incentive and its trend over time are open questions, but they are certainly among the most important open questions affecting the future evolution of conventional forces and of international security generally. As yet, no military establishment has dedicated itself explicitly to a countervailing strategy based on small-scale conventional operations to the extent of organizing a technical development program with that strategy primarily in mind. And it is unlikely that the Iraqi incident alone would move anyone to do so. Iraq under the rule of Saddam Hussein was sufficiently isolated in political terms that few other countries were inclined to identify with its fate, and that is undoubtedly the primary reason why the broader implications of the 1993 incident were not contested. The conception of a countervailing strategy remains latent in most of the world, and the possibility is discussed most actively not by those most likely to implement it, but rather by U.S. military planners as an element of the threat assessments they present in justifying their proposed budgets. And in that context, it usually has been associated with the use of nuclear weapons or chemical and biological agents on a limited scale rather than with advanced conventional munitions. Clearly articulated strategic conceptions typically emerge only at the more advanced stages of their technical and operational development, however, and the process is driven at the initial stages primarily by technical opportunity. Since substantial technical opportunity is being provided on a global basis as a consequence of commercial development, there is a serious question as to how it might be exploited. Whatever the outcome of that question proves to be, new features of security policy are likely to be formulated in the process of producing it.

The opportunity derives not only from technology itself but also from the manner in which it is being developed. The basic elements of information technology in particular are being driven by commercial applications on a scale and at a pace that dedicated military programs simply cannot match. The development cycle for a major weapons system typically is measured in many years and frequently extends over more than a decade. The development cycles for major consumer products incorporating information technology and produced in large numbers typically are measured in months and rarely extend over more than a few years. Major industrial products produced for commercial markets, such as passenger aircraft, have longer development cycles than consumer products but shorter ones than weapons systems. All that means that commercial applications have been better able to keep up with the inexorable march of Moore's much-cited law—the supposition advanced in 1965 that the number of components that could be embedded in an integrated electronic circuit would double every two years.[23] As a result of the disparity in product cycles, the basic electronic components used in the most advanced weapons systems are typically a decade or more behind those used in the most advanced commercial products. And since the magnitude of investment generated by global commercial markets is much larger than in any military program, in areas where the end products are similar the commercial versions are a great deal more advanced. This creates a situation in which a smaller military establishment less encumbered by the elaborate bureaucratic machinery of dedicated weapons procurement might be able to adapt to commercial technology more readily than the United States and thus to assemble a sophisticated and intrusive small-scale conventional capability. Such a capability might be fashioned on the basis of cruise missile technology, and the potential for doing so has not yet been exploited to its technical limit.[24]

Pressures for Revision

The United States has both the economic capability and the political inclination to sustain its conventional force advantage indefinitely. In the Balanced Budget Act of 1997, which provided for a federal government surplus for the first time in almost thirty years, the basic defense budget was set at $270 billion in 1998 dollars and was projected to continue at that level through 2002. That level of financial commitment absorbs an appreciable but tractable 3.2 percent of the total economic product, less than the 6.3 percent average for the cold war period, and it is not considered to be either a detriment or a major stimulant to economic growth. Allocational imbalances within the budget have not been resolved, most notably in the level of procurement necessary to replace and upgrade basic military equipment on a steady schedule.[25] That problem involves amounts in the range of $10 billion to $20 billion a year, however—less than 8 percent of the total defense budget. It can be resolved or absorbed without any fundamental change in policy. The absence of what is politely called a peer competitor is often noted, but that has not been translated into any politically significant concern that the national defense effort might be excessive for the circumstances. The most dedicated proponents of the effort, who dominate the formal channels of decisionmaking, are now driven more by absolute standards of capability than by relative ones, and general public opinion basically accepts the rationale that an advantage of whatever size is a prudent hedge against the future rise of some great power inclined to pose a standard aggressive threat. The security posture of the United States consolidates what is believed to be the weight of historical experience, and there is powerful momentum behind it. The American political system, one can reasonably surmise, will not voluntarily relinquish the acquired advantage or abandon its justifying logic—will not spontaneously embrace the implications of discontinuity.

But it assuredly will be compelled to adapt to them. Big environmental shifts can be counted on to have big effects. The question is not so much whether they will occur, but what their character will be and how they will be brought about. The dinosaurs in their time dominated the planet, but their time did not endure indefinitely. Presumably the current situation is a lesser case, but the same questions apply. Presumably as well, evidence of the emerging answer will first appear in those societies most directly and most powerfully affected. If so, then Russia is the prime candidate.

The Leverage of Weakness

Under the logic of contingency planning—a logic as deeply ingrained in Russia's military legacy as it is in that of the United States—the military requirements of territorial defense are determined by potential threats as distinct from probable ones. Since the exact circumstances that might generate an aggressive attack are difficult to anticipate, the ones that conceivably might do so are used for reference, and the range of possibility seriously considered is broader than what is judged likely to occur. For the same reason the available capabilities of potentially opposing military establishments are weighed more heavily than the immediate intentions attributed to their governments. The aspiration is to assure that a major conventional assault never becomes probable by preparing a defense robust enough to defeat any plausible threat.

The application of that standard planning logic to the territorial defense of Russia presents the most burdensome set of requirements of any country in the world. The Russian Federation has the longest and most exposed physical perimeter of any nation-state. Fourteen countries are arrayed along the 19,917-kilometer land portion of that perimeter. Eight of those were constituent republics of the Soviet Union and are still very sensitive about their sovereign prerogatives. Three of the others consider themselves to have been subjugated by the Soviet Union, and many of those that were not, most notably China, nonetheless have been entangled in disputes serious enough to produce armed conflict within living memory. Despite the extensive transformation occurring within Russia, virtually all of the neighboring states still attribute to Russia primary responsibility for the burden of Soviet history. So does the U.S. alliance system positioned just beyond the border area and potentially involved in many of the conceivable confrontations that might arise along it. There are substantial Russian minorities in the Baltic states whose civil rights are not solidly established, and any political dispute arising from that situation has a significant chance of involving the members of NATO. Similarly 22 percent of the population of Ukraine is ethnically Russian and is disproportionately concentrated in the eastern regions contiguous to Russia. The Crimean peninsula has historically been Russian. The relationship between the Russian Federation and Ukraine so far has been managed responsively by both sides, but the potential for conflict is high, and the region is one of the most volatile in the world. In the Russian Far East, a population of 7.5 million people, declining through migration to other regions, occupies a land area of 6,216 square kilometers containing large concentrations of natural resources.[26] The large population concentrations in northern China—120 million on the Chinese side of the border in Heilongjiang—are much closer to this region than are the European portions of Russia, and significant numbers of ethnic Chinese have migrated across the border in recent years.[27] Along the southern border a series of chronic and especially violent civil conflicts are potentially intensified by struggles for access to the large oil and natural gas resources believed to be contained in the Caspian Sea area.

When conventional force deployments are connected to this set of circumstances, Russia confronts at least two major problems that could arise on short notice. First, any dispute in the European area that seriously engaged NATO could generate a monumental problem of air defense. If the members of NATO were maximally energetic about it, they could mobilize within a week or so a tactical air operation capable of undertaking 700 attack sorties daily against targets more than 800 kilometers into Russia and also capable of mounting 300 defensive sorties against any Russian counterattack. An operation of about 450 attack sorties and more than 230 defensive sorties might be sustained indefinitely, generating 3,000 or more attack sorties a week. Given the technical advantages the United States in particular could bring to bear, such an operation could devastate the infrastructure of military capability located in the western portions of Russia. And, second, in Siberia a ground incursion from China, developing over a somewhat longer period of time, could require a response from Russian forces actively prepared for the purpose. In principle China might be able to bring at least forty standard-maneuver brigade units through the 100-kilometer border zone, within which military deployments have been controlled by mutual agreement, over the course of a four-week period.[28] From the perspective of a Russian contingency planner, these two problems could occur at the same time. Moreover, if either or both of them did occur, some portion of Russian forces could be engaged in civil conflict from which they could not be redeployed.

Although Russia has not discussed its contingency planning in much detail, it is evident that some attempt has been made to respond to traditionally conceived requirements. In July 1997 the recently installed and professionally respected Russian defense minister General Igor Sergeyev announced a reform plan for the Russian military meant to preserve basic mission capabilities while conforming with the broader process of economic reform.[29] In acknowledging the need to restrain military spending, the plan provided for a 30 percent reduction in the overall size of the military establishment and a controversial consolidation of its separate services, its regional military districts, and its operational commands. The main thrust of the effort, however, was to preserve or, more candidly, to restore the capacity to perform the missions associated with global deterrence and territorial defense. The target figure provided for the deployed forces—1.2 million people—is a minimal number for these purposes under traditional assumptions, but the claim it levies on government resources documents the underlying intention. The plan for a 1.2 million–person establishment clearly was not designed to fit the existing budget. At a Duma hearing in February 1998 the chief of the General Staff and first deputy defense minister, General Anatoly Kvashnin, revealed that the Russian military establishment projected under the reform program would need an annual budget of 400 billion rubles—the equivalent of $67 billion—to meet its basic needs. The actual defense budgets of the Russian Federation have been less than half of that amount over the course of its existence.

Whatever its fine details might be, it is evident that the 1997 military reform plan is fundamentally infeasible. There is no realistic prospect that the Russian economy will be able to provide the financial resources even to sustain a 1.2 million–person military establishment, let alone to make it capable of defeating quality opposition. The Russian Federation has a population of 146 million people on its 17,075,200 square kilometers of territory, roughly the same population as the United States in 1950. But its 1998 total economic product had only about 25 percent of the value of the U.S. economic product in 1950.[30] Since 1950 the U.S. economy has grown at an average annual rate of 3.3 percent: 40 percent of that increase has been due to growth in the U.S. population and 60 percent to growth in per capita productivity. In the unlikely event that Russia, whose population is not projected to increase and has recently been declining, could match that 3.3 percent annual growth rate, the value of its economic product would not match the 1950 level of the United States until 2040 or so. In essence, Russia is running more than a century behind the United States in overall economic performance and is not even keeping pace, let alone catching up.

Moreover, Russia still faces tremendous barriers to productive growth. The number of enterprises that are operating under market conditions is a small segment of the overall economy, geographically concentrated in the Moscow area and functionally concentrated in the provision of financial services that are, in effect, a capitalization of political influence. Most of the major commodity-producing enterprises still are operating under conditions deeply affected by the old system. Using the network of personal relationships derived from that system, they have set up elaborate barter arrangements that allow them to sustain production under conditions highly buffered from market discipline. They induce state orders for traditional products and use them to meet federal tax obligations. Similarly they provide goods and services for local governments in lieu of tax payments, and they trade commodities among themselves in order to acquire the material inputs they need for their own production. These transactions occur under attributed prices two or three times higher than plausible market values. That practice exaggerates the reported value of the Russian economic product—an effect that cancels out much and perhaps all underreporting of the informal economy in the official statistics.

The most effective Russian enterprises also produce some products for cash sale at market prices, but they consciously regulate that activity well below its potential and are careful not to show an overall profit. Virtually all cash receipts not used for direct wage payments are taxed or extorted away, and cash earnings undermine the ability to negotiate the exchange of products and services for tax obligations. As an insight into the relative magnitudes involved in this process, in 1997, 210 of Russia's very largest enterprises, employing among them 25 percent of the industrial labor force, paid nearly 85 percent of their federal tax obligations—well over the 70 percent average for all enterprises—but only 8 percent of that amount was in cash. The rest was in the attributed value of products delivered and services performed.[31]

Since there is very little historical experience with this situation, no one can claim to understand its dynamics very well. Nevertheless, it seems unlikely that standard macroeconomic policies of the sort espoused by the International Monetary Fund will be sufficient to bring about the transition to market conditions. Deep structural reforms of the large enterprises that developed under the planned economy eventually will be necessary. These reforms have not begun in Russia. Until that transformation is demonstrated, it will not be possible to know what rate or pattern of growth is reasonable to project. In the meantime this transitional situation will severely limit the capacities of the Russian government. As of early 1999 total cash tax receipts for the Russian Federation were running at an annual rate equivalent to less than $10 billion at the then-prevailing exchange rate, and it is doubtful that they ever have exceeded $50 billion. That is a small fraction of what the military establishment alone would need for the barest of basic needs, let alone what would be required to make it competitive. In order to compensate for technical deficiencies carried over from the Soviet period and compounded under the Russian Federation, a military establishment of 1.2 million people would require annual expenditures substantially in excess of $100 billion, with an investment component that is some appreciable fraction of the $90 billion the United States spends each year to upgrade and replace its military equipment.[32] Even with internal barter arrangements taken into account, annual defense expenditures of the Russian Federation almost certainly have been less than $30 billion, and under the severe austerity thereby imposed the investment component of that effort has been disproportionately low.

These circumstances virtually assure that the territorial defense of Russia eventually will have to be conducted on some basis other than the traditional logic of contingency planning. For an indefinite period of time, Russia simply cannot meet the most basic mission requirements of the traditional conception with the resources at its disposal, and the effort to do so will have dangerously perverse effects. Chronic underfinancing of the Russian military establishment inexorably produces internal deterioration—the progressive decay of equipment, infrastructure, and managerial capacity. Although no one has devised a comprehensive measure of this process, there are many anecdotal indications that it is occurring.[33] At some uncertain point in the process of internal deterioration, the degradation of control over large weapons inventories and the austerity imposed on military personnel will threaten the entire process of political and economic reform within Russia and the control of weapons proliferation internationally. Beyond that lies the possibility of massive civil violence. The specific implications of deterioration cannot be visualized as clearly as the standard assault scenarios used in contingency planning; for that reason they are fundamentally more threatening, not only to Russia itself but also to the international community generally.

Given the overriding imperative and inherent difficulty of economic reform, Russia will have to reduce its military establishment probably to a level of 300,000 people or less over a period of time likely to last at least two decades if the process of deterioration is to be contained. At that level it can aspire to preserve professional competence and internal coherence but will not be able to prepare for any major combined-arms operation arising on short notice. Russia will have to relieve itself or be relieved of that perceived requirement. Russia's external security relationships, especially those with the United States and China, will have to be rendered less confrontational and more reassuring than they now are or ever have been. Those are demanding requirements that Russia cannot accomplish alone but can motivate independently. Russian weakness is a determining condition of international security—a formative influence potentially as consequential as American power.

The Implications for Safety

The implications of disadvantage, moreover, extend well beyond the leading instance of Russia. Because of its large geographic exposure and small economic base, it is especially obvious that Russia cannot meet the standard requirements of contingency planning as the United States has defined them. But the same can be said of virtually all countries not included in the U.S. alliance system. For any country that does not consider itself protected by the combined assets of the dominant alliance and particularly for those that can imagine a hostile engagement, there are conceivable conventional threats that could not be defeated decisively at feasible cost. Countries that react to this practical fact will be driven to rely on some variation of deterrent practice involving the presentation of a countervailing threat sufficiently destructive to dissuade an attack that could not physically be prevented.

It has long been recognized that this situation encourages more expansive application of nuclear weapons by the countries that possess them and their ultimate acquisition by those that do not.[34] The first of these concerns already is being demonstrated in the Russian case. As discussed in chapter 2, the Russian military planning system has proclaimed the principle of relying on nuclear weapons to compensate for the deficiencies of conventional forces, an extended deterrence doctrine whose operational implementation increases the risk of accidental or inadvertent actions and thereby degrades overall standards of safety. That natural effect is compounded by the process of internal deterioration. With grossly inadequate resources for training and investment throughout the Russian military establishment, it is highly questionable whether the established mechanisms of operational control are being preserved to historical standards and very unlikely that they are being developed to the extent that the new extended deterrence doctrine would require. The second concern remains more of a potential problem than an immediately active one, but the potential clearly has been enhanced by the nuclear weapons tests conducted by India and Pakistan in the spring of 1998. Those tests were the first explicitly proclaimed breach of the proliferation barrier since the signing of the nuclear nonproliferation treaty (NPT) in 1968.[35] They were not legal violations of the treaty since neither India nor Pakistan had signed it. Moreover, it had long been assumed that both countries had developed weapons programs. But the frontal challenge to what has been a central provision of international security will affect national judgments throughout the world. Many countries are better able to develop nuclear weapons programs than either India or Pakistan, and a cascade of national programs is certainly a technical possibility. If that were to occur, there would be many deterrent relationships rather than a single dominant one, and standards of safety would be much more difficult to assure. It is prudent to assume that any increase in the number of active deterrent forces independently operated would decrease the global balance of safety. That might even prove to be an exponential process, with each newly deployed national force adding disproportionately to the overall risk that some deterrent operation will trigger a catastrophe.

That is not the full extent of the problem, moreover, and not necessarily even its most ominous feature. In anticipating how the incentive to develop compensation for inherent disadvantage might interact with technical opportunity, there is reason to be worried about a potentially dangerous coupling between familiar deterrent operations based on agents of mass destruction and innovative variants based on small-scale conventional operations. The reasons for concern have to do with the problems encountered in attempting to wield a large threat in an unbalanced situation.

In the established conception of deterrence devised as a rationale for large nuclear arsenals, an operationally credible threat of mass attack has been broadly accepted as an appropriate and even as a necessary means for achieving the deterrent effect. The legitimate scope of application has been qualified, however, by problems of proportionality. The more massive the threat that is evoked, the more it deters itself, and even the most limited use of mass destruction agents would be disproportionate to most human disputes. The theory of deterrence has established the legitimacy of displaying a massive threat, but the actual conduct of an attack is much more of a question. For a country attempting to compensate for a large-scale disadvantage in conventional force, this poses a serious dilemma. If the threat of mass retaliation to conventional provocation does not work—and the historical record suggests that it will not in most circumstances—the state issuing the threat will encounter the burden of initiating a military action that is likely to be received not only as disproportionate but as criminally so. There is a substantial chance that, whatever the justifying provocation, an inherently weak country daring to use an agent of mass destruction in a manner that can be documented immediately will be charged with the equivalent of genocide, will lose any presumption of legitimacy, and will be exposed to the worst that the dominant alliance can do. The worst is very bad indeed and will most likely be fatal to any ruling regime and its military establishment. By comparison, small-scale conventional operations conducted with high precision over long range offer countervailing threats that can be quite disruptive without risking the absolute loss of legitimacy. It is therefore much more realistic to imagine that such operations might occur. That type of response probably will not stop a large conventional force operation, however, whereas a limited use of nuclear weapons has some appreciable chance of doing so. Disadvantaged states that are exposed to intimidation and dedicated to developing a countervailing capability can generate a rationale for pursuing both options in strategic tandem, with small conventional operations seen as the usable instrument and a mass-effect deterrent force as the reserve threat necessary to make the conventional instrument credible.

It is difficult to predict how many states might make that judgment and undertake the programs necessary to implement it. The logic involved is not so compelling as to be inevitable, but it is at least as plausible as the deterrent formulations that emerged from the cold war. But as with the business of contingency planning, the fundamental implication of the logic depends less on exact prediction than on the possibility and its consequences. It is technically feasible for Russia, China, and India to develop a two-stage countervailing strategy of this sort with global reach. Over a more extended period of time, it will be similarly feasible for Iran and Iraq to do so within their region. All have some reason to consider it. The outcome of such considerations is not a matter that can be left to chance. Any extensive development of a two-stage countervailing strategy can be expected to degrade the overall conditions of operational safety very severely. The unprecedented intrusiveness of highly precise conventional operations extended over intercontinental ranges operationally coupled with a mass-effect deterrent operation would create a volatile combination—a potential source for forms of warfare well short of a full nuclear exchange or a continental-scale conventional contingency, but highly disruptive nonetheless. However likely that line of evolution might be, it is a looming problem serious enough to induce a significant revision of the conventional force configuration and the associated security arrangements that emerged from the precipitous ending of the cold war.

Catalytic Circumstances

As important as they are in determining the fundamental conditions of international security, the consequences of large and enduring disparities in conventional military capability are probably too diffuse to reshape the configuration of forces directly. There are many ways in which the process of internal deterioration in Russia and the general incentive for countervailing reaction might play out, most of them quite different in character from the standard conceptions of an aggressive threat, which drive contingency planning. At least in the initial stages of adaptation, it will be very difficult to achieve the consensus required to adjust the deployment pattern and operational practices of conventional forces without reference to some specific circumstance that connects to established conceptions of threat. It also is difficult to anticipate the exact issues that might play this catalytic role, but it is nonetheless evident that activities in space provide one of the most prominent possibilities. Virtually all of the RMA schemes currently being advanced depend heavily on space assets for observation, navigation, and communications relay, and the latter two functions increasingly overlap the rapidly developing support structure for commercial activities. Under the well-established pattern of technical development, the assets in question are exceedingly valuable and highly vulnerable. That combination provides very high leverage for the more limited military establishments to counteract the superior capabilities of the United States without violating well-established international rules. The potential consequences are obvious enough and troublesome enough to motivate some form of accommodation.

As of 1998, 550 operational spacecraft were revolving around the earth accompanied by an overall population of nearly 10,000 associated objects large enough (more than 10 centimeters) to be subjected to continuous surveillance.[36] The rate at which new missions are being undertaken has declined from the level of 120 space launches a year during the cold war period, largely because Russia has not sustained the Soviet Union's military effort, but commercial communication ventures are on the rise and beginning to substitute for the reduction in number of dedicated military missions. A total of eighty-six successful space launches were conducted in 1997, including ten undertaken for the commercial satellite constellations Iridium and Orbcom.[37] At that rate the overall number of orbiting objects undoubtedly will continue to increase, as it has with minor fluctuations since the first satellite was launched in 1957. The design, purpose, and orbital pattern of the operational satellites vary a great deal. Particularly for those dedicated to military use, elaborate efforts are made to conceal the technical details. For all the complexity and mystery thereby created, however, the laws of physics and of economics establish several determining features of the situation.

First, space is an inherently transparent environment. Objects in space of the size required to perform important functions are readily observed, and their orbital parameters can be calculated over the spans of time—days, weeks, and months—within which military interactions typically unfold. Official surveillance currently is conducted through a large global array of optical sensors and radar installations, and those advanced capabilities are necessary to track relatively small orbiting objects 1 meter or smaller in size. Nonetheless, the satellites that conduct critical support activities for military operations—imaging, electronic intercept, navigation, and communications relay—are typically larger than a meter in size and can be monitored by more modest methods. They are monitored by networks of amateurs who regularly broadcast their orbital parameters and identify their basic purposes on the basis of that and other generally available information.[38] That spontaneously available service might not be absolutely comprehensive or completely reliable, but it does demonstrate that space assets can be identified independently with sufficient precision to be attacked. With a modest surveillance effort focused on strategically chosen assets, a lesser military establishment could support a very effective threat.

Second, space also is an inherently exposed environment. Assets placed in orbit are highly susceptible to deliberate interference by a variety of means ranging from hostile illumination in some suitably chosen portion of the electromagnetic spectrum, to physical collision at the very high relative velocities that can occur with intersecting orbits, to assault with explosives directed either at space objects themselves or at their supportive ground installations. Standard methods of protection—concealment, deception, redundancy, evasive maneuver, physical hardening, and active defense—can be applied to some extent, but the results that can be realistically achieved are dramatically more limited than they are on the surface of the earth or beneath it. Thirty-two megajoules of kinetic energy must be imparted to every kilogram of material placed into a minimal-altitude orbit—a change in velocity of 8 kilometers per second, requiring approximately 30 kilograms of rocket propellant. That necessary expenditure of energy imposes pervasive restrictions on the mass of material that can be used and the amount of maneuver that can be undertaken. For the foreseeable future, those restrictions assure that the task of creating and protecting a network of assets performing any of the basic services will be a great deal more expensive than the task of disrupting those services. Basically the mass required to inflict damage is much less than the mass required to do anything else. Extreme miniaturization of sensing, storage, processing, and transmitting capacities might eventually diminish the inherent leverage, but those developments would have to be truly extreme and would have to be achieved at implausibly low cost to eliminate or reverse the expenditure of energy and the resulting cost advantage that the attacker would have over the defender in any direct battle over space assets.

And, third, space is increasingly an interactive environment. Although a large area around the earth might, in principle, be occupied by orbiting satellites, the functions to be performed dictate that most of them will be found in one of four basic orbital patterns. High-resolution imaging systems, for which the angle of orientation to the sun is important, are concentrated at low-altitude polar orbits where natural orbital dynamics keep the orientation to the sun constant without requiring the satellite to expend any energy. Navigation satellites use mid-altitude orbits of 20,000 kilometers to achieve a twelve-hour period with an inclination of precisely 63.4 degrees where orbital dynamics are uniquely stable.[39] Highly elliptical orbits with a perigee (low point) at 550 kilometers and apogee (high point) at 42,000 kilometers are used by Russian communication satellites in particular to achieve twelve-hour periods with eight hours of direct line-of-sight visibility in the northern latitudes, and these also use the naturally stable 63.4 degree inclination. Geosynchronous orbits of 36,000 kilometers and 0 degree inclination are used by communications relay and other types of satellites to preserve a fixed position over a single point on earth and a constant angle of vision to some 40 percent of the surface. The desirable slots for operational satellites already are becoming scarce in the geosynchronous band, and the accumulation of debris is beginning to pose an appreciable problem in all of the bands used.[40] Although techniques are being developed to avoid and remove incidental objects, it is apparent that battles over space assets, particularly those fought with high-velocity impact or explosive means, could generate a surge of debris dangerous to all satellites within the orbital pattern involved. In 1996 the upper stage of an American Pegasus rocket exploded, generating 700 objects large enough to qualify for continuous tracking and an estimated 300,000 objects large enough to damage operational spacecraft. Within a year, the initial concentration of this material had dispersed to a nearly random pattern.[41] Space, it can be said, is quintessentially a global environment that may well be the first to compel comprehensive management.

The pattern of space development shaped by these considerations clearly is shifting from the dominant focus on strategic confrontation characteristic of the initial phase, which coincided with the cold war period, to a much broader array of purposes associated with the process of globalization. The overriding priority given to the support of rapid-reaction deterrent operations in a context of strategic confrontation is being progressively diluted, not only by the military's interest in tactical support for more limited contingencies but even more by commercial operations. A substantial portion of all voice, data, and video communication traffic currently depends on satellite relay, and depending on how technical competition with terrestrial landlines works out, that dependence might increase over coming decades. The navigation services originally designed for military use have become integral elements of commercial sea and air transportation and are being extended gradually to individual consumers. Other than for weather observation, which has become a routine global service, imaging systems have not yet been as extensively extended, but it is probable that high-resolution monitoring of the earth's surface will become more important in managing land use patterns and environmental effects and that the resulting information will necessarily be broadly available. These continuing trends have profoundly changed the context of space development. What was once a military preserve for the preparation of massive warfare is rapidly becoming an essential venue of daily life. That change will inexorably affect the governing rules, which are only partially developed. The opportunity for countervailing leverage has as much to do with the working out of regulatory rules necessary to protect the large and diffuse general interest in space activity as it does with the development of a physical threat for military purposes.

The principal implication has not yet been prominently acknowledged but can be anticipated. Space assets are the natural hostages that almost certainly will be used, implicitly or directly, to regulate the imbalance in conventional force capability. They provide critical ingredients for the conventional missions destined to be of greatest international concern—those involving extreme precision and rapid timing over global ranges. If not absolutely necessary for all operations of that type, space assets are nonetheless important enough that their potential loss provides a strong motive for restraint, a deterrent effect not readily discounted. They can be attacked without directly causing any loss of life on earth and without violating any legal rule that has yet been formalized. The dedicated capacity to conduct such attacks has not been developed extensively, but it can in principle be done within the legitimizing context of developing a space launch capability. It is prudent to assume that it would be done if the United States attempted to realize the visions of national dominance that have been projected by the more exuberant RMA advocates. The highly intrusive actions that would be possible with full development of RMA projections and that have been demonstrated in the retribution operations undertaken against Iraq, Afghanistan, and the Sudan and in the coercive operation undertaken against Yugoslavia in the 1999 crisis over Kosovo eventually would generate countervailing antisatellite operations from the countries threatened by such actions. Should that process develop, it would induce commensurately vigorous efforts to impose formal restraints. It is one thing for the international community to tolerate single acts of retribution against a politically isolated country in response to furtive actions generally considered to be despicable or against actions that fit the definition of genocide. It is quite another to tolerate an extended process of retribution warfare in space where even the inadvertent consequences would menace large investments and cause havoc to commercial operations.

In the first instance, efforts to devise protective regulations undoubtedly would depart from proposals to ban antisatellite weapons that were last discussed formally by the United States and the Soviet Union in the 1970s. That initiative was suspended and effectively abandoned under the impetus of the Reagan administration's efforts to develop a ballistic missile defense system for the United States. Any comprehensive prohibition on the capacity to attack satellites would preclude many of the space components of the potential ballistic missile defense system that the Reagan administration especially wished to emphasize. For its part the Soviet Union made it apparent that antisatellite capability would be developed to negate any missile defense system deployed by the United States in violation of the antiballistic missile treaty. Even without that political and strategic complication, however, which remains unresolved, it is unlikely that a realistic technical demarcation could be established in the evolving context of conventional force interactions. Any intercontinental ballistic missile and any space launch vehicle with suitable choice of payload and launch parameters could be operated against satellites. Access to that capability cannot be restricted to currently approved recipients over an extended period of time. Reliable regulation of the potential for retribution warfare in space eventually will have to be based on broadly accepted arrangements for protecting legitimate security interests.

Extended Reassurance

Although it is conceivable that the Russian military establishment might drift safely to a sustainable level without organized relief, it would hardly be prudent to count on that. The odds certainly appear to run the other way. And, similarly, although general disparities in standards of protection might be tolerated indefinitely without triggering troublesome countervailing strategies, that outcome cannot be considered either reasonable or likely. The U.S. alliance system, whose dominant capabilities establish preferential protection for its members, includes only 15 percent of the world's population, and the proportion included will decline over time.[42] Regardless of the exact consequences, minority privilege on a matter as vital as security cannot be preserved forever; eventually a more equitable outcome will have to be fashioned. Under the impulse of globalization, in fact, such an outcome would appear to be a compelling interest of the minority itself, whose standards of protection would be enhanced rather than diminished by the process of extending them.

Principles of equity are obviously not a substitute for weapons and could not directly replace the traditional calculations of relative capacity that have been used to design and to defend conventional force deployments. But equity considerations do affect the determination of legitimate purpose that has always been an essential ingredient of military capability and is likely to become even more important in a world of expanding spontaneous interactions. There is never enough raw power to determine human events by that means alone. The physical coercion involved in the exercise of military power operates through channels of justification, and without the organized consent thereby established no military operation could act coherently or achieve its intended objectives. The logic of justification creates the circuits, as it were, through which power can flow, and the design of the circuitry becomes ever more important as the pattern of human interaction becomes ever more diffuse and ever more intricate. When contemplating the capability for destruction, to stretch the analogy just a bit, it is natural to calculate the magnitudes of energy provided by generating plants and transmitted by high-voltage wires. When it comes to doing something useful, one begins to notice the network of integrated circuits and to ask about their specific purposes. Although there is no accepted way to quantify the contribution that the definition of purpose makes to the determination of military power, it is arguably as important as the amount of explosives available or the handling of information. The rules of legitimacy that regulate the purposes to which military forces are applied have significant practical effects, and they are likely to be an increasingly important means of shaping international security conditions in the emerging environment.

The most fundamental rule of legitimacy for the operation of conventional forces derives from the primacy accorded to national sovereignty: it is legitimate to defend self-determined national territory and illegitimate to violate it. Virtually all military operations are rationalized as a defense in some sense of legitimate sovereign jurisdiction, and virtually all of the enduring results achieved reflect the credibility of that connection. With the advantage of retrospect it seems apparent that Hitler's grandiose exercise of aggression could not possibly have been sustained—that it was from the outset a colossal strategic misjudgment—primarily because it extended so far beyond any plausibly legitimate claim. And the effect appears to hold on a lesser scale as well. Argentina's assault on the Falkland Islands in 1982 and Iraq's attack on Kuwait were less massive violations of the rule but nonetheless were stark enough to trigger international reactions well beyond anything that had been prepared in prior contingency planning. The size and decisiveness of those improvised reactions document the strength of the underlying principle.

If the defense of national territory is the primary legitimate purpose of military forces, then the ultimate standard of equity is the equalization of physical protection for all sovereign entities. That idea is implied by the formal commitment to general and complete disarmament incorporated in the NPT. If the 187 signatories of the treaty did disarm and managed to induce compliance of the four countries that have not yet signed it, then at least as far as external assault and remote bombardment are concerned the territorial integrity of all states from the largest to the smallest would be assured and their broader interests would have to be pursued by means other than the use of force.[43] Since it is obvious that such an end result will not be achieved or even approximated anytime soon, the broadly ratified commitment to disarmament often is dismissed as an empty diplomatic piety. That common attitude misconstrues its significance. The commitment expresses a basic sense of fairness that has practical importance even if it cannot be fully achieved. It generates an operating principle that affects the detailed workings of international politics—if anyone is to accept restraint, then everyone must do so. This implies that there are limits to the legitimate pursuit of national advantage. The practical problem is to embody these meaningful but imprecisely specified guidelines under circumstances where the capacities and vulnerabilities of nation-states cannot be equalized in physical terms within any foreseeable time.

At its very powerful emotional wellspring, that problem is related to the more general one of harmonizing relationships between different ethnic and racial communities, a problem that has been the source of continuous agony and relevant policy. Over the course of its history and at the cost of a massive amount of human grief, the United States has developed inclusive principles of social organization that apply to its internal affairs. It has abolished slavery, has largely overcome the practice of segregation that survived it, and has at least engaged the more subtle forms of discrimination that survive formal segregation. Were it possible to measure the weight of these accomplishments, incomplete as they are, they probably would prove to be a far more important determinant of American influence in the world than the physical capacities of the U.S. military establishment. They are a major element of what the United States stands for and would be a justifying theme in virtually any application of military power.

Despite their underlying importance, however, the principles of inclusiveness used to formulate international security relationships are not as advanced as those applied within the United States. The formal alliance commitments of the United States are based on perceptions of cultural or at least ideological similarity, and discrimination against those excluded is defended as assertively as segregation once was. But the relentless implications of inclusiveness are not confined to national borders, particularly not in a globalizing society. In 1954, the U.S. Supreme Court in one of its seminal decisions determined with regard to public education that separate cannot possibly be equal when there is a gross disparity in assets and that at any rate it is not inherently desirable for any of the separated communities. The same principle applies to international security as well. It is a fair judgment that the United States, however reluctantly and with whatever amount of dispute, will be driven by its core purposes and its practical interests to develop international security arrangements that are more inclusive and less discriminatory than the ones created over the course of the cold war. That in all probability will prove to be a central imperative of the era.

If so, then the implications will require a much more substantial revision of historical attitudes than has yet occurred. If all societies are to be conceded an equal right to protection from massive assault or illegitimate intrusion, despite disparities in capacity and exposure that cannot be removed entirely, then all would have to be granted equal access in principle to the most advanced standards of protection established within the U.S. alliance system, and that system could not continue to be systematically exclusive, as it unquestionably has been. The dominance that it has acquired, it can be said, entails an obligation to aspire to the principle of universal inclusiveness articulated in the UN Charter. States may disqualify themselves for inclusion by violating the standards of legitimacy on which the system is based, but those standards must be truly universal. It is not appropriate to exclude states from the protection of the dominant alliance on the basis of location or a set of attributed characteristics that amount to the equivalent of racial, cultural, or political discrimination. The burden for extending privileged protection, moreover, should lie at least proportionately with the advantaged members. Arguably, on the analogy of affirmative action, that should be a disproportionate burden. Even to state those implications is to make it intuitively apparent that the process of adjusting underlying attitudes is likely to be difficult and lengthy.

Nonetheless, it is not outlandish to expect that process to be accompanied in its immediate stages by visible and consequential shifts in the logic of contingency planning. For members of the U.S. alliance system, prevailing conventional force deployments are more than adequate for exercising a supplemental deterrent effect and for undertaking any contingency reaction that could be required. It is appropriate that the force deployments dedicated to the main designated contingencies be reduced in size and in immediate readiness status and that the annual rate of investment be set to sustain a somewhat more relaxed posture. That has been the trend among the European members of NATO since 1992–93 and eventually can be expected among the Asian allies and the United States itself. Although that trend, like any other, could be taken too far, for a decade and more it can be considered a healthy adjustment, despite the predictable alarms raised by the advocates of traditional contingency planning. Moreover, to the extent that reductions in force size and readiness status are embraced as appropriate adjustments and not merely suffered as a sin against prudence, they will encourage a more important shift in the balance of operational conception. Standard contingency planning relies on principles of active confrontation requiring that large-scale capabilities be rapidly available at all times. The contrasting principle is that of systematic reassurance, whereby military establishments deliberately convey to each other convincing evidence of constrained capability and benign intention in order to minimize the burdens and avoid the dangers of unmitigated confrontation. Security policies always involve some balance of these conflicting principles, even during the conduct of warfare.[44] And the commonly shared interest always has been to enhance the more refined and more efficient principle of reassurance and to subordinate the more primitive and more costly principle of confrontation. Under emerging global conditions the incentive to strengthen reassurance is increasingly powerful for strong and weak alike.

Enhanced reassurance is a vital matter for Russia, and that alone makes it a vital matter for everyone else as well. Russia does not have and cannot reasonably develop the conventional force capability that its geographic exposure would require under stark confrontational assumptions. The country is attempting to cover that vulnerability by the extended deterrent effect of its nuclear operations. This configuration could be dangerously volatile under crisis conditions, and the danger would be increased if Russian forces were reduced to bring them in line with financial capability without changing their operational practices.[45] If those forces were not reduced, however, the process of deterioration would threaten their internal coherence. Any constructive resolution of these pressures would require that both the size and operational management of Russian forces be shifted progressively from reliance on principles of confrontation to reliance on systematic reassurance. The same is true to a lesser extent for all of the military establishments outside the American alliance system. At the moment Russia is the only country where contingency planning for conventional forces has serious and immediate implications for internal coherence and for the safety of nuclear weapons operations, but there are many potentially troublesome variations of the fundamental problem. To the extent that India and Pakistan develop active nuclear weapons deployments in the context of their regional confrontation, as both have promised to do, they will present additional instances.

Provisions for reassurance have been developed most extensively in the relationships among members of the U.S. alliance system, where there is continuous operational engagement of deployed forces and an extensive exchange of information involving current and projected levels of deployment, budget allocations, technical development projects, intelligence assessments, operational plans, and virtually all of the other matters involved in managing military forces. The national command channels remain intact and protect their innermost deliberations, but the deployed forces are so interpenetrated that they have intimate knowledge of each other and are able to exercise mutual influence in considerable detail. The overall effect is that some of the deepest and most violent historical antagonisms have been subordinated—most notably, those that have occurred among the United States, Britain, France, Germany, and Japan. This has not prevented spirited political disagreements from arising among these countries, but it has established an overriding presumption that they will not attack one another even though they are capable of doing so. They are reassured in detail about that presumption on a daily basis, and the exercise of reassurance pervades their operational practices. They do not visibly display a deterrent capability against one another or prepare conventional contingency reactions. To be sure, all of this was developed in the context of conducting an active confrontation against a common external opponent, but it defines the most advanced practice of reassurance and has become in its own right a major feature of current international security arrangements.

Less-extensive provisions for reassurance regarding conventional force deployments also have been developed as a means of moderating rather than replacing direct confrontation. The major instrument for this purpose—the conventional armed forces in Europe (CFE) treaty—asserts "an obligation to refrain . . . from the threat or use of force against the territorial integrity or political independence of any State" and commits its thirty signatories to the objective of "eliminating . . . the capability for launching surprise attack and for initiating large-scale offensive action." With those purposes in mind the treaty sets overall ceilings and area limitations on five categories of military equipment that would be used in any major ground offensive—tanks, armored combat vehicles, combat aircraft, artillery, and attack helicopters—with associated rules for reporting and inspection designed to document compliance. An associated agreement considered to be politically binding but not legally ratified establishes corresponding ceilings on military manpower. Almost 51,000 individual weapons were removed from active service in the course of implementing the treaty:

— 19,456 tanks,
— 9,417 artillery,
— 19,305 armored combat vehicles,
— 332 helicopters, and
— 2,434 aircraft.

Most of these weapons were destroyed under formal observation, and basic compliance with the limitations has been achieved.[46] In 1999 the parties to the treaty finalized an agreement to transform the original arrangement, which was based on the two cold war alliance systems, into one that imposes individual ceilings on each of the thirty signatory states generally at lower levels than the original ceilings.

This treaty establishes a framework of meaningful restraint but does not create a standard of protection commensurate with NATO membership. The CFE treaty limitations do not eliminate NATO's capacity to conduct a highly debilitating tactical air offensive against Russia or against any of the other parties to the CFE treaty that do not belong to the alliance, and they do not apply to Asia at all. Nor do they eliminate Russia's potential for intimidating its smaller neighbors within Europe. Some of those neighbors, including especially Ukraine, have been assured that they will not be subjected to any hostile NATO operation, but they have not received the guarantee against other sources of assault that applies within NATO. Transformation of the CFE treaty into a multinational arrangement has not been accompanied by any provisions compensating signatories for their disparities in capability. The treaty codifies an intermediate practice of reassurance that is not sufficient to displace the confrontational requirements of contingency planning and does not create an equitable arrangement.

Apart from the difficulty of overcoming entrenched attitudes of discrimination and the corresponding resentment they inspire, there is no fundamental reason why the more advanced standards of reassurance practiced within NATO cannot be extended with mutual benefit. For the advantaged, it is a matter of efficiency. Just as it is much easier to preempt an aggressive military operation that eventually could be defeated, so it is more efficient to preclude the circumstances under which such an operation might be prepared. Reassurance is a matter of enabling preemptive reaction earlier in the sequence of a developing confrontation before it has to be characterized as a preemptive reaction. For the disadvantaged, it is a matter of effectiveness as well. Territorial defense is far more assured, at whatever cost, if the capacities of the dominant alliance are involved than if they are not. During the course of the cold war, it was presumed that political ideology and the impulse to impose imperial rule so overrode the legitimate concern for territorial defense that it was categorically impossible to extend reassurance across the division of alliances. It certainly was not accomplished. Some hard-line adherents to the realist school come close to arguing that the properties of great power status preclude the general extension of reassurance, whatever the reigning ideology might be. If the process of globalization means anything, however, it assuredly means that the comprehensive extension of reassurance will have to be attempted before it is declared impossible. The obvious deal is for the stronger states to provide protection and the weaker states to provide access so that the legitimate missions associated with territorial defense can be accomplished more efficiently and more safely. If that were the general practice, as it is within the U.S. alliance system, then large-scale contingencies could not arise on short notice for anyone.

A serious attempt to develop an arrangement of this sort would involve more than simply issuing a declaration of principle, which, at any rate, the UN Charter and the NPT already provide. It would involve working out the detailed provisions of cooperative engagement between operational forces in the specific circumstances where it matters most. Since Russia presents the most acute problem, that country would constitute the most definitive case—the venue where the most demanding and most comprehensive set of requirements are encountered. But North Korea, Taiwan, Iraq, and Kashmir are significant as well. These situations present common themes and generally applicable principles. In all these instances, the routine surveillance and active defense of airspace is probably the single most important operational activity determining whether a pattern of confrontation or reassurance prevails, and the management of brigade-size ground force maneuver units would be the most significant supplementary determinant. For Russia, North Korea, Taiwan, and Iraq the management of naval and air assets covering the close sea approaches would have to be included. The relevant details have not been developed for any of these cases. They are perhaps most advanced in application to Iraq, where they have been imposed by force—have had to be imposed, most would say—with virtually no provision for the reciprocal application necessary to establish their legitimacy within Iraq. The current practice of reassurance is incomplete, and its extension is inchoate at best. It nonetheless is likely to emerge as the central organizing theme shaping the evolution of conventional forces.

The North Korean situation appears to be the most obvious and most likely venue for further development of the theme. It is increasingly evident that North Korea cannot sustain indefinitely the active conventional force confrontation that has existed for fifty years. Despite its proclaimed ideology of self-reliance and the extensive efforts made to adhere to that standard, North Korea's economic and security policies both depended on outside support from Russia and China derived under the circumstances of the cold war. Neither of these policies is viable outside of that context. Its conventional forces have one major item of military leverage—more than 260 artillery batteries, many maintained in hardened positions, within firing range of Seoul.[47] The most meaningful measure of reassurance that North Korea could undertake would be to remove those weapons to positions from which they could not strike South Korea. Since that is the primary threat they pose, the corresponding measures of reassurance they receive in exchange would have to be comprehensive to produce an equitable result—basically a guarantee of protection issued by the U.S. alliance system physically manifested in a new configuration of deployment. That could involve the stationing of American forces in the current demilitarized zone. A comprehensive arrangement of that sort undoubtedly would include a substantial reduction and more benign deployment of North Korean ground infantry as well as artillery units. It also would include substantial provisions for operational transparency. There has been no indication in the public record that such an arrangement has been officially discussed, but it certainly could be designed, and it might emerge as a major exercise of reassurance not only for the Korean peninsula but for the surrounding region as well.

It is much more venturesome to speculate that such an exercise involving the U.S. alliance system might be extended to Siberia, but if that were to be done it would have greater global significance. There is no immediately acute problem to inspire such an effort, and the regional states themselves have developed explicit measures of reassurance that appear adequate to prevent border clashes of the sort that occurred in the 1960s and 1970s over disputed river islands. The Soviet Union and China completed an agreement in 1991 legally demarcating most of their 4,300-kilometer eastern border, and a second agreement between Russia and China in 1994 formalized the shorter western border. Three of the disputed islands were not covered by these agreements, but the danger of active conflict over them is regulated by restrictions on military deployment in the border areas and a set of associated transparency arrangements established by an agreement in 1996 among Russia, China, Kazakhstan, Kyrgyzstan, and Tajikistan.[48] Constructive as they are, however, these arrangements are not sufficient to remove from Russia the burden of contingency planning for the defense of Siberia, and Russian conventional forces are not sufficient to meet the standard planning criteria. Russia's compensating reliance on nuclear weapons for the defense of Siberia under a doctrine of extended deterrence sets an important constraint on the prospects for achieving an inherently safer configuration of its nuclear forces. It also imposes operational pressures that could be dangerous in any situation of apparently imminent confrontation in the region. One can discount heavily the possibility of such a situation arising from deliberately aggressive policies in either Russia or China. One cannot discount so heavily the possibility of significant trouble emerging from spontaneous migrations of population.

The principal provisions of a more robust extended reassurance arrangement for Siberia are much less evident than they are for Korea, and some major conceptual and institutional innovation undoubtedly would be required to develop the idea. One possibility would be to extend CFE treaty provisions to the region as a means of establishing agreed ceilings on military forces and operational transparency rules not merely for the border areas but for the region as a whole. That would have both the virtue and the difficulty of engaging China in the more advanced arrangements devised for Europe, and it would provide a natural context for justifying U.S. involvement. Another complementary possibility would be to create a regional development commission designed to provide major investment assets but also agreed guidelines for employment practices, environmental management, and infrastructure development. The transparency and policy coordination involved in an institutionalized activity of that sort could preempt many of the potential sources of conflict and might be even more important than the direct regulation of military forces.

In the end, a wealth of substantive detail and institutionalized procedure in areas of potential conflict among conventional forces is necessary to make the principle of reassurance effective, and that is not readily reduced to a summary form corresponding to tables of force balances. But in the beginning—and, in the critical areas of contention, the state of the art is still embryonic—it is the concept itself that begs for recognition.

CHAPTER FOUR

Containing Civil Violence

Security policies traditionally have made a sharp distinction between organized forms of warfare conducted by legitimately established military forces and civil violence perpetrated by individuals and illicit organizations. Warfare is designed to be systematically intentional. It involves explicitly conceived operations prepared or undertaken in order to accomplish some visualized outcome. It also is conducted primarily between designated combatants who are distinguished from civilian populations. Civil violence is more spontaneous, less calculated, and less discriminating. It principally involves citizens rather than soldiers. And although some motivating purpose and intended outcome usually can be attributed to the individual events involved, the overall rate of occurrence and the social consequences inflicted usually are not considered to be deliberate. Civil violence may have a coherent underlying cause, but rarely an organized intent.

Under existing international rules, civil violence generally is assumed, virtually by definition, to be a phenomenon generated primarily from within the society in which it occurs, and legal responsibility for managing it is assigned exclusively to the sovereign entity legitimately representing that society. In addition most societies reinforce that legal distinction with an institutional one. Primary jurisdiction for responding to internal violence generally is given to local police units rather than national military forces, a division of purpose that is widely considered to be an important means of protecting democratic government against the misuse of military power. The feasibility of that division rests on the normally valid presumption that civil violence occurs on a lesser scale than organized warfare and is not systematically concentrated at locations that have strategic consequence for the society as a whole.

In part because this distinction between organized warfare and civil violence has been drawn so sharply in conceptual, legal, and institutional terms, intermediate instances of conflict that cannot be assigned readily to either category historically have caused a great deal of difficulty. Dedicated dissidents incapable of undertaking a standard military campaign but able to sustain a political cause repeatedly have demonstrated the effectiveness of stealthy guerrilla operations against formal military and police units conducted from an organizational base within the society whose policy or distribution of power is being contested. The pattern of violence generated is certainly deliberate and usually involves some expressed purpose. It is not symmetrical, particularly not when there is a large disparity in the capacity of those involved. Although some instances do approximate standard battles between similar combatants for the control of some asset, the more troublesome variants involve assaults on unarmed and unprotected victims where violence is itself the immediate purpose. An important subset of what are broadly labeled terrorist actions fits this pattern. Conflict of this sort rarely matches the physical destructiveness of standard warfare, but it can have devastating effects on living conditions.

The difficulty of controlling these intermediate forms of violence was the most painfully demonstrated defect of the cold war security arrangement. Some 22 million people were killed over the course of the cold war in conflicts that were contained largely within the jurisdiction of a single sovereign state.[1] Many of those conflicts did not have the symmetrically organized characteristics of standard warfare and might be called communal to reflect their intermediate character. In one of the earliest and most gruesome instances, a massive dislocation of populations produced an estimated 800,000 violent deaths in India from 1946 to 1948 in the aftermath of establishing its formal independence and the negotiated separation of Pakistan.[2] Britain, as the retiring colonial power, was precluded from attempting an intervention of the size required to contain the violence, and the embryonic UN Security Council, with its major members entangled in the formative stages of their cold war confrontation, was not remotely in position to contemplate such a venture.[3] By default a precedent was set that social convulsions on that scale were not a prime concern or direct responsibility of the international community and were not a fundamental qualification to the claim of national sovereignty. In later instances, with the contending alliances more fully developed, a yet more permissive rule was implicitly established. Numerous communal conflicts were sustained by the respective alliances through indirect assistance in the form of weapons supplies, financing, training, and clandestine participation. Those conflicts became proxy battles in what was conceived to be a global struggle for allegiance. In Mozambique between 1981 and 1994, that process interacted with South Africa's violent efforts to preserve minority rule with particularly devastating consequences. More than a million people died, an estimated 95 percent of them civilians, with damage done to the process of economic development that is measured in decades. In other instances conceded to be driven more by internal forces, somewhere between 1.5 million and 2 million civilians have been killed in two civil wars in the Sudan extending over nearly four decades, and a comparable number died in Cambodia in a four-year period in the late 1970s as a result of murderous repression systematically imposed by the government on its own citizens.[4]

Eventually Vietnam forcefully contained the violence in Cambodia but was not given an international mandate to do so or thanked for its efforts after the fact, particularly not by the United States or its allies. The dominant legacy of the cold war on the subject of direct international intervention in civil conflict was set by the U.S. experience in Vietnam and the Soviet experience in Afghanistan, episodes that are estimated to have produced 2 million and 1.5 million casualties, respectively.[5] In both cases the interventions were conceived primarily as an exercise in strategic positioning rather than as an attempt to control violence for the sake of doing so. And for both, the results were judged to be disastrous beyond any doubt, an error of policy never again to be repeated. Throughout the period, international efforts were made to assist the individual victims of internal conflicts, but the right of humanitarian intervention—the qualification of sovereign prerogative with the deepest legal roots—was not asserted for the purpose of stopping them. Nor was the Genocide Convention applied to the conflicts that occurred after it was promulgated in 1948. Scholars of the subject have estimated that more than 10 million people have died under circumstances that would appear to trigger the international commitment expressed in the convention to prevent, suppress, and punish acts of genocide, but it was not evoked in any of the major instances.[6]

With a single alliance system now dominating the capacity to conduct major military operations, there is less reason than there was during the cold war to fear that episodes of communal violence might inadvertently trigger standard forms of warfare. A truly spontaneous outbreak that happened to affect deterrent force interactions could generate a serious problem, as could one that occurred at critical points of engagement in the Persian Gulf or on the Korean peninsula. But the heavily skewed balance of capability, reduced expectations of global conflict, and operational legacy of the cold war clearly have diminished the potential for that particular catalytic effect. Moreover, the contest for allegiance is a great deal more muted, and the means used to pursue it have more to do with money than with weapons. The major military establishments, the governments that direct them, and the electorates that empower the governments have emerged from their cold war experience not fundamentally inclined to become involved in problems of communal violence and not systematically poised to react to them. In particular the control of such violence has not been established as a central mission for the U.S. military establishment, whose support capabilities are necessary for virtually any long-distance military operation of significant size. As a practical matter, U.S. involvement in several relevant episodes—most notably in Bosnia, Haiti, Kosovo, and Somalia—has produced a substantial amount of experience that is now reflected in military training and in operational doctrine, but that activity has remained clearly subordinate to preparations for the standard contingency missions.

The most revealing measure of this legacy was provided by the massive outbreak of communal violence in Rwanda in April 1994 following a fatal attack on an aircraft carrying the presidents of Rwanda and Burundi as it was attempting to land in the capital area. That event initiated a violent assault undertaken by political extremists belonging to the majority Hutu community against moderate politicians of the same community and against all people identified with the minority Tutsi community. The population of Rwanda at the time was 85–90 percent Hutu, 9–14 percent Tutsi, and 1 percent Twa, with the Tutsi generally considered the historical elite.[7] The immediate purpose of the assault was to preempt the imminent implementation of a power-sharing arrangement between the communities that had been signed in August 1993, but the underlying intent involved a comprehensive attack on all Tutsi individuals. This attack fit the definition of genocide as well as any event in half a century. That intent was well enough understood and the principal protagonists well enough known that close observers warned of the impending calamity in specific terms in its earliest stages. A UN force, officially named UNAMIR (United Nations Assistance Mission for Rwanda), that had been formed in October 1993 to oversee implementation of the August agreement already had some 2,500 personnel in the country, including 1,660 infantry troops under the operational command of a Canadian general. That force would have been enough to stop the slaughter of civilians but was considered to be only half of what would have been required to control the fighting between Hutu government and insurgent Tutsi military forces that was also triggered by the plane crash.[8] Instead of reinforcing UNAMIR and committing it to decisive intervention, as requested by its commander and recommended by the UN secretary general, the UN Security Council authorized the withdrawal of its combat troops in response to concerns about their safety. The bedrock reason was that the United States, the only country capable of undertaking the rapid reinforcement required, was not willing to do so. As the crisis played out, Tutsi military units supported from bases in Uganda seized control of the country, but not before some 500,000 to 800,000 people had been killed, including a significant portion of Rwanda's Tutsi population. The Tutsi counterattack drove 1.1 million Hutu refugees, including many of the perpetrators of the original assault, into what was then Zaire. The reverberations ultimately were fatal for Zaire's ruling regime and still generate resonant violence throughout the region.[9]

That episode would appear to confirm a precedent of nearly categorical international disengagement. If the UN Security Council, adequately warned and with an established operational presence, could not commit the single brigade required to save hundreds of thousands of innocent victims in Rwanda, then it seems that virtually no amount of civil violence would generate a decisive response for that reason alone—that is, without some other driving concern such as oil or the perceived threat of a violent ideology to motivate the effort. But the protagonists at the time did not draw such a stark implication and indeed acted in contradiction to it, albeit belatedly and ineffectively. After voting to enable the withdrawal of UNAMIR on April 21, fifteen days after the plane crash, the Security Council tried to reengage on May 17 with a resolution authorizing the requested doubling of its personnel level. And on June 22, having been unable to secure the commitment of forces less implicated in the conflict, the United Nations authorized French forces on the scene to protect civilians and assist humanitarian relief efforts. The United States eventually provided support services. The commitment made and the results achieved were hardly decisive, but they were enough to document discomfort with the consequences of detachment. When President Clinton visited Rwanda in March 1998, he acknowledged that the episode had been an act of genocide and that in failing to stop it the international community bore some responsibility for its occurrence.[10] Minimal as they may seem, the belated reaction and the implicit apology give some hint that the management of communal violence is not entirely a settled matter.

The observable elements of the globalization process suggest, moreover, that communal violence may not be a matter that can be settled by the cold war legacy, however well entrenched that legacy may appear to be. Again, rapid shifts in the movement of capital and in the location of basic economic functions are generating unusually rapid shifts in the structure of employment in most societies and creating areas of endemic austerity throughout the world. With economic growth concentrated among the wealthy and population growth among the poor, vastly expanded flows of information have made widening disparities in basic standards of living and associated cultural differences more apparent and broadly accessible than ever before. Although the root causes of communal violence are poorly understood, endemic austerity and perceived inequity have something to do with it.[11] If their effect proves to be strong, then underlying susceptibility to civil violence of all kinds can be expected to increase as the global economy forms and as the means of conducting it increase. The world is awash in the light weapons that are used to inflict most of the casualties in communal conflicts, and the porous forms of regulation currently in effect are not capable of imposing limitations on the flow of supplies binding enough to restrain even a major instance.[12] These circumstances mean that there is some as yet unmeasured potential for the problem of communal violence to become substantially more serious than it has been in the past, conceivably serious enough to alter the legacy of disengagement.

Admittedly the problem would have to be very serious indeed. Any limit to the international tolerance of communal violence implies some qualification of sovereign authority and some exception to the principle of noninterference by one state in the internal affairs of another. Those are the fundamental principles of the traditional order—the primary rules established and defended as the basis for preventing direct aggression and colonial subordination. Although they never have been absolutely categorical principles, most established governments would consider any new qualification to be a greater danger than any imaginable threat of communal violence. Even those willing to entertain the possibility would find it difficult to imagine an example sufficiently compelling to require a revised formulation of general international principles. Virtually no one would argue that civil violence might be prevented as completely as organized warfare. Virtually everyone would concede that it occasionally is a necessary means of overcoming oppression or unlocking other restraints on social progress. Some would defend even major instances as a natural part of the life cycle—the social equivalent of a flood or fire or volcanic eruption in which destruction sets the conditions for subsequent regeneration. These are deeply established presumptions, and together they provide strong support for the legacy of disengagement.

Nonetheless a potential development is capable of forcing major revision against the most entrenched resistance. There is reason for concern that the process of globalization might generate contagion effects powerful enough to undermine the legal foundations of the international economy and of its constituent societies and that sudden surges of civil violence might occur both as a manifestation and as a contributing cause of that pathology. To the extent that this proves to be correct, then vital legal standards would have to be defended everywhere if they are to be preserved anywhere, and principles of security would have to be adjusted to enable that to happen. Human societies could not indefinitely tolerate any sanctuary for the gestation of a process that seriously threatens the operating rules necessary to sustain a global economy.

The Contagion Hypothesis

In its most familiar application, the word contagion refers to the spread of an infectious disease among members of a susceptible population, but the underlying process of propagation underlies many of the recurring cycles of nature in which one event generates another of the same kind and sometimes more than one. Contagion processes routinely occur at a moderate pace well adapted to normal daily life, but they can accelerate suddenly and rapidly, with sharply discontinuous consequences, most of which are highly destructive. The chain reaction that generates the explosion of a nuclear weapon is a contagion process in the phase of rapid acceleration, as is the chemical reaction that detonates a conventional explosive. By its very nature, an explosively accelerating contagion cannot be sustained indefinitely or even for very long. It eventually encounters or itself generates some limiting condition that halts the process, and in most practical examples this occurs quickly enough for the effects to be highly localized both in space and in time. Even in the case of a nuclear weapon, the process is confined to very small units of time, and the consequences, although large on the scale of human vulnerability, are minor on the scale of nature. Some of the contagions coherently conceived and actually observed in nature, however, are truly massive on any scale. A type Ia supernova, for example, is a naturally occurring thermonuclear explosion generating light pulses of galactic proportions, and the theoretical concept of vacuum collapse defines a potential contagion originating at a single location that might in principle engulf the entire universe.[13] With such large possibilities displayed in nature, it seems plausible to assume that human societies might themselves generate major instances of explosive contagion, and in the case of infectious disease they certainly have been subjected to such events. Although the outbreak of most of the infectious diseases that affect human societies are confined within a limited area and a limited segment of the affected population, a few are substantially more extensive and a very few are globally extensive.

If it is accepted that one violent action can readily generate another, then it follows that civil violence can in principle be contagious, and something like that clearly occurs in a spontaneous riot or the outbreak of an unintended battle where some small initiating event produces a cascading reaction. Normally this is an infrequent occurrence routinely controlled by controlling the preconditions. Governments have long taken care to prevent the gathering of mobs in an angry mood, for example, and to avoid the positioning of armed military units in close proximity under circumstances of political tension. Normally an instance is highly localized, but an inadvertently triggered engagement of the deterrent forces is an obvious example of one that would be massive. World War I is a plausible example of one that was in fact massive. In that instance, a single act of violence—the assassination of the Austro-Hungarian Archduke Ferdinand—triggered an extended and extremely destructive war whose timing and characteristics none of the participants had accurately anticipated. Historical explanations naturally have focused on the background diplomacy and disposition of military forces that set the preconditions for the war and on the deliberate judgments made in the course of prosecuting it. But a distant observer of the episode as a whole could perceive it as a sudden surge of violent contagion initiated by circumstances that even in retrospect are not fully understood and terminated only when the process ran to exhaustion. That is not the conventional view, but it is difficult to refute.

In both of these examples—the conceivable breakdown of deterrence and the actual outbreak of World War I—the deployment of military forces systematically organized for large and rapidly enacted operations constitutes a determining condition for explosive contagion. If it could be established that this is a necessary condition, the problems of communal violence would be largely exempt from that concern other than as a potential triggering circumstance. Although standard military operations can inflict extensive civilian casualties as a collateral result, the major instances of conflict that are considered to be primarily communal in character do not involve counterpoised military operations. Nor are they the result of spontaneous frenzy between individuals and communities differentiated by some cultural or ethnic distinction. The carnage in Rwanda, for example, was not the work of spontaneously assembled mobs and not the result of a general engagement between the Hutu and Tutsi communities with comparable numbers of perpetrators and victims. Although the average population density in Rwanda at the time of the 1994 episode was among the highest in the world, people were not so crowded together that individually generated acts of violence could propagate swiftly and widely among them in a cascading chain reaction.

Unfortunately, however, the direct propagation of violence either between individuals or between organized military units is not the only model of how an explosive contagion could occur, and it is not necessarily the one to which human societies, as distinct from their military establishments, are most susceptible. The more serious possibility has to do with more subtle, less visible, more indirect forms of propagation affecting the fundamental elements of social coherence—the sense of legitimacy on which government authority rests and the basic rules of behavior that regulate routine social interactions. These are imprecise concepts that cannot be measured directly, but they are as important to any grasp of political and social events as the concept of gravity is to any comprehension of the physical world. Whatever the direct motives of communal violence might be, it is reasonable to assume that its incidence is regulated by the operating rules of a society and that a shift in those operating rules, whether sudden or gradual, allows it to occur. The more serious episodes reflect a common organizational pattern in which a relatively small number of armed predators brutalize a much larger population whose normal protection has broken down. These marauding bands, composed largely of young males with tenuous connections to normal social structures and led by people with criminal inclinations, operate outside of normal political institutions to a degree that varies with circumstance. They are virtually always activated by the effective collapse of such institutions. The mass killings and wanton communal destruction in Rwanda, for example, was done by such groups interspersed with regular military units who preyed with impunity on the general population from the time of the plane crash in April to the consolidation of control by Tutsi military forces in mid-July. Although they had been formed by Hutu extremists in the period prior to the event, the sudden activation of these groups reflected the collapse rather than the expression of Rwanda's governmental institutions, and the reign of terror corresponded to the period when no government was capable of exercising normal authority. In other instances, such as in Bosnia as the Yugoslav Federation disintegrated, groups constituted as militia were more integrated into the functions of normal government and produced a more systematically organized form of brutality. In 1992 concentration camps emerged in Bosnia practicing virtually all known acts of human degradation, and in the assault on Srebrenica 1995 there were highly organized executions of thousands of civilians in complete disregard for normal standards of law.[14] If one accepts small indications as evidence, virtually all societies are susceptible to this phenomenon. All can and do generate street gangs at times and in places where legal rules cannot be enforced effectively, and it is at least a strong possibility that all would generate progressively more serious forms of predatory violence at more advanced stages of legal decay. There is recent evidence to suggest that the inclination is a genetic characteristic of the human species as a whole.[15] It seems prudent to assume, therefore, that the combination of determinants that controls adherence to basic legal standards also sets the most fundamental conditions for controlling civil violence. Hence a contagion process affecting the overall balance of legal adherence could pose a threat of monumental proportions.

The stark fact is that not enough is known about the determinants of legal adherence to assess its intrinsic robustness in any society or the degree of threat to all societies that might emerge from the process of globalization. A spirited debate on this topic has extended deeply into the history of philosophy and broadly into the commentary on current events, with one prominent line of thought arguing that human nature is fundamentally benign and another that it is inherently violent.[16] Each strand has spawned variations, with one strand arguing that the institutions of democracy offer general protection against major outbreaks either of war or of civil violence but another doubting whether the general extension of peaceful democracy will be the enduring historical trend.[17] A completely informed and absolutely unbiased referee undoubtedly would rule that the conflict between these contending perspectives and their many variations has not been resolved. At any rate any historical resolution would have to be reconsidered as the consequences of globalization unfold. Several systematic efforts to measure the incidence of civil violence have recorded a decline in the post–cold war period.[18] But the trend of aggregate measures does not provide decisive reassurance to those concerned about the potential implications of an emerging process whose full effects have not yet been experienced and whose indirect effects may be as significant. Nor is the aggregate level of violence the exclusive concern. The intensity and international resonance of specific episodes also matter. In one of the more thorough recent reviews of the topic, the Carnegie Commission on Preventing Deadly Conflict, while acknowledging the uncertainty involved, issued a warning about the possibility of violent contagion. In the first paragraph of its executive summary, the commission stated:

> The rapid compression of the world through breathtaking population growth, technological advancement, and economic interdependence, combined with the readily available supply of deadly weapons and easily transmitted contagion of hatred and incitement to violence, make it essential and urgent to find ways to prevent disputes from turning massively violent.[19]

Many of the members of that commission had been involved in efforts to mediate some of the more serious recent episodes of civil violence and were attempting to summarize the judgments they had derived from that experience.

The warning was echoed by the Asian financial crisis that was triggered in the fall of 1997. Although that crisis was a market phenomenon ostensibly unrelated to the problems of civil violence, it demonstrated a contagion process having a great deal to do with underlying legal standards. Particularly in Indonesia, it quickly generated a serious episode of communal violence. The crisis emerged from an unanticipated interaction between exchange rate policies and banking system conditions in Indonesia, Malaysia, Thailand, and South Korea against a background of strong aggregate economic growth in those countries—an average of 8 percent a year between 1992 and 1995—and macroeconomic fundamentals that were considered to be very good—low inflation, low unemployment, and internal fiscal conditions at or near balance. The core problem was in the banking system where a tradition of loose regulation and rampant political favoritism had produced the predictable accumulation of bad loans. However, that was a long-standing problem, and no one anticipated that it could produce a sudden financial crisis. Indeed up to the onset of the crisis Asian banks were attracting large amounts of foreign capital by offering high interest rates in the context of strong economic performance and also by encouraging the inference that national governments would cover their risk. Although that belief apparently was based on political judgment rather than legal definition, it produced large inflows of short-term debt denominated in foreign currencies—largely dollars—that the Asian financial intermediaries then translated, rather carelessly, into longer-term obligations in the national currencies. That in turn drove up the value of internal assets and made the banking system simultaneously vulnerable in all four countries.

As is now realized in retrospect, the triggering condition for a devastatingly sudden market adjustment was the exchange rate mechanism that all four countries were using simultaneously—an intermediate system between a rigidly set rate and a free-float rate that would continuously reflect market assessments of relative currency values. In attempting to hold their exchange rates within a determined band, Thailand, Indonesia, and South Korea depleted their currency reserves, maintaining what the capital market considered to be unrealistically high values and creating a cumulative buildup of speculative pressures. The international financial institutions, most notably the International Monetary Fund (IMF), did not track this process, nor did they monitor the growing use of overnight offshore credit to manage the internal strains associated with it. The IMF was not aware of total debt accumulation of the countries in question, since the borrowing of subsidiaries in foreign markets was not being counted as international transactions. When the dam burst, speculation against the currencies rapidly eroded their market value. In the space of two months in late 1997, the Korean won was devalued 114 percent against the dollar; the Thai baht fell 140 percent against the dollar between June 1997 and January 1998, while the Indonesian rupiah fell 489 percent against the dollar between July 1997 and January 1998. Although these currencies regained some of their value, these precipitous drops rendered the underlying debt inherently unmanageable and virtually halted further investment. Reacting primarily to contain the financial contagion and to avoid a continuing cycle of defaults, trade restrictions, and competitive devaluations, the IMF imposed high interest rates and severe austerity measures as a condition for new credit, causing standards of living to fall dramatically throughout the region. In evident reaction to the economic shock, communal riots broke out in Indonesia in May 1998 directed against the country's ethnic Chinese communities. In a few days the commercial food distribution system that those communities had long operated was effectively destroyed. In the summer of 1999 marauding militia evidently assisted by rogue army units terrorized the civilian population of East Timor in the wake of a referendum on independence, eventually triggering an international intervention. The full details and the ultimate implications of this sequence will undoubtedly be debated for quite some time, but its obvious features convey a warning. This was an unanticipated, sudden, and surging contagion that simultaneously engulfed major societies and put them at heightened risk of internal violence. At the center of it were the operating rules of the banking systems long treated as a matter of sovereign prerogative. It turns out that disparities in basic standards on that point could not be sustained.

With the exception of the serious but so far fairly limited episodes in Indonesia, the recent occasions of catastrophic legal breakdown sufficiently serious to generate major communal violence have been confined largely to relatively small single countries, and the international effects, at least the readily observable ones, have occurred largely in nearby regions. But that hardly means that major societies are immune, particularly not Russia, which will be subjected to crushing economic pressures for an extended period of time and where the balance of legal adherence is clearly an unsettled issue. In most countries, including the United States, there are incipient reflections of legal decay—areas where at least at certain times individuals cannot rely on basic legal standards for protection. It is questionable whether any society can afford to be categorically confident about its ability to preserve those standards under the pressures of globalization. Any sustained breakdown of legal jurisdiction in any part of the world provides both a stimulus and a redoubt for criminal organizations—a profitable opportunity for smuggling weapons, a base for conducting the drug trade, a venue for training terrorists. Those organizations can and do extend their activities well beyond the areas of immediate conflict. No one of them alone is likely to pose a significant global threat, but the overall process of criminalization might well do so.

Taking all of this into account, the contagion hypothesis in its more sophisticated form posits that, with intensifying interactions occurring across all societies, the global balance of legal adherence might be subject to suddenly accelerating degeneration if access to economic opportunity does not expand in reasonable balance with population dynamics or if antagonism rather than adaptation is the more prominent reaction to dramatically increased cultural exposure. Were strains of that sort to accumulate, civil violence might be the visible manifestation of the underlying process, but much more than violence itself would be at stake. A rapidly progressing degeneration of legal standards would endanger essential determinants of economic performance and social coherence.

In terms of bare logic with no emotional coloring, that image of contagion might well be considered as plausible as the traditionally postulated threats of deliberate aggression and as even more ominous. If such a process were to start, it is not at all clear how it would end or what its natural limits would be. Without a more compelling demonstration than has yet occurred, it seems unlikely that natural contagion could match or replace organized aggression as an organizing concept of threat. A diffuse process does not evoke the emotional resonance of a designated opponent and does not provide as strong a unifying focus. Nonetheless whatever its exact degree of validity or immediate practical status, the contagion hypothesis does identify a major implication of the globalization process. The emerging problems of security, it is prudent to assume, are not merely and not even primarily about the defense of territory; they concern more generally the defense of vital legal standards.

Common Standards

That supposition has extensive implications for the configuration of military forces, beginning with their most basic conceptions of their missions and extending through to the most intricate details of equipment, training, and operational design. The exercise of seizing or defending territory in conflict with a commensurate opponent is different from that of preempting the breakdown of legal order or restoring it once that has happened. To be sure, at the extreme, the one problem can be reduced to the other by brute force. The complete occupation of a country, defeat of its military establishment, and forceful replacement of its government does enable legal order to be imposed thereafter. If that is done with reasonable judiciousness, the results can be successful, as they were in Germany and

Japan in the wake of World War II. But if the problem emerges from a diffuse global process rather than from a particular belligerent government, then more refined and more broadly applicable methods are required. These generally involve much less force applied much more rapidly and in a much more discriminating manner. The brigade that was judged to be required in the Rwanda situation, for example, would have had to conduct some standard field operations to fix the positions and control the movements of Hutu government and insurgent Tutsi military units, but the essence of the problem was the timely arrest of probably less than 100 individuals who were the principal organizers of the violence—a police function that military units would have had to perform.[20] Beyond that, most of the task involved reassuring the general population that their physical safety would be equitably protected and that the exercise of basic protection would not be extended to the imposition of political rule. Information and legitimacy are much more critical assets than firepower in such a situation, for the simple reason that it is critical to inspire voluntary collaboration from most members of the affected population. Otherwise the amount of coercion required would begin to approximate the brute force method.

Under the presumption that military forces are not to be involved in matters of civil violence, they generally have not been mandated to prepare refined operations for the purpose of defending or restoring legal order and have not done so with the systematic effort devoted to standard military missions. In particular, the capacity to perform police functions has not been developed systematically, and the foundations of political support for intervention missions with this purpose have not been established.[21] These are not matters that can be improvised on short notice. The U.S. military did have ready brigades that were flexible enough to undertake initial pacification of the Rwanda situation even though they had not anticipated it. But the United States as a whole did not have the concept of interest necessary to justify the effort or the capability for extended consolidation. In that sense, the country was unprepared to respond when the situation arose. Of all the missing ingredients, the foundations of justification would appear to be the most critical. If the reasons to do so were recognized and accepted, military operations certainly could be adapted and supplementary capabilities could be developed to undertake an assertive defense of vital legal standards.

Under prevailing international rules, the management of civil violence is based on the principles of sovereign jurisdiction and nonintervention.[22]

The legislative actions of a legitimately established nation-state are considered to be the principal and most authoritative source of law for a given society, and formally enacted statutes are generally given priority over the broader moral standards, largely based on religion, that span national jurisdictions. Responsibility for defining and implementing internal law is left to the society itself and is protected from outside interference. That basic formulation was qualified from the very beginning of the nation-state system, however, by an asserted right of humanitarian intervention acknowledging that all societies have some stake in each other. Over the course of the current century and particularly in recent decades, that qualification has been appreciably elaborated.[23] In its initial declaration of purpose, the UN Charter speaks of the importance of defending "the principle of equal rights and the self-determination of peoples" and manages in various passages to suggest that its sovereign members are to uphold common standards having to do with the composition of their laws, the procedures they use in establishing them, and their effectiveness in enforcing them.[24] The Universal Declaration of Human Rights promulgated by vote of the UN General Assembly in 1948 enumerates these common standards, and two supplementary covenants on human rights adopted in 1966 attempt to embody the main provisions of the universal declaration in treaty obligations covering economic, social, and cultural rights in one document and civil and political rights in the other.[25] Although national sovereignty remains the reigning principle both in practical and in formal legal terms, the aspiration to extend universal standards of legal protection to all individuals imposes a clear constraint on the doctrine. In principle the concept of sovereignty already has evolved to encompass not only the right to be protected from outside interference but also the obligation to uphold universal legal standards.[26] And, again in principle, it is a natural extension of this development to make the right of protection contingent on the effective exercise of this fundamental obligation.

In practice the connection between sovereign rights and sovereign responsibilities has not been solidly established or operationally enforced. Nation-states that are generally accepted as legitimate have effective legal autonomy within their own society, and this has produced differing standards of legal protection for their citizens. It is possible that the underlying processes of economic globalization and intensifying cultural interactions eventually will harmonize these standards, but presumably this will occur over a very extended period. Most immediately the issue of common legal standards and the locus of responsibility for defending them is posed by the instances of radical breakdown. It is one thing to accept substantial variation across societies in the degree of protection that citizens routinely enjoy and quite another to absorb the cascading violence that occurs when a national legal system fails and cannot be regenerated from within. If there is widespread potential for radical legal disintegration under emerging international circumstances, then a practical doctrine of sovereign responsibility will have to be developed to accompany the rhetorical aspirations that already have been expressed. Such a doctrine would impose a serious requirement on recognized members of the nation-state system to preserve the most basic legal standards within their jurisdiction and a residual obligation on the international community as a whole to do so if a member state fails to meet the requirement.

Some demanding ingredients would have to be assembled in order to establish a practical doctrine of sovereign responsibility. From the broad array of human rights that have been asserted, a critical subset would have to be identified that are so fundamental and so broadly accepted that their preservation can be made a condition of sovereignty and their sustained violation a justification for the intrusive assertion of international authority. Similarly the conditions would have to be identified that constitute such a dire threat to these basic legal standards that they demonstrate the need for exceptional action. Unless the concept of sovereign responsibility can be protected from misapplication, it cannot be established at all.

This means that the definition and enforcement of responsibility would have to emerge from a broad international coalition. The process might be initiated in general and in specific instances by the more influential states, but it could not rest exclusively on a regional or political grouping that does not reflect the international community as a whole. It also means that measures of prevention would have to be far more consciously and more effectively mastered than they currently are. The highly coercive actions required to control mass violence once a legal system has failed are inherently so difficult and so contentious that they would have to be established as the conceivable but improbable extreme—the political equivalent of war. The range of actions normally used to enforce a doctrine of sovereign responsibility, even in exceptional circumstances, would have to be more legitimate and more constructive in character.

At least in a logical sense, this sequence of requirements begins with the definition of fundamental standards, and that in turn begins with the Universal Declaration of Human Rights. Both in its content and its process of development and promulgation, the universal declaration is the most comprehensive and most authoritative document of relevance. It is a strong presumption that any legal standard with sufficient standing to carry the burden of defining sovereign responsibility would have been included in that document. It is an important fact that the declaration was the product of broad collaboration and that it emerged from the world's most inclusive voting assembly.

The declaration includes more than is likely to be considered truly fundamental in the sense that a practical doctrine of sovereign responsibility would require, but it does advance the most basic human standards, for example:

> Everyone has the right to life, liberty, and security of person. [Article 3]
> No one shall be held in slavery or servitude. [Article 4]
> No one shall be subjected to torture or to cruel, inhuman, or degrading treatment or punishment. [Article 5]
> All are equal before the law and are entitled to equal protection of the law. [Article 7]
> Everyone has the right to own property . . . No one shall be arbitrarily deprived of his property. [Article 17]

Whatever else it might do, a legal system worthy of the name must protect all individuals against murder, robbery, rape, enslavement, and torture. No state claiming legitimacy can avoid this set of commitments. Although crimes of this sort cannot be absolutely prevented, whenever they occur or threaten to occur on a large and sustained scale, all societies have good reason for active concern. As specified in the Genocide Convention, they have especially compelling reason for concern whenever such crimes are directed systematically against groups of people defined in ethnic, racial, or religious terms. If the members of the nation-state system come to recognize a common interest in undertaking an assertive defense of basic legal standards, the problem of identifying those standards is not likely to be a decisive impediment.

Anticipation

It is more of an impediment to identify the conditions of incipient threat that require assertive international action, particularly if effective and legitimate action is to occur in anticipation of mass violence rather than in reaction to it. Once hundreds of thousands of innocent people have been killed and millions of others driven from their homes, as occurred in

Rwanda, the conditions of legal breakdown are apparent to even the most reluctant of observers.[27] By then, however, the objective of prevention largely has been forfeited, and the actions required to master the situation are very extensive and very intrusive indeed. The residual sovereign entity is loath to suffer them, and the international community is equally loath to undertake them. A successful doctrine of sovereign responsibility depends on early detection and rapid reaction with a low rate of error. That appears to be the requirement most difficult to achieve.

In recognition of the importance of that problem, extensive efforts have been made both to explain and to predict the occurrence of communal violence by examining the statistical correlates. The most systematic of these efforts was undertaken by the State Failure Task Force, a consortium of prominent specialists organized by the U.S. Central Intelligence Agency in 1994 to summarize available evidence on the occurrence of violent episodes associated with what they called state failure—a phrase that expresses the idea of legal breakdown.[28] The group identified 113 relevant cases that occurred between 1955 and 1994 in all countries other than the United States with populations greater than 500,000 people. Those cases were compared with a randomly chosen set of countries and years in which no comparable episode occurred, and more than 2 million items of data were examined to determine the characteristics distinguishing the instances of failure from the randomly chosen set. The single best statistical model to emerge from that exercise used three variables—openness to international trade, infant mortality, and democracy—to distinguish 70 percent of the cases of state failure from the randomly chosen set two years in advance. The more open and more democratic countries with lower rates of infant mortality were less prone to violence. That result offers some insight, but it clearly is not refined enough to distinguish an imminent explosion from a chronic problem with the reliability that an effective policy of prevention would require. Were the same statistical performance to be achieved projecting forward rather than in retrospect—a feat not yet demonstrated—it would generate on average fifty false alarms a year (statistically expected episodes that do not occur) and would miss one actual event. Moreover, the 113 episodes that were included in the exercise were not of equal importance. The policy problem requires correctly identifying the much smaller number of especially egregious outbreaks that would justify the unusually assertive actions required to prevent them.

That exercise provides sober insight into the current limits of analytic understanding, but it does not mean that the problem is intractable in practical terms. In most of the recent instances of mass violence, the danger has been perceived accurately in advance, particularly by the humanitarian relief organizations and human rights observers that generally become involved as serious legal disintegration begins to occur within a society. In the Rwanda case, in 1993, long before the plane crash, the human rights organization Africa Watch warned that Hutu extremist leaders had compiled lists of persons to be targeted for retribution and issued rapid notification of the organized murders in progress.[29] Their assessment was reinforced by the local diplomatic community before they themselves were driven from the country. In Somalia, in 1992, the growing inability of the humanitarian relief organizations to assure the security of their own operations provided the immediate stimulus for U.S. intervention. The relief organizations are the best established and most legitimate of the increasingly large number of private groups that have come to be known in bureaucratic jargon as nongovernmental organizations. Despite the term, they usually operate with the financial backing and loose cooperation of the major national governments and are nearly always the initial frontline agents of the international community in major episodes of violence. As a by-product of their efforts to deliver food, clothing, shelter, and medical services to stressed populations, they generally develop the most detailed assessment of incipient legal breakdown, and the systematic disruption of their operations is one of the most reliable indications of an impending outbreak of mass violence.[30] In principle the collapse of relief operations provides a natural justification and practical trigger for assertive international actions to prevent violence. That rule would not provide a completely reliable means of discerning the truly critical cases, but it is good enough to suggest that effective anticipation is not an absolute impediment to a practical policy.

Evolving Experience

On June 10, 1999, the UN Security Council issued Resolution 1244 by unanimous vote with one abstention, which formally determined that the violent displacement of the civilian population in the Yugoslav province of Kosovo occurring over the previous year constituted a threat to international peace and security. That formulation established the legal basis for forceful intervention under Chapter 7 of the UN Charter, and the resolution specifically authorized both an international military presence in the province and the formation of an international civil administration.

The combination in effect imposed comprehensive international authority in Kosovo to be exercised until an indigenous government could be established on the basis of legitimate consensus. Under the terms of the resolution, all Serbian military and police units were to be removed from the province and reintroduced only with international permission. The insurgent organization internationally known as the Kosovo Liberation Army was to be demilitarized. Together the military and civilian international authorities were to assume direct responsibility for assuring equal protection to all segments of the population. Continued sovereignty of the Federal Republic of Yugoslavia was acknowledged in principle, but its exercise was suspended categorically and indefinitely.

Those provisions were implemented by a military force of some 60,000 people supplied and operated primarily by the North Atlantic Treaty Organization (NATO). The language of the resolution combined with forceful implementation clearly entailed a much more assertive standard of international responsibility for the preservation of civil order than had been accepted up to that point. It was accompanied, moreover, by a remarkable, if largely implicit, display of support. Despite vehement and continuing objections to the NATO bombing campaign against Yugoslavia that preceded the resolution, Russia voted in favor of it and joined the implementing force. Despite the provocation of an attack on its Belgrade embassy in the course of the bombing campaign and despite grave concern about any act of international intervention, China enabled the resolution to be enacted by abstaining on the Security Council vote and thereby withholding its veto. Despite a universal expectation that the international commitment to Kosovo would be lengthy, dedicated isolationists in the U.S. Congress made no major attempt to prevent U.S. participation in the intervening force or to impose a termination date on that participation. It would require the passage of time, sustained mastery of violence in Kosovo, and additional applications as well to determine that a new doctrine of responsibility had in fact been established, but that is the implication of Resolution 1244. It was reinforced three months later by Resolution 1264, which provided a peacekeeping force to halt a surge of militia violence in East Timor that was triggered by a referendum on independence from Indonesia and abetted by local units of the Indonesian military. The process of intervention in East Timor was distinctly more expeditious than it had been in Kosovo.

At the time that Resolution 1244 and Resolution 1264 were enacted, the United Nations was conducting fourteen peacekeeping operations in other parts of the world, and NATO was conducting a separate one in Bosnia larger than the others combined. Altogether that set of activities provided the primary base from which the international practice of contending with civil violence was evolving. Each generated formative experience for those who were involved, but their significance was difficult to judge even by those who were conducting them. Certainly size and political attention are not reliable indicators. In instances where preventive action is taken and does succeed, the character and magnitude of what otherwise would have occurred are not demonstrated, and the effort is not likely to be widely recognized as a major accomplishment. By contrast, preventive efforts that fail in some important respect or are not even attempted create a historical record whose prominence is roughly proportional to the failure. That natural bias in the interpretation of experience is often called the paradox of prevention, and its consequence is that the more notable failures, especially those involving the United States, have a disproportionate influence on what is perceived to be the state of the art.

The systematic brutality in Kosovo that generated Resolution 1244 was a failure of prevention, the fourth such episode in the post–cold war period prominent enough to be globally recognized by a simple geographic label. Bosnia, Somalia, and Rwanda were the others. All of these occasions involved either the disintegration or legal degeneration of normal government, a condition that emerged in at least three of the instances after a lengthy process in which the accumulation of international debt played a major role. All generated the characteristic pattern of predatory behavior that was tolerated through the formative stages when effective prevention would have been most feasible and then, in the case of the earlier three, entrenched in a belated attempt to contain the consequences with minimal effort. All have left festering residues that indict the original actions and suggest that the revision of international practice finally promulgated in the Kosovo resolution will have to be consolidated there and generally extended. None of these episodes can be considered completed, and their full implications undoubtedly will be debated for quite some time to come. Nonetheless, at least two enduring lessons are apparent. Experience in the four episodes indicates that there are distinct limits to the international tolerance of communal violence, no matter how culturally or geographically remote any instance may seem. There also are significant opportunities for prevention.

The first of these lessons is neither a precise nor an absolutely universal rule. Civil war continues in the Sudan for a fourth decade without exceeding the bounds of international tolerance. Chronic violence in Afghanistan and two acute episodes in Chechnya have commanded more attention but not assertive reaction. Nonetheless, in the four noted cases, visual display of communal violence—the fabled CNN (Cable News Network) effect—drove reluctant governments into reactions they initially were determined to avoid because the consequences of complete disengagement were not acceptable to the voting public. Although the full set of conditions that determine which events become the focus of news coverage and which do not are somewhat mysterious, it is reasonable to expect that instances emerging from an extensive breakdown of legal order are likely to attract attention, not only because atrocities are generated but also because collapsed and criminally degenerate governments cannot prevent international access. If unrestrained slaughter cannot be ignored, neither can it be tolerated; most people register the threat it represents. This presumption may be vague and open to exceptions, but it is powerful.

The second lesson turns on inherently disputable interpretations of how actual events might have been altered by more judicious policies, but it also is strong enough to shape evolving practice. As careful scholars have recognized, especially in the cases of Bosnia, Kosovo, and Somalia, the collapse of political institutions and the surge of communal violence were preceded by a lengthy process of economic deterioration in which the international community as a whole was heavily, if unwittingly, implicated as a by-product of the cold war. The western governments provided extensive financial credit to the Yugoslav Federation, with Bosnia a constituent republic and Kosovo an autonomous region, because its communist government was assertively independent of the Soviet Union. The credit was designed to encourage an indigenous military capability that would preclude Soviet occupation without direct assistance from NATO forces, and it was not accompanied by provisions for access to western markets that might have enabled it to be invested profitably. As a natural consequence, Yugoslavia in the latter phases of the cold war had increasing difficulty servicing the more than $20 billion in hard currency debt it had been allowed to accumulate and was subjected to a series of IMF stabilization programs that imposed increasingly severe internal economic austerity. With the ending of the cold war, the NATO governments and especially the United States abandoned political support for Yugoslavia's communist government and did not notice that the austerity measures imposed on behalf of market discipline were eroding the intricate arrangements for internal resource allocation that enabled the Yugoslav Federation to manage its ethnic diversity. There was essentially no appreciation of the corrosive effects of western policy, no effort to preserve the political integrity of the federation, and no attempt to design a graceful dismemberment either.[31]

In Somalia, the process had somewhat different features, but the outcome was comparable. Somalia was one of the rare cases of a country that switched its alignment in the later stages of the cold war, primarily because its original patron—the Soviet Union—backed Ethiopia in a 1977–78 war over the Ogaden, a region of Ethiopia populated by one of the Somali clans. With Soviet military aid and the direct assistance of Cuban troops, Ethiopia repulsed Somalia's assault on the Ogaden, and the defeat seriously undermined the political standing of the highly authoritarian Somali leader, Siad Barre. The western alliance, acquiring Somalia as an aspiring client state largely by default, was not enthusiastic about the exchange and not willing to make the Ogaden a matter of strategic significance. However, it did provide some $500 million in military assistance and $2 billion in financial credit over the course of the 1980s.[32] In contrast to Yugoslavia, the credit was accompanied by market access, but that proved to be more of a curse than a blessing. The access in question mostly involved the sale of agricultural products to Saudi Arabia, which did not pose anything like the difficulty involved in giving Yugoslavia access to European markets, but along with it came exposure to international competition and to the price fluctuations to which agricultural commodities are notoriously susceptible. The adaptive balance of Somalia's communal agriculture was seriously disrupted by this exposure, and the government did not have the capacity to provide indigenous buffers. The result was a large accumulation of debt, reaching levels over 200 percent of gross national product by 1990, with annual debt service obligations near 125 percent of export earnings.[33] Again a series of IMF stabilization programs imposed stark economic austerity. Under this grinding process, the authority of the Somalia government and the internal rule of law visibly deteriorated throughout the 1980s. When Siad Barre finally abandoned any pretense of rule and fled the capital, Mogadishu, in January 1991, there was no comprehensive government to replace him. At that point the prevailing pattern of marauding militia became the exclusive form of political organization. Some 350,000 people were killed between 1988 and 1992—virtually all of them civilians rather than active combatants—as a direct and indirect result of the warring militia.[34] As in Yugoslavia, the accumulating danger was not recognized as the commanding security problem it proved to be, and there was no dedicated effort to preempt it—no program for what the Carnegie Commission labeled structural prevention.[35] Since yet larger societies are subject to the same degenerative process—Russia and Indonesia in particular—the experience has imposing implications.

Bosnia

The failures of longer-term anticipation in Yugoslavia and in Somalia were compounded by failures in immediate reaction as well. Despite having long been the subject of political speculation, the formal disintegration of Yugoslavia caught the international community without responsive policies when it began in 1991. The conflicting patterns of ethnic identification that immediately drove the process pitted established principles of territorial integrity and national self-determination against each other, and no one had authoritatively worked out how those principles might be reconciled in that situation. The process also evoked historical associations—between the French and the Serbs, for example, and the Germans and the Croats—that had been highly divisive over the course of the two world wars and had not been harmonized with the new context of European integration. In reacting to the rapidly unfolding situation without coherent preparation, the major governments made a series of what proved to be glaring misjudgments. They attempted to evoke the principle of sovereign territorial integrity with no commitment to defend it by force and no provisions to assure legitimate self-determination. Specifically they recognized the sovereign independence of Slovenia—the only one of the Yugoslav republics with homogeneous ethnic composition—with no conditions for the internal protection of minority rights. At German insistence, they extended that unconditional recognition to Croatia, which contained a substantial Serb minority already reacting violently to the impending dismemberment of the federal government. The same unconditional recognition was then further extended to Bosnia, this time at American insistence, against the ubiquitous warnings of knowledgeable specialists that this would precipitate factional fighting among its intricately interspersed Serb, Croat, and Muslim communities, as indeed it did.

In the initial stages of this sequence the United States under the Bush administration refused to use readily available and applicable air power to halt direct attacks on civilian populations when they first occurred—the artillery assaults on the Croatian cities of Vukovar and Dubrovnik undertaken by Serbian units of the Yugoslav army in the summer of 1991. At that point the United States proclaimed, in the words of Secretary of State James Baker, "We've got no dog in this fight."[36] In subsequent stages of the conflict under the Clinton administration, the United States openly sided with the Muslims and the Croats against the Serbs but refused to commit the ground troops that would have been necessary to contain the fighting that had erupted in Bosnia in the spring of 1992.[37] It persisted in that refusal for three years as ethnic militia systematically brutalized the civilian population and progressively humiliated a UN peacekeeping operation that had been inserted without the means to perform its mandated functions or to defend itself. It finally was compelled to commit ground forces in 1995 to prevent the precipitous withdrawal of the allied troops that had formed the core of the UN operation. At that point the United States brokered an agreement that in effect ratified the violent separation of ethnic populations—an arrangement that is blatantly inconsistent with general standards of law and indeed with the terms of the formal agreement that produced it and that is likely to require active international policing for an indefinite period of time.[38] Although there is plenty of room for argument about important details, it is evident that an international intervention at the start of the sequence, beginning with the issue of independence for Slovenia and Croatia, could have prevented most of the 250,000 deaths that occurred and could have avoided the coerced displacement of nearly 3 million people with no greater a commitment of assets than was ultimately made.[39] Unwelcome as that lesson may be, the enduring grievances that have been created are likely to make it difficult to ignore.[40]

Somalia

A corresponding lesson is embedded in the very different circumstances of the Somalia episode. The progressive degeneration of the Siad Barre regime into lawless brutality against opposing Somali clans was sufficiently apparent by the late 1980s that the U.S. State Department commissioned a special consultant's report to document systematic assaults by the army on Issak villages in northern Somalia. That basic comprehension was not translated into a dedicated effort to organize a stabilizing settlement. A coalition of the insurgent clan leaders known as the Manifesto Group issued a joint declaration in April 1990 calling for the formation of a provisional government and negotiations for political reconciliation. Italy, with strong ties to one of the insurgent factions, did attempt mediation and did join with Djibouti and Egypt after the collapse of the Barre government to convene two conferences intended to facilitate the formation of a new government. These efforts did not have the scope or intensity of international support that would have been required to make them effective, however. The UN machinery was first engaged a year after Barre departed Mogadishu, when it became apparent that the Somali population faced not only uncontrollable militia violence but also mass starvation. Even then the efforts made were so inadequate to the requirements of the situation that the UN representatives were exposed to intimidation and manipulation by the local militia, as they were in Bosnia. In January 1992 the UN Security Council invoked Chapter 7 of the UN Charter to declare the internal violence and humanitarian emergency in Somalia a general threat to peace and in April formally established a peacekeeping operation (United Nations Operation in Somalia—UNOSOM I) with instructions to send fifty observers to monitor the situation. It did not authorize military forces to enforce its resolutions until July, however, and did not deploy them until September when a lightly armed contingent of 500 Pakistani soldiers was sent to Mogadishu under orders to operate only with the consent of the local parties. It quickly became apparent that they could not prevent the plundering of humanitarian relief supplies and were, in effect, hostages of the militia leaders. In March 1992 James O. C. Jonah, a representative of the UN secretary general, negotiated a cease-fire agreement between the two principal leaders in the Mogadishu area whose forces were responsible for the most serious violence—Ali Mahdi Mohamed and Mohamed Farah Aideed—but that effort did not include the less-belligerent clan leaders in other parts of the country, whose participation clearly would be necessary for the reconstruction of a viable government. A subsequent attempt to broaden the mediation effort by a UN special representative, Mohamed Sahnoun of Algeria, was absorbed largely in negotiating the terms of deployment for UNOSOM I with Ali Mahdi and Aideed. It took him several months to work out agreement for the September deployment. Sahnoun resigned in October 1992, complaining that his difficulties with the Somali clans had been compounded by acerbic relations with the UN bureaucracy. For an entire decade, international reaction to the increasingly serious communal violence in Somalia was consistently too little, too late. The obvious misery could not be entirely ignored, but there was no adequate attempt to overcome it either.[41]

That pattern was suddenly amended by the United States in late 1992 as it became evident that UNOSOM I could not protect humanitarian relief operations in Somalia and that a catastrophic level of starvation loomed. According to a U.S. Centers for Disease Control and Prevention report of December 1992, the crude mortality rates reported in the Somalia villages of Baidoa and Afgoi were "among the highest ever documented by a population survey among famine-affected civilians."[42] The various nongovernmental organizations involved in the relief effort were assertively warning of an accelerating disaster and the imminent collapse of their own efforts—a situation that promised to generate stark images of emaciated children at Christmastime and to offer an appalling display of international haplessness.[43] The U.S. government was in the midst of a presidential transition at the time—not normally the moment for a major initiative. It nonetheless managed to react swiftly in a manner sufficient to overcome the immediate problem. On November 25, the United States offered to organize and undertake a military operation to ensure the delivery of relief supplies in Somalia if such an action were to be authorized by the Security Council. On December 3 the Security Council passed Resolution 794 providing the authorization, and, on December 9, the first elements of a UN Unified Task Force (UNITAF) arrived in Mogadishu under the command of a U.S. Marine Corps general operating through the national command channels of the United States. A total of 37,000 troops were assigned to UNITAF by more than twenty countries, including NATO allies France, Canada, and Italy, but its primary combat capability was provided by an authorized force of 28,000 U.S. troops spearheaded by a marine expeditionary force.[44] Reflecting the national character of the operation, the United States also supplied its own coordinating official, Ambassador Robert Oakley, to manage the associated diplomacy. With far more authority and operational capacity at his disposal than Sahnoun had enjoyed, Oakley arranged the uncontested deployment of UNITAF six days after the authorizing resolution, and by the end of January UNITAF had established sufficient control over the southern third of Somalia, where militia violence and exposure to starvation had been concentrated, so that effective humanitarian operations could be resumed. The action is believed to have saved the lives of hundreds of thousands of people, including many of the children whose anguished faces would otherwise have haunted the world's television screens.

As the initiative evolved over the ensuing year, however, it came to be perceived in the United States as a political disaster, primarily because eighteen American soldiers were killed in a battle with Aideed's militia in October 1993. In response to public outrage at that event, inflamed by television images of an American soldier being dragged through the streets of Mogadishu, U.S. military operations associated with the UN force were restricted to prevent any additional casualties, and all American troops were ordered to withdraw from Somalia by the end of the following March. The implication, repeatedly articulated in public commentary, was that no casualties could be tolerated in conducting humanitarian operations, and residual UN operations were aligned with that rule. Some 30,000 troops from twenty-eight countries constituted as UNOSOM II and operating under UN command authority remained in Somalia following UNITAF's withdrawal.[45] With neither the capacity nor the mandate to control the predatory militia, they were compelled to survive by accommodation, and the continuing violence that had to be tolerated overshadowed whatever was prevented. Both UNITAF and UNOSOM were judged to be decisive failures of the sort never again to be attempted.

That attitude continues to be prominent and may be enduring, but it appears to have been amended in the subsequent Kosovo episode and is susceptible to retrospective reassessment in the case of Somalia as well. In its initial phase, UNITAF clearly demonstrated the international capacity to suppress militia operations and to restore some approximation of normal life at feasible levels of effort. That was particularly apparent in rural areas outside Mogadishu.[46] However, even there, at the major point of contention between the Aideed and Ali Mahdi forces, the situation was not militarily unmanageable up to and including the fateful battle on October 3 and 4, which U.S. forces initiated. Had the United States chosen to prosecute that engagement rather than withdraw from it, Aideed's forces would have been severely degraded and the United Nations would have been in a commanding position to negotiate political accommodation. Moreover, had UNITAF's operations been more assertive from the start and more systematically coordinated with a diplomatic effort to reconstruct a viable government, there is good reason to believe that a direct battle of that intensity could have been avoided. UNITAF's uncontested arrival was negotiated with the militia leaders that might have resisted it, but the speed with which that was accomplished against the background of contempt for UN operations clearly indicates that those leaders were chastened by the large and sudden commitment of the United States. That effect was quickly dissipated, however, by the extremely limited purpose that the United States projected and by the correspondingly cautious behavior of the UNITAF operation. In announcing the action, President Bush emphasized that it would be devoted exclusively to the delivery of humanitarian aid and would be completed within a few weeks, a formulation so outlandishly impractical under the circumstances that it signaled fear of excessive entanglement rather than a determination to succeed. No statement of purpose was issued either at the outset of the operation or at any point thereafter that would justify combat casualties, and that fact was reflected in the decisions of American commanders on the scene. UNITAF's actions were forceful enough to compel the militia to move major weapons out of the urban areas where they could be used to tax and otherwise control the delivery of food supplies, but there was no effort to disarm the militia despite insistent pleas from Secretary General Boutros-Ghali that it be done.[47] The militia leaders could discern from the unfolding pattern of the operation that the U.S. commitment was politically fragile and not likely to be sustained.

That impression was reinforced by the fitful diplomacy associated with the operation. In the immediate aftermath of the UNITAF deployment, UN mediators were working in concert with Oakley to stage two conferences in Addis Ababa involving the clan factions that had been identified as the principal sources of most of the militia operations. On March 27, 1993, the second of these conferences produced a document committing the fifteen signatory organizations to a program of disarmament and political reconciliation including the creation of transitional institutions intended to produce a national government within a two-year period. That document was not a complete political settlement, but it was a significant enough step in that direction to suggest that an internationally negotiated reconstruction of the central government was feasible in principle and might actually occur. The Somali factions were compelled to take that possibility seriously, since none of them was capable of establishing a comprehensive authority on its own terms. The United States refused to accept responsibility for fashioning a political settlement, however. That was construed to be an exercise in nation-building, a derisive term in the American political lexicon at the time. Without the military capacity of the United States, the United Nations could not impose the practical discipline required to manage the delicate transition between coercive and consensual methods of acquiring power. Oakley resigned before the Addis Ababa agreement was issued, and primary responsibility for security in Somalia was shifted from UNITAF to UNOSOM II a few weeks thereafter. With the departure of the cautious but imposing and nationally commanded U.S. combat forces that had formed the core of UNITAF, the Somali militia resumed their operations, and in June elements of what was assumed to be Aideed's militia ambushed Pakistani troops assigned to UNOSOM II, killing twenty-four. On June 17, in an apparent effort to establish the operational credibility of UNOSOM II, the special representative of the secretary general in Somalia, retired American Admiral Jonathan Howe, issued a warrant for the arrest of General Aideed, setting off an extended manhunt that culminated in the October 3 battle. Over the course of that sequence, efforts to develop the Addis Ababa agreement were suspended, and they collapsed thereafter.[48]

Although it cannot be demonstrated what the result would have been if UNITAF had been instructed to support the process of political reconstruction over the two-year period mapped out in the Addis Ababa agreement, it is reasonable to believe that in Somalia, as in Bosnia, a substantially better outcome could have been achieved with less grief on all sides than was actually suffered. Five years after the watershed battle, no government had yet been established in Somalia, malnutrition was endemic, and the relief agencies were again warning of massive starvation.[49] A judiciously extended and moderately more willful UNITAF could have exceeded that standard and presumably would have done so had the assertive attitude subsequently embodied in Resolution 1244 been applied in the earlier instance.

Kosovo

In terms of casualties inflicted and individuals at risk, the violence in Kosovo that generated Resolution 1244 was substantially less than what had occurred in Rwanda and not markedly greater than that in Bosnia or Somalia. The number of people arbitrarily killed appears to have been less than 10,000; hundreds of thousands were driven from their homes into life-threatening conditions. Because of its history and location, however, Kosovo was considered from the outset to be a particularly sensitive international problem. The division between Serbian and Albanian communal identities had more extensive historical roots, sharper definition in linguistic and religious terms, and stronger external resonance than comparable distinctions in any of the other countries, including Bosnia. Kosovo was understood to be one of the world's major cultural fault lines.[50] Moreover, the surge of atrocities committed during the period of acute crisis from January to June 1999 was perceived to be a campaign of expulsion dangerous to the surrounding region. The international community reacted late in Kosovo, as it had in the other instances, but not as late and much more assertively when it did act, in part because it was more inclined but also because it was reacting to the earlier experience.

From the time the autonomous status of the province within the Yugoslav Federation was withdrawn in 1989, the situation was especially ominous. That became ever more apparent as Slobodan Milosevic systematically consolidated power on the basis of Serbian nationalism using the symbols, fears, and grievances of the Serb minority in Kosovo as a primary emotional engine. The withdrawal of autonomy was itself a major provocation to the Albanian majority, which comprised an estimated 90 percent of the Kosovo population. The ensuing campaign of Serbian national assertion subjected the Albanians to such egregious mistreatment that it was virtually assured to evoke a violent reaction if it was sustained long enough. The Albanian language was completely suppressed in the public education system. Blatant job discrimination was practiced in favor of the Serbian minority. The police were almost entirely Serbian, and their behavior was unabashedly partisan and repressive. Dating back to the treaty of Berlin in 1878 when the boundaries of Balkan political jurisdiction were set by agreement among the great powers of the time, the Albanian communities in Kosovo had staged repeated revolts to establish or defend local autonomy under Ottoman rule. They also had experienced repeated episodes of communal violence and policies of forced expulsion under direct Serbian rule between 1912 and 1941. The principle of autonomy for the province had been proclaimed in 1945 to provide reassurance against violent and discriminatory treatment, but the actual terms had been contested within Tito's communist regime up to its legal consolidation in the 1968 and 1974 revisions of Yugoslavia's federal constitution.[51] That experience made both the degree of provocation and the nature of the expected response quite apparent. In the first paragraph of his book, published in 1998 just before the acute phase of the crisis that culminated in Resolution 1244, the historian Noel Malcolm identified Kosovo as the most intractable of all the Balkan political conflicts and warned that it was capable of producing the most intense violence.[52]

It was widely understood from the outset that any sustained outbreak of communal violence in Kosovo could not be contained within the province. Albania itself would become involved, whatever its government chose to do, as would the substantial Albanian community in Macedonia, which nursed communal grievances of its own. The viability of coherent government was simultaneously in question in the two neighboring states as well as in Kosovo itself, and political stability in the entire region was threatened even more than it was by the civil war in Bosnia. The sharply etched danger was encased, however, within an acknowledged sovereign jurisdiction that was much better established in practical terms than it had been in the other instances. Serbian authority over Kosovo had been imposed by military conquest in 1912, and formal sovereignty of the conglomerate Yugoslav state was proclaimed internationally in 1918 as part of the rearrangement of Europe following World War I. Both the Serbian and the federal Yugoslav claims were universally accepted even though neither had been legally ratified.[53] Fearing the stimulus that might be given to separatist movements elsewhere, none of the European governments wanted to contemplate Kosovo's independence. In the initial stages of Yugoslavia's disintegration, even the dissident Albanian community in Kosovo accepted the principle of Yugoslav, as distinct from Serbian, sovereignty. Moreover, everyone acknowledged that, reprehensible as its internal policies clearly were, the government in Belgrade dominated by Milosevic did exercise practical authority in Kosovo right up to the point that Resolution 1244 was adopted. It never collapsed to the degree that the governments of Somalia and Rwanda obviously did. Most of the ethnic violence in Kosovo appears to have been inflicted by irregular militia, as it had been in the other instances, but they were universally believed to be operating with at least the implicit approval, if not the direct instruction, of Serbian army and police forces. To override the sovereign authority of a government still capable of exercising it and to do so by assertive military action would set a precedent of very serious concern to many states contending with active or potential internal dissension. To tolerate indefinite repression, however, would invite a cascading disaster.

The dilemma resulted from yet another failure of prevention. Although the threat of violence in Kosovo became increasingly apparent as all the other events associated with the dismemberment of the Yugoslav Federation unfolded, the most obvious opportunity to head it off was forfeited. In December 1989, in reaction to the removal of constitutional autonomy voted by the Serb Assembly in Belgrade the previous March, the Democratic League of Kosovo was formed with an Albanian academic, Ibrahim Rugova, as its acknowledged leader. Known by its Albanian initials as the LDK, the league proclaimed a policy of establishing the status of Kosovo as an autonomous republic through nonviolent means and explicitly appealed for international assistance in doing so. That formula sidestepped the delicate issue of independence and could be seen to be primarily a restoration of what had just been taken away. For the ensuing five years it commanded largely uncontested support from the Kosovar Albanians. In the light of what ultimately happened, it clearly would have been prudent for the major states concerned with the Balkan situation to provide material support for that formula, including positive incentives for Serbia that might have competed with Milosevic's brand of belligerent and repressive nationalism. No serious effort of that sort was made, however, and by 1996 the Kosovo Liberation Army (UCK in the Albanian acronym) was beginning to emerge as an insurgent force primarily committed to violent resistance. The UCK quickly developed from obscure origins as the primary agent of the Albanian cause—materially assisted, it appears, and perhaps directly generated, by networks that long had run drug operations in Southern Europe. By 1998 a classic pattern of communal violence was well entrenched in Kosovo. The lightly armed UCK learned, after some early bravado about protecting their Albanian compatriots, that they could not win pitched battles against Serbian police units or against the Yugoslav army units that reinforced them, but that they could inflict casualties on these forces that, in turn, provoked indiscriminate retaliation against the Albanian villages assumed to be supporting UCK operations. The evident brutality of Serbian retaliation generated recruits and material support for the UCK not only from within Kosovo but also from Albanian communities in the surrounding states and from the Albanian diaspora more generally. It also attracted international attention and cast the Albanian insurgency in the morally superior role of victim, a critical asset in the battle for international political approval.

International diplomacy did not become seriously active until 1998, and by that time the momentum of violence had been established so thoroughly that it was doubtful that any of the indigenous political leaders could control it. Nonetheless, the central premise of the various diplomatic efforts made was that Milosevic, as the acknowledged locus of sovereign authority and the presumed political source of the expulsion campaign, was to be held primarily responsible for ending it. In March 1998, the major power coordinating committee established during the Bosnia crisis—generally known as the contact group—issued two statements on the crisis in reaction to a series of Serbian police raids in the Drenica region of Kosovo where the UCK had been especially active. The statements condemned both the excessive use of police force and terrorist actions by the UCK but urged that a comprehensive embargo be imposed on all arms transfers to the Yugoslav government—a recommendation that clearly signaled where the principal responsibility was judged to lie.[54]

On March 31, those judgments were embodied in UN Security Council Resolution 1160 and thereafter were supported by a number of visitations to Milosevic by emissaries of the contact group governments—the most prominent of whom was Richard Holbrooke, architect of the Dayton agreement on Bosnia. The net result of that activity was the outline of an agreed arrangement for a cease-fire in Kosovo, a direct dialogue on political accommodation, a specified reduction in the number of Serbian police and army units present in the province, and unimpeded access for humanitarian relief organizations—a set of provisions that were to be verified by unarmed observers operating in Kosovo through the Organization on Security and Cooperation in Europe (OSCE) and by air surveillance conducted by NATO from its bases in Western Europe. These terms were issued as demands by UN Security Council Resolution 1199 on September 23, which also warned of unspecified "further action and additional measures" if the demands were not complied with. In mid-October the Yugoslav government signed formal agreements with the OSCE and with NATO providing for the monitoring provisions specified in Resolution 1199 and implying some degree of substantive compliance as well. On October 24, UN Security Council Resolution 1203 specifically endorsed those agreements and demanded compliance. Resolutions 1160, 1199, and 1203 were all issued by the same 14 to 0 vote, with China abstaining, that subsequently produced Resolution 1244 as well.

On September 24, the day after Resolution 1199 passed, NATO formally initiated the preparation of two contingency plans, one for air strikes against Yugoslavia in the event of continued defiance and another for a ground monitoring and enforcement operation in the event that a formal agreement for a cease-fire and force withdrawal was reached. On October 13 after some ten days of negotiating with Milosevic in Belgrade on the specific terms of the envisaged agreement, Richard Holbrooke flew to NATO headquarters in Brussels and publicly stated that progress in the negotiations depended heavily on the threat of air strikes. In response, the North Atlantic Council, NATO's governing body, voted an activation order giving the organization's civilian secretary general, Javier Solana, authority to order such strikes. The formal agreements with NATO and the OSCE on monitoring arrangements followed on October 15 and 16, and 4,000 Serbian police forces withdrew from Kosovo on October 27, giving the impression that the prospect of air attack was indeed effective, whether as a motivating threat or as a bit of political theater covering controversial terms of accommodation.

Over the course of the following months, it became apparent, however, that air strikes were neither the commanding nor the facilitating instrument imagined in October. Despite its nominal acquiescence to the Security Council resolutions, the Milosevic government did not halt its military operations in Kosovo or withdraw its forces as required. Instead it prepared a campaign of violent repression evidently designed not merely to destroy the UCK but to force mass emigration of the Albanian community, presumably in order to establish the ethnic base for secure Serbian rule. As the pattern of defiance emerged in November and December, it became evident that the unarmed OSCE monitors could not physically protect Albanian civilians but did protect Serb forces against air strikes by providing ready hostages that could be taken in retaliation. On January 15, 1999, forty-five bodies were discovered in the village of Racak, and the head of the OSCE's Kosovo Verification Mission, the American William Walker, judged them to be murdered Albanian civilians, while admitting his limited ability to investigate. By the end of January the United Nations High Commissioner for Refugees estimated that 20,000 people had fled Kosovo in the course of that winter month, 5,000 of them from the Racak area.

With the Racak incident attracting the attention of the international press and crystallizing a general perception that an expulsion campaign was being conducted, the contact group issued an ultimatum to the Serbian government and to Albanian political representatives to attend a conference at the Chateau Rambouillet in France in order to work out a political arrangement to halt the violence. In support of that demand, the North Atlantic Council once again authorized air strikes at the discretion of the NATO secretary general, indicating that it was prepared to compel political accommodation by force if necessary. But, at the repeated insistence of the U.S. and German governments, NATO determined that it would not commit ground troops to control the conflict directly without formal agreement of the involved parties to accept them. The Rambouillet conference was held in February, and in a series of extended negotiations a general agreement was outlined. The Albanian community would be given political autonomy short of complete independence with protection provided by an international peacekeeping force led by NATO—something like the original LDK program. Milosevic did not personally participate at Rambouillet, however, as he had at the Dayton conference on Bosnia, and he did not at any point accept serious accommodation with the Albanian community. On March 18 diplomatic efforts to complete the agreement were suspended, and on March 22 the U.S. State Department confirmed that widespread military actions were being conducted in Kosovo by Serb police and Yugoslav army units.[55] On March 24, NATO initiated an air offensive against Yugoslavia that ultimately involved more than 37,000 sorties, more than 10,000 of which were strike-and-attack sorties against a wide array of military and civilian infrastructure targets.[56] The bombardment ended in June with Resolution 1244 and effective termination of the Milosevic government's rule in Kosovo.

Some of the major implications of this sequence are immediately evident. As in the previous episodes, there clearly was a failure of reaction as well as a failure of prevention. The danger of an intolerable explosion of violence in Kosovo was recognized well enough by March 1998 to produce UN Security Council Resolution 1160, but the civilian population was not protected until fifteen months later, after a large fraction of the civilian population had been violently dislodged and thousands murdered. It can be argued that a more rapid reaction would not have been politically feasible and, in particular, that the assertive override of Serbian sovereignty could have been accomplished only after the humanitarian calamity had been demonstrated. The projections of a few knowledgeable specialists, it can be said, would not have been broadly accepted as a valid basis for unusual, indeed nearly unprecedented, assertiveness. That argument discounts the warning provided by the earlier incidents as well as by the unusual features of the Kosovo situation, but the thought that the eventual intervention might have been undertaken earlier clearly involves a disputable judgment.

Whatever one concludes about timing, however, it is difficult to justify the methods used to react to the violence in Kosovo, despite their apparent success. The longer-term reverberations assuredly will provide strong reason for critical reassessment. From the outset there was never any reasonable prospect that air bombardment could protect the civilian population. The process of intimidation and expulsion to which they were subjected was conducted by small units whose most relevant actions could not be detected by remote observation and at any rate were too intricately interspersed with their victims to be controlled by that means. Even at the highest standards of feasible performance, air power cannot be applied directly to the fine scale of violence entailed, and the commitment to use it therefore required the indirect theories of effect that were applied—the general assault on the military establishment and civilian infrastructure of Yugoslavia was rationalized as coercive pressure on the political leadership. Previous efforts of that sort had never been rapidly decisive and had always produced substantial social damage of their own. Since this one culminated in acquiescence, it is being hailed by those who conducted it as an exception. That judgment assuredly will be contested in retrospect. The general bombing campaign did a great deal of damage but did not have any decisive physical effect and appears to have done more to rally than to undermine immediate political support for the Milosevic government, as had happened in most previous instances. Agreement on Resolution 1244 came at a moment when the air campaign was inflicting its greatest damage on Yugoslav units in Kosovo, but that was enabled by the fact that UCK ground operations had forced the concentration of their forces. Moreover, NATO was beginning to contemplate a ground operation of its own, and that prospect is an alternative explanation for the timing of Milosevic's acquiescence. As an issue of fact, it is a fair presumption that air bombardment intensified the danger to Kosovo's population in the initial stages, and it is not evident that it achieved the eventual agreement to enact and enforce Resolution 1244. As an issue of principle, it is highly questionable whether that agreement would justify the air campaign even if it were assigned full credit. In effect the NATO air operation accepted as many as 11,500 civilian fatalities in order to minimize the risk to its own military personnel.[57] It is speculative but reasonable to suppose that the net number of fatalities and overall scale of social dislocation could have been reduced substantially by a timely ground intervention in Kosovo. An international force intervening against dedicated resistance would have suffered combat losses of its own but could have saved lives on balance.[58]

For the seventy-eight-day duration of the NATO air campaign, the policy of coercing compliance by that means was accepted without major dissent within the countries that directly participated. The fact that their forces suffered no combat casualties undoubtedly had a great deal to do with the degree of consensus displayed by the alliance as a whole. The differential weighing of life and risk entailed by that policy was not endorsed outside the alliance, however, and it seems evident that it never would be. The NATO campaign was conducted on behalf of the most basic human rights but in violation of international legal procedure. It was an offensive operation initiated beyond its designated treaty area by an alliance proclaiming to be exclusively defensive in character. There was no attempt to establish explicit approval of the UN Security Council, despite the sequence of votes clearly suggesting the Security Council would contemplate some form of coercive action under Chapter 7 of the charter. For an action that is overriding one set of legal standards in defense of another, justification depends heavily on the net effect achieved, and protection of the Kosovo population was the only plausibly valid basis for such justification. The consequence for NATO forces providing the protection could be considered an important constraint, but not an absolute one. If there are valid reasons for inflicting casualties, then there are valid reasons for suffering them as well, and the latter effect cannot be made an overriding consideration without bringing the former into question. The legitimacy of the air campaign was threatened by the indirect and arguably perverse effects it had on the incidence of violence in Kosovo and by collateral damage inflicted on the civilian population of Yugoslavia. That fact eventually would have been registered within the NATO democracies. Even if it is assumed that air bombardment did produce political capitulation, it does not follow that such a policy could have been sustained long enough to guarantee that outcome.

Even less could coercive bombardment be advanced as the appropriate method of choice in any similar circumstance, and reassurance to the contrary is likely to be a significant issue of international security generally. The NATO air campaign was perceived in Russia as a dire threat to Russia itself—a demonstration of the alliance's willingness to use its imposing capabilities for offensive purposes at its own initiative and to bypass the UN Security Council in doing so. The implications for Russia are extremely serious given that country's burdensome problems of contingency planning. It suggests that Russia could be subjected to similar coercion on matters that it considers entirely within its own jurisdiction. It further suggests that political agreements with NATO cannot be trusted and that the legal procedures embedded in the UN system do not provide reliable protection. In Russia's reading of the diplomatic record, the United States under the Bush administration promised at the time of German unification that NATO would not be expanded eastward, but under the Clinton administration it did so anyway. In accommodating to that broken promise, Russia was then told that the alliance would never attack unless it was itself attacked. The air operation against Yugoslavia defied that promise against vehemently expressed Russian objections, and neither NATO's consultative machinery nor the UN Security Council appears to have provided an effective means of reconciling those objections. In its inner deliberations the Russian government probably was reluctant to defend Milosevic's actions in Kosovo and for that reason might have found it convenient to avoid a Security Council vote. The result set a precedent, however, whose implications for Russia are too ominous to be absorbed without attempting some major strategic response—either more credible reassurance or more effective deterrence. Although not directly engaged in the Kosovo situation, China and India have had similar reactions.

If the more assertive doctrine of responsibility advanced in Resolution 1244 is to be developed as a new standard of international security practice, therefore, not only will a viable form of civil order have to be achieved in Kosovo, but a more broadly acceptable match of methods and objectives will have to be established for incidents of this type and NATO will have to be more reliably subordinated to the UN Security Council. If a civilian population is ever again endangered to the extent that decisive international intervention is required, then direct protection must be the dominant criterion of action, a timely ground operation must be the presumed method, and Security Council procedures must be the primary process of justification. It is one thing to act indirectly without formal authorization, if a more justifiable response is seriously attempted and cannot be achieved for whatever reason. It is quite another to do so without having made such an attempt.

Although all four of the prominent episodes eventually produced an international ground intervention of some sort, each was belated and haphazardly designed. None of them can be considered an adequate demonstration of effort. The failures in all of the situations appear to have been much more a matter of conception than of capacity or even directly of political will. The many opportunities to practice effective prevention at reasonable effort were neglected primarily because at every point there was no developed formulation of interest to motivate and to shape the more than routinely assertive actions that would have been required. Fear of lengthy, bloody, and ultimately ineffective entanglement in another society's internal conflicts was much stronger than any sense of danger associated with the process of conflict in general, so much so that the presumption of disengagement was seriously contested only by dedicated partisans—those who perceived themselves to have, in the telling imagery of Secretary Baker, a dog in the fight. The debate between skeptics and partisans overshadowed any discussion of the importance of defending general legal standards until the manifestation of violence became sensational enough to generate a broad public reaction. At that point the underlying interest in general standards of human behavior became visible in the immediate context, and an imperative to react developed under conditions of high risk and likely misfortune. The concerns of the skeptics were partially overturned at a moment when they were particularly valid, but as a consequence of that fact they were reinforced in the aftermath.

This sequence may be destined to be repeated many times, but that has to be considered an open question under the impulse of globalization. Whether directly acknowledged or not, there is tension between the traditional principle of nonintervention and the spontaneous process of international integration that is obviously occurring. It is increasingly doubtful that vital interest can be defined in compartmentalized terms—ones that are selective with regard to geography, culture, or national identity. It is increasingly likely that security and prosperity for all societies will depend on coordinating rules resting on legal foundations that must be generally defended if the integrity of the rules is to be maintained. Control of violence is an essential element of legal order, and for that reason it is a vital and general human interest. Even the unfortunate episodes of recent experience indicate that, if this interest were to be acknowledged and the implications accepted, a more refined balance could be set between sovereign prerogative and international involvement and more effective practices of prevention could be developed. The pressure of events will continuously drive international security policies in this direction.

Experience in Kosovo is likely to add new dimensions to international practice. In the Kosovo instance, the international community intervened with military forces readily able to control standard forms of combat and to halt the operations of marauding militia, but not prepared to perform normal police functions or to regenerate viable civil administration. The latter nonetheless are clearly critical to restoring legal order in circumstances where prevention has failed as decisively as it did in Kosovo. Since even the most advanced practice of prevention will not succeed in every instance, the assertion of international responsibility proclaimed in Resolution 1244 clearly implies some systematic preparation, not merely for halting violence but also for restoring order. At a minimum, that implies the preparation of international police and civil administration capabilities, including all the intricate diplomatic coordination that would be involved in their creation and deployment. No one country would or should agree to bear exclusive responsibility, and no country has in fact developed dedicated assets for this purpose. It is inherently an international responsibility not yet acknowledged to that extent. Sustained mastery of the Kosovo situation, however, will certainly require the development of police capability and civil administration under international direction. If the lessons of the episode are drawn accurately, then some degree of contingency preparation for other instances can be expected, if not immediately, then eventually. That is a predictable requirement for the control of civil violence and the protection of legal standards under the circumstances of globalization.

CHAPTER FIVE

Preventing Mass Destruction

No threat has been as compelling in the public mind as the prospect of global war between the United States and the Soviet Union once was. Nor have the lesser threats of conventional invasion and communal violence been considered imminent within the countries of the U.S. alliance system, which set the prevailing terms of international security policy. To the limited extent that there has been a central public fear within the predominant countries, it would be the possibility that the proliferation of access to agents of mass destruction might induce extreme forms of terrorism. That has been a prominent theme in the popular imagination, and it has been reflected as well in official statements of security policy. In 1994 President Clinton declared a national emergency based on his determination that the process of proliferation "constitutes an unusual and extraordinary threat to the national security, foreign policy, and economy of the United States."[1] That declaration established what has become in effect an indefinite extension of emergency powers to undertake various forms of sanction against suspected threats. In 1998, reportedly after reading a popular novel, the president initiated a series of measures for responding to a major terrorist incident and amended the earlier executive order to expand its scope of application.[2]

The sense of imminent danger has been sustained, despite the fact that no event or documented attempt would qualify as an instance of mass destruction terrorism. The limited use of the chemical agent sarin in the Tokyo subway by the Japanese sect Aum Shinrikyo in 1995 suggested the possibilities, however, and even skeptics have to concede that convincing details about threats of this sort are unlikely to be available in advance. Perpetrators of highly destructive terrorism and agents dedicated to resisting it both can be expected to practice such elaborate secrecy that no one ever could be fully informed about the actual state of danger. The underlying potential nonetheless is apparent. Conceivable motives and access to the relevant means are both endemic in contemporary societies, and the combined incentive is amplified by prevailing imbalances in standard military capability. Terrorism is a method that the inherently weak use against the inherently strong, and there are features of the process of globalization that might drive it to extreme forms. One can hope that the probability is quite low; but, as with the critical parameters of deterrence, there is no valid means of measuring that probability. Hence there is a diffuse but insistent public demand for a responsive policy.

Efforts to defend against extreme forms of terrorism naturally intersect efforts to defend against the ordinary variety, which does occur regularly and has inspired elaborate forms of surveillance and counteraction. Nonetheless there are important conceptual and organizational reasons for maintaining a sharp distinction between the forms of terrorism that have been experienced so far and the mass destruction possibilities that are as yet only imagined. Not only are the magnitudes very different, but so is the operational situation. For conventional terrorism it is more feasible to contain the actors than to control the means; for the imagined variety, which has been termed catastrophic terrorism, it is the other way around.[3]

In the case of conventional terrorism, there are active practitioners whose actions, including the acquisition of weapons and explosives, provide a practical means of identifying who they are and what they do. It is not practical, however, to restrict access to the means they use so much that the capacity to cause damage is meaningfully contained. Access to conventional munitions is ubiquitous, and much of it is legally legitimate. In contrast to that situation, no practitioners of catastrophic terrorism have been unambiguously identified as yet. It obviously is possible that conventional terrorists and the belligerent states that sponsor them might extend their activities to larger scales of violence, but there is no guarantee that they are the exclusive or even the principal suspects in that regard. In fact there are reasons to doubt that they are. However vicious or deranged the actions of conventional terrorists are considered to be by their victims, they usually do make some sense from within the perspective they inhabit. Up to this point at least, they have adhered to limitations in service of objectives that extend beyond the violence inflicted. Terrorist operations that are too large and too frequent risk exposure virtually certain to be fatal to the immediate organizers and potentially so to whatever cause they are pursuing. Intuitively it would seem that an incident of catastrophic terrorism is most likely to be the unique act of a previously unknown person or organization. If directly monitoring the perpetrator is not feasible, however, preventing the acquisition of a mass destruction agent is more so, even if it cannot be absolutely assured. For the problem of deliberate mass destruction, control of the means is necessarily the dominant focus of policy.

The technologies that would enable a small clandestine operation to cause mass destruction generally are understood to include nuclear explosives, chemical agents, organically produced toxins, and living pathogens, all of which can generate a larger number of human deaths with a smaller amount of material than can be accomplished with bullets and conventional explosives. The distinctive characteristics of these agents are more important than that common property, however, and individually they present substantially different problems of control. In terms of sheer destructive power concentrated in time and in space, nuclear weapons present by far the largest threat, but not the most distinctive problem. Control over the means of wielding a nuclear threat is incorporated into the management of deterrent operations discussed in chapter 2. The fact that the current state of control over fabricated weapons and fissionable material falls well short of feasible standards is a practical problem that could contribute to an incident of catastrophic terrorism, but it does not pose a separate conceptual issue. An effort to establish higher standards of safety for deterrent operations would include all the measures that might be used to prevent terrorist acquisition or use of nuclear material along with any other form of unauthorized access.

That is less true for chemical agents where the question is whether existing and projected control arrangements designed to manage militarily significant quantities are adequate to cover potential use by terrorists as well. But as a first approximation, that is more a problem of extension and refinement than of conception. The Chemical Weapons Convention, which entered into force on April 29, 1997, categorically prohibits the production, stockpiling, or use of chemical agents that might be used for mass destruction purposes, commits its signatories to imposing criminal punishment on any individual who violates those provisions, and establishes an international organization to monitor compliance.[4] More than a dozen countries have neither signed nor ratified the convention, and some of these are accused of conducting hidden chemical weapons programs. The holdouts are not sufficient in number or in prominence to overturn the standard set by the convention, however, and complete implementation of its terms would constitute systematic control over terrorist application. At any rate, at the relatively small volumes and modest weights suitable for clandestine operations, chemical agents are substantially less threatening than nuclear explosives. In terms of sheer destructive potential, they do not belong in the same category, even though they commonly are listed together.

By contrast biological pathogens pose a problem that is fundamentally different in character and potentially very large.[5] Pathogens are alive; explosives, toxins, and noxious chemicals are not. Nuclear and chemical weapons do not invent themselves, do not reproduce themselves, and do not independently engage in adaptive behavior; pathogens do all of these things. They are generated in nature, and they spontaneously evolve in a process whose critical intricacies are only imperfectly understood. Those that are especially virulent—less than thirty or so of the thousands that are known—provide the potential basis for an emergent pathogen that might in principle cause a devastatingly swift and massive global contagion. One can imagine killing more people with an advanced pathogen than with the current nuclear weapons arsenals. That possibility cannot be precluded on scientific grounds, and the current weight of uncertain judgment probably would have to admit it. Such a catastrophe might be the act of an apocalyptic terrorist, but it also might be a spontaneous act of nature. And, of course, the two sources of danger might interact. Deliberate manipulation of a pathogen might induce further natural evolution and vice versa.

The scientific basis for comprehending both natural and deliberate biological threats is developing very rapidly, and the momentum of the research effort is producing results that could be highly menacing or highly protective depending on how they are applied. As scientists determine the mechanisms of pathology in increasingly greater detail, they simultaneously identify potential offensive and defensive technologies, and the distinction between the two at the research level is a knife-edge of intent rather than intrinsic to the work itself. Reflecting that fact, the main impetus of the relevant research effort comes not from weapons projects but rather from the large, inherently international, and necessarily open enterprise of medical science. The natural threat and the potentially deliberate one are so intertwined that it is neither feasible nor desirable to rely on standard methods of controlling weapons technology. Access to basic scientific information and to the pathogens themselves cannot be restricted either in principle or in practice to the degree that it is for fissionable material or even for chemical agents.

It is primarily the distinctive features of biological pathogens, then, that make the possibility of catastrophic terrorism a distinctive policy problem. Since overwhelming retribution cannot be inflicted on an opponent that cannot be identified, it has to be assumed that the problem escapes the bounds of deterrent policy. The natural threat certainly does. Moreover, since access cannot be restricted by standard methods of security classification and physical isolation, direct preventive protection has to be based on different methods than those developed for nuclear materials and chemical agents. By default, biological agents are controlled much less effectively under current policy than are the other potential agents of mass destruction. Fortunately it is not as easy as commonly imagined to produce dangerous pathogens or to use them for deliberately destructive purposes. Those who are not adequately trained to do so are not likely to succeed or even to survive the attempt. But the knowledge and the training are available, and individuals who have them only require a small home brewery to generate a potentially devastating capability. The public sensation virtually guaranteed to accompany the use of a biological agent creates an ominous incentive. In combination, natural and deliberate sources of biological threat constitute powerful pressure for innovation in security policy.

Relevant History

The principal means of defending against both types of threat is provided, of course, by the passive barriers of the human body and the active response mechanisms of its immune system—the product of several million years of evolution. Any security policy can only be a marginal supplement to those natural mechanisms of protection whose interactions with harmful pathogens are more intricate than anything that could be consciously designed or even, as yet, fully understood. There is evident need for supplement, however. Natural protection is strong, but not invincible. Despite the best efforts of public hygiene and medical practice, individuals are lost to uncontrollable infections, and there are occasional epidemics during which human immunity breaks down on a social scale. In the documented record there have been three major incidents of this sort, one of them recent and one current. An infectious agent believed to have been the plague bacterium killed an estimated 20 million people over a four-year period in the fourteenth century, including nearly a quarter of Western Europe's population at the time. Another 20 million were killed worldwide in less than a year by a virulent strain of the influenza virus that appeared in 1918.[6] And in the fifteen-year period following identification of the AIDS virus in 1983, some twenty variations of the virus have infected nearly 22.6 million people worldwide, more than 8 million of whom have contracted the disease. As of 1996, the annual rate of death from the disease was 1.5 million people.[7] These episodes define the boundaries of experience to date, but not necessarily the limits of what is possible.

Of these three major historical contagions, the 1918 influenza is the most ominous from a security as distinct from a medical perspective. The plague bacterium and the AIDS virus have relatively cumbersome mechanisms of transmission that are vulnerable both to preventive and to acute care measures. Deadly as both of them can be, the full sequence of characteristics from propagation through incubation and disease pathology offers time and opportunity for reaction. The natural threat of plague has been contained by public health practice, and it is reasonable to expect that AIDS eventually will be contained as well without requiring significant assistance from a dedicated security effort. But influenza is another matter entirely. The mechanism of transmission of the influenza virus from an infected host to a prospective victim is extremely effective, the best yet identified. Virus particles are carried on aerosol droplets that take at least seventeen minutes to fall the height of a room when an infected host coughs or sneezes, and their size, ranging from 5 to 10 microns, is nearly ideal for penetrating the physical barriers that guard entry into human lungs. As a result, without comprehensive measures to filter the air intake of individuals, the propagation of an influenza strain cannot be stopped once it has started. One strain infected an estimated 80 percent of the world's population in a six-month period. Normally the incidence of disease among those infected is relatively low, as is the mortality rate of those who contract the disease. However, aviary strains of the virus have killed virtually all of the birds infected, which suggests the possibility of highly lethal human strains as well.

There are inherent trade-offs between virulence and the efficiency of propagation in that a strain that kills its host too ruthlessly restricts its opportunity to be transferred. But the dynamics involved are not so well defined or so restrictive that the boundaries of possibility can be specified exactly. Fatalities from the 1918 epidemic were estimated to be about 4 percent of the number of people infected, implying that somewhere between 500 million and 1 billion people were exposed to the virus. If it is accepted that a 10 percent fatality rate is conceivable for a virulent strain without dramatically altering its efficiency of dissemination, then a contemporary episode involving the deaths of hundreds of millions of people is imaginable. If natural evolution has not yet done such a thing, one can suppose, then it is not likely to happen anytime soon, but unfortunately it recently has become feasible to manipulate the influenza virus with such a result in mind. Like nuclear war, that thought is not unthinkable, strong as the inclination to declare it so may be.

The 1918 influenza epidemic straddled the end of World War I, beginning six months prior to the armistice and continuing for six months thereafter. Although the first identified cases occurred at a military training base, no one ever suggested that the outbreak was a deliberate act of war, but the statesmen of the era were quite impressed with the potential that had been demonstrated. Over four years, the armies of Europe had managed to kill 8 million soldiers and nearly as many civilians while barely moving their front lines. The influenza virus exceeded the combined total of war fatalities in a single year and demonstrated global reach in doing so. When the Geneva Protocol was issued in 1925 to ban the use of poison gas, which had been used on the World War I battlefields and had inspired special revulsion, the provision was extended to include what were then called bacteriological agents as well. The protocol affirmed that weapons of both types were "justly condemned by the general opinion of the civilized world." "Civilized" is one of the most powerful words in the international lexicon of approval and condemnation. To declare a person, group, or country uncivilized is to come very close to denying any claim to legitimacy or human consideration.

The categorical prohibition of the Geneva Protocol applied only to the hostile use of biological agents, however, leaving the major military establishments legally entitled both to develop and to deploy weapons applications of such agents if they so wished. Many of them, including the United States, systematically explored the possibility, but the results were sobering. The effects of a live agent are less direct and less immediate than those of an explosive or a lethal chemical and proved to be much less predictable. An explosive dominates its immediate vicinity and instantaneously propagates its shock wave regardless of the specific circumstances encountered. The process of dispersing either a chemical or a biological agent from its delivery container to a broader area is much more affected by intricate details of terrain and weather and is therefore subject to much wider variation. For biological agents an incubation period imposes some delay on the intended effect under all circumstances and also is subject to wide variation in timing and ultimate outcome. To compound those natural uncertainties, moreover, it is much easier to protect combat soldiers against a dispersed agent than against bullets or explosives. Soldiers can be trained to wear masks in immediate battle situations much more reliably than civilians can be induced to wear them throughout their normal daily routine. That simple device would significantly enhance natural protection against aerosol dispersion of biological agents—the form of dissemination most likely to be effective for military purposes.

In contending with these difficulties the military establishments came to realize that they could not entirely eliminate uncertainty as to whether a biological weapon would accomplish its intended military purpose and that most of what might be done to diminish that uncertainty also would increase the risk of catastrophic collateral effects. They pursued both offensive and defensive development programs, but not on the scale or with the intensity that would be associated with central mission commitments. Their offensive efforts focused primarily on agents such as anthrax and tularemia that are highly lethal to the persons directly exposed but do not spread from one victim to another and thus will not trigger an uncontrollable contagion. As best can be judged from the public record, biological weapons programs did not attempt to develop the type of agent that would be most sensationally destructive—one that combines lethality with efficiency of propagation. Moreover, with the exception of what appears to have been some significant operational experimentation by Japanese forces in China prior to World War II, military establishments have not used biological agents in actual battles and have not deployed them to the extent that they did with both nuclear and chemical weapons. They remained respectfully fearful of biological weapons, but on the whole skeptical that they ever would be an effective instrument of war.

That ambivalent attitude was codified in the Biological and Toxin Weapons Convention (BWC) in 1972. The BWC extended the existing prohibition on the use of biological weapons to cover the development, testing, and stockpiling of weapons for offensive purposes, but it was considered from the outset to be a legal formalism subject to undetectable violation. The BWC was promulgated nearly a half century after the Geneva Protocol, largely at the instigation of the United States, which unilaterally terminated its offensive weapons program in 1969 and wanted to establish a corresponding international standard. The BWC explicitly acknowledged the legitimacy of defensive measures, however, and conceded that it is exceedingly difficult to distinguish between defensive and offensive intent by means of readily observable activities.[8] It did not include provisions for enforcement of the sort that have accompanied formal limitations on nuclear and chemical weapons, and that was a striking omission for the American president at the time, Richard Nixon, who generally denigrated unilateral restraint and insisted on robust verification arrangements for the other types of weapons. Biological warfare was considered to be illegitimate and ineffective for the leading military establishments, but not for individuals or groups unwilling to honor rules of legitimacy—it provided a means, as it were, of moral and operational insurgency.

There was, however, a troublesome exception to that professional military attitude. After the dissolution of the Soviet Union, it was revealed that Soviet military planners had reached very different conclusions about the military utility of biological weapons. In March 1992 the newly formed Russian Federation admitted that the Soviet Union had conducted a clandestine offensive weapons development program in conscious defiance of the BWC and ordered the program to be terminated. Details of the program were not revealed, but it evidently was large, involving many tens of thousands of people, and was connected to an actual concept of military operations. The best guess from what is available on the public record at the moment is that Soviet military planners, instructed to prepare a decisive assault against Western Europe in case an unavoidable war should break out, thought they might have to use biological agents to complete such a mission. Presumably they realized that biological weapons could not substitute for conventional munitions in direct battles against NATO (North Atlantic Treaty Organization) forces, but they might have calculated that, with judicious selection of the agents and timing of their delivery, the urban populations of Western Europe might be sufficiently weakened to allow an occupying army to accomplish an otherwise impossible task. In dealing with a balance of conventional capability that assuredly would have turned against them in a protracted war, as discussed in chapter 3, Soviet military commanders would have been driven to desperate measures to the extent that they took their strategic assignment seriously. It appears that biological weapons were one of the options prepared.

This revelation has cast a dark shadow over contemporary efforts to strengthen the BWC in response to rising concerns about terrorism and about the suspected development of biological weapons by so-called rogue states. The unelaborated candor of the Russian government about the Soviet effort has not been rewarded with a presumption of its own adherence to the BWC. On the contrary, the United States has bluntly questioned whether the offensive weapons program Russia inherited from the Soviet Union truly has been terminated and, with the expressed intention of resolving that doubt, has attempted, together with Great Britain, to arrange for the direct inspection of suspect facilities. While accepting that effort in principle in a trilateral declaration issued in September 1992, Russia clearly has resented the accusation and resisted implementation of the agreed declaration. Efforts to negotiate the details of inspection stalled in the trilateral channel, and that impasse in turn retarded a broader diplomatic effort initiated by all the signatories of the BWC to provide the convention with specified enforcement mechanisms. The parties to the convention have designated an ad hoc group to work out a legally binding instrument that would set objective criteria for compliance, establish formal reporting requirements to provide reassurance of compliance, and define rights of inspection in the event of suspected violations. As of 1999 the ad hoc group had generated a draft text, but that draft did not settle the basic elements of an agreed arrangement, let alone the legal details. As a practical matter, until Britain, Russia, and the United States—the three governments with the most prominent historical programs—come to terms, there is not much chance that the others will do so, and there would be insufficient effect if they did.

The situation reflects the difficulties of dealing with historical residues. It required many years of dedicated effort after 1969 for the United States to root out and redirect the last vestiges of an offensive weapons program that was never as large or as deeply implanted as the Soviet one was. In light of that experience it must be considered unlikely that the Russian government, caught up in a massive internal transformation, will be able with its own resources to meet the standards that the United States and Great Britain are attempting to impose. The American and British stance is hardly gracious, but it does represent an inevitable reaction to the historical revelation. Russian intransigence is hardly reassuring, but it can be attributed to an inherited problem.

Constructive Regulation

It is reasonable to expect that the trilateral impasse eventually will be resolved and that the BWC will be provided with provisions for international inspections. That outcome is a natural extension of established methods of arms control, and diplomatic efforts to achieve it are likely to persist until there is some presentable result. Whatever the exact details prove to be, a formal inspection arrangement undoubtedly will help the BWC to evolve from a formal declaration of principle to an enforced regime, but it is unlikely to resolve suspicions aroused by the historical Soviet program or by the secretive programs widely attributed to some twenty other states. Nor would it erect a barrier to confine catastrophic terrorism. Any organized operation capable of surmounting the technical difficulties involved in developing pathogens for deliberate mass destruction probably would be able to evade a standard adversarial inspection. That is the implication of the lengthy, intrusive, and ultimately frustrated inspection exercise that the UN Security Council imposed on Iraq in the aftermath of the Gulf war. Over a seven-year period, that effort, which was backed by drastic economic sanctions and in the end by direct bombardment, did not succeed in determining the fate of some 200 munitions that Iraq apparently had filled with biological agents during the war.[9] An uncertainty of that magnitude after an effort of that intensity provides stark testimony to the limitations of adversarial inspection.

But adversarial inspection is not the only applicable method of control or the limit of reasonable aspiration. Although the predominant public discussion of biological agents has concentrated on speculation about their deliberately belligerent use in the context of some security confrontation, the public health aspects of the subject provide a different context with different prevailing attitudes and a wider range of applicable methods. It long has been recognized that infectious disease is quintessentially a global problem in that pathogens are largely unaffected by the politically significant distinctions of culture, nationality, ethnicity, or sovereign jurisdiction. Given the continuous mixing of populations produced by air transportation, an infectious agent appearing in any part of the world might well be transferred to any other part within the time limits of its incubation period. Although most outbreaks of infectious disease do remain localized and, by well-developed institutional tradition, are handled by local medical practitioners and public health officials, there is growing recognition of the global character of the natural threat and of the need for better global coordination. Several authoritative reports recently have warned that the international practice of disease monitoring and epidemiological response is well short of what would be required to handle the threat of naturally emerging infections. These reports have issued a series of recommendations for strengthening these mechanisms.[10] The underlying principles of systematic monitoring, protocols of disclosure, and epidemiological collaboration provide the basic design of an arrangement that might be extended to cover deliberate sources of threat as well.

A strategy of using the natural threat to contain the deliberate threat has some significant advantages. The science and technology of infectious disease emerges primarily from medical rather than military culture; diffuse as that observation may appear to be, it has meaningful implications. The driving purpose of medical science is to preserve life, and that fundamental principle affects the prevailing attitudes of those most directly involved. This was strikingly demonstrated during the cold war period. In 1958 and 1959, as the initial commitments were being made to exceedingly large nuclear weapons deployments and as an acute confrontation raged over the status of Berlin, large-scale field trials for the Sabin polio vaccine that had been developed in the United States were initiated in the Soviet Union involving 15 million administered doses. By the summer of 1960, Soviet scientists and health officials had inoculated 77 million persons in their own country and another 23 million in the allied countries of Central Europe with vaccine produced from the seed viruses provided by Albert Sabin. In 1962, the year of the Cuban missile crisis, the results of the Soviet trials became a primary basis for licensing the vaccine in the United States.[11] In these transactions, conducted without direct agreement between the governments, Soviet citizens absorbed the risk of experimentation, and American citizens were vaccinated on the basis of the evidence provided. Both enjoyed the benefits of the vaccine. That accomplishment was remarkably more advanced than what the political relationship at the time generally allowed. It was based on the personal relationship between Albert Sabin and Mikhail Chumakov and on the medical culture within which they operated. By virtue of their training, those who are knowledgeable enough to be at the frontiers of research on infectious pathogens have considerable exposure to that culture, and much could be done to bring the effect of that exposure more specifically to bear.

The fundamental principle of the BWC—protective measures are legitimate, and offensive ones are not—is widely accepted among the research professionals and medical practitioners who are directly engaged with the most dangerous pathogens. With dedicated effort, that distinction could be developed into a professional norm of major significance, making it difficult to conduct dangerous lines of research and development without triggering the critical scrutiny of professional peers. That would not preclude the possibility of capable individuals willing to violate the norm, but it could make such actions explicitly unethical and indeed criminal and could reduce substantially the chance that deviant individuals could operate without detection. If the fundamental standard were to be set more explicitly at the level of practicing research scientists and if it were to be continuously reiterated and reinforced by international monitoring, scope for the development of dangerous pathogens by alleged rogue governments or extreme terrorists would be significantly constrained—not absolute protection, to be sure, but much better than the prevailing situation. It probably would not impose a major barrier to terrorist adaptation of a well-known agent such as anthrax, which can be found in many parts of the world and whose properties are well documented. Anthrax can be used to put tens and perhaps hundreds of thousands of people at risk, but it cannot produce the higher levels of catastrophe associated with an efficiently contagious agent. An organized standard of practice among research scientists is a more promising and in fact a vitally important method of preventing the development of agents more dangerous than the ones currently known.

The completion of an inspection regime for the BWC would contribute, of course, to the explicit setting of a professional standard at the individual level. There are proposals to reinforce the convention at that level by making acts of violation an international crime that could be prosecuted in any jurisdiction regardless of who did it or where it occurred.[12] Criminal sanctions against individuals are potentially quite powerful, as are economic sanctions against governments to the extent that violations can be convincingly demonstrated, and that would apply to any documented use of a biological agent for destructive purposes. But the ambiguity of the research process limits the applicability of criminal sanctions at the critical stage of developmental research just as it limits the effectiveness of adversarial inspection. Moreover, quite apart from their clarity and enforceability, the prohibitions articulated in the BWC and the sanctions associated with them are negative instruments. "Do no harm" is often presented as the first rule of medical practice, but it is not the only one. There is an abiding concern for healing as well and for assertive prevention. A strategy of control resting on the standards of research professionals would not only emphasize concern for natural as well as deliberate threat but also embed the necessary prohibitions in an arrangement with positive incentives.

In broad outline, such a program would internationalize the management and the financing of all research efforts relating to a designated set of pathogens determined to be most dangerous. The basic purpose would be not only to assure compliance with the BWC but to establish more effective collaboration in the prevention of infectious disease. A credible scientific entity, in effect an oversight commission, would be created to set constructive research priorities and general guidelines for responsible practice and to adjudicate any dispute arising from specific research efforts. All individuals and research institutions dealing with the designated pathogens would be required to register with the commission and to inform it of their basic purposes and results. All known strains of the designated pathogens also would have to be registered with the commission. The commission would develop research priorities and arrange for international collaboration in pursuit of those priorities. It would dispense a budget of financial support for these efforts that would be an appreciable fraction of total research expenditures for the listed pathogens. It would focus primarily on provisions for the voluntary but systematic disclosure of information about research activities but also would work out protocols for inspecting research facilities and for conducting the epidemiology associated with the incidence of any disease caused by the designated pathogens. Were such a commission to be created and operated by leading scientists, it would provide much more advanced protection against both types of biological threat. That combination of constructive purpose, comprehensive oversight, and positive incentives is likely to be necessary to achieve high standards of compliance with the BWC.

International practice at the moment is admittedly very far from a comprehensive arrangement of this sort. Some of its provisions have been established within the United States. In April 1997, operating under the authority of antiterrorism legislation enacted in 1996, the Centers for Disease Control and Prevention of the U.S. Public Health Service issued regulations specifying twenty-four infectious agents and twelve toxins that pose an unusually great risk to human health and requiring all individuals and organizations dealing with any of these agents or toxins to be registered with the federal government.[13] An estimated 200 research and medical facilities in the United States fall under these regulations. In some other countries, including Russia, national legislation imposes a legal obligation on individuals to uphold the prohibition on offensive application of biological agents with criminal penalties for violation. In general, however, direct regulation of the most dangerous pathogens is restricted largely to imposing standards for biosafety containment. International guidelines for biosafety containment practices are issued by the World Health Organization, but effective administrative authority resides at the national level. Environmental surveillance for the incidence of disease is done primarily at the national level, with widely varying degrees of attentiveness. Reaction to outbreaks is coordinated between local and national officials in different ways in different countries. In 1995 the World Health Organization established a division to strengthen international disease surveillance, but at the moment only three diseases—plague, yellow fever, and cholera—must be reported. There is extensive exchange of information as a result of normal science and medical practice, but no codification of obligations in that regard. Proprietary rights increasingly are being asserted in relevant areas by individuals and commercial corporations. Appropriate boundaries between these rights and the larger public interest have not been defined.

The basic idea of a combined arrangement has been advanced, however, in the context that might be most expected to induce its development. In 1997, as an extension of the assistance the United States has provided to Russia for the deactivation of nuclear weapons and the maintenance of secure control over fissionable materials, a series of collaborative research projects was established between scientists of the two countries on subjects relating to both the natural and the deliberate threat of biological agents.[14] The participants on the Russian side were located at two of the principal research institutions that had supported the Soviet Union's biological weapons program, and that was understood to be the principal point of the exercise. The projects were intended to demonstrate that scientific expertise derived from the historical Soviet program has legitimate and important public health application and that procedures for collaboration can be worked out that preclude any reasonable suspicion of diversion to offensive application. They also were meant to explore a sustained collaboration between the United States and Russia that might provide the embryo of global oversight.

The extended implications of the collaborative projects have encountered predictable resistance from the security bureaucracies on both sides, who remain locked in their impasse over inspections, but there is some chance that the process of deterioration in Russia eventually will penetrate even the most recalcitrant bureaucratic attitudes. Economic austerity in Russia is so dire that it is quite outlandish to suppose that a major offensive program from the Soviet era still is being secretly sustained and would systematically resist incorporation in a collaborative effort that enforced legitimate restraints and provided sustained financing. Far more likely is the possibility that vestiges of the Soviet effort have been cut off both from financial support and from coherent central direction and that the individuals involved are vulnerable to exploitation by anyone willing and able to pay them. Moreover, public health standards in Russia have been so degraded that the population, especially the prison population, is becoming a potentially dangerous reservoir of infectious disease. The standardized death rate for all Russian males was 27 percent higher in 1993 than it was in 1991 and 15 percent higher than in 1980, rates of decline that are unique in the world. Within those total figures, the standardized death rates due to tuberculosis in particular and infectious and parasitic diseases in general were 59 and 51 percent higher, respectively, in 1993 than they were in 1991.[15] As of 1998, 10 percent of the prison population throughout the former Soviet Union had active tuberculosis, and 12 percent of these—about 18,000 cases—were infected with drug-resistant strains. At one penal colony at Mariinsk, 40 percent of the inmates were found to be infected with drug-resistant strains, the highest incident rate ever recorded for those strains.[16] With overall public health expenditures declining to 2.5 percent of a gross domestic product that itself has declined by as much as 50 percent since the inception of the Russian Federation, there is danger that Russia might lose control over infectious disease in its increasingly stressed population. The weakening of control over both dimensions of threat in Russia creates reasons for assertive international assistance that are already strong and could rapidly become compelling. Any attempt to provide assistance would have to feature strong constructive incentives and be based on equitable reciprocity if it is to have any hope of acceptance.

Protective Oversight

As long as there is no event to validate it, the catastrophic potential of biological agents is not likely to become a primary focus of security policy, despite the situation in Russia and despite the fact that political concern about the belligerent use of virulent pathogens has intensified in the aftermath of the cold war. Response to that concern has been directed largely to contingency preparations for hypothetical incidents of small to modest size compared with the outer reaches of what can be imagined, and it is difficult to quarrel with the practical judgment implied. Smaller incidents appear to be more probable, and they certainly would be more tractable. The possibility of a massive contagion that would overwhelm any prepared response does loom in the background, however, and the momentum of scientific investigation will provide a continuously evolving reminder of the underlying danger.

That relentless fact was exemplified by a recent dispute over an experiment done at the State Research Center for Applied Microbiology in Russia—one of the major institutions formerly involved in the Soviet-era biological weapons program. The experiment was inspired by a line of research attempting to understand the genetic basis for large variations in the virulence of naturally occurring anthrax strains. The experimenters produced three genetically altered strains of anthrax, one virulent strain and two mild strains suitable for use as the basis for vaccines.[17] They demonstrated that for the experimental animals, gold hamsters, the altered virulent strain overrode immunity provided by the natural vaccine strains, but that the altered vaccine strains restored immunity. The experiment was described at an international conference in the United Kingdom in 1995, and it inspired some discussion of the scientific interpretation of the results, but no questions about its basic propriety. When it was published in the journal *Vaccine*, however, in December 1997, it generated a great deal of alarm in the international press.[18] The United States was engaged at that moment in active confrontation with Iraq over the inspection of facilities related to their historical effort to develop biological weapons, and several articles speculated that the genetically altered strain in the experiment might be able to defeat the immunity provided by the vaccine administered to U.S. troops in the region and that it might have been sent to Iraq. No evidence for either supposition was cited in the articles, and no mention was made of the fact that the experiment was done on animals not considered to provide a reliable model for judging human effects. The speculation had no reasonable scientific basis, but the controversy revealed that there are no agreed professional standards to determine the bounds of propriety. The deliberate genetic alteration of virulent pathogens is acknowledged to be a very sensitive matter, and it is doubtful that the experiment would have been considered appropriate at USAMRIID, the U.S. Army's biological research program at Fort Detrick, Md. But it is also very difficult to say that natural variation in the virulence of anthrax strains should not be investigated, and no one had suggested that to the Russian scientists who developed and published their work in normal fashion. Other experiments of this sort might be done on agents that entail a much greater risk of contagion. The more experiments that are done, the more compelling is the reason to develop common professional standards and to embed them in protective oversight practices.

In regulatory practice at the moment, the term oversight does not have the broad recognition or legal standing established for the term verification, and the distinction is not sharply drawn. But the underlying principles are different. Verification is a process that occurs between adversaries and is delimited strictly by formal agreement and associated rules of procedure. The obligations subject to verification are established explicitly by ratified treaties, and the methods used depend primarily on remote observation. The parties in such an arrangement are not expected to share direct access to the activities in question. Oversight is more of a collaborative arrangement conducted on behalf of commonly shared purposes. It is less bound by legal specifications and depends more on voluntary disclosure rules and on the assertive interest of the participating parties in conveying mutual reassurance. It also depends less on the exercise of central authority and more on the spontaneous effects of consensus. It is a dispersed form of regulation applicable when there is no fundamental barrier to direct and detailed collaboration. States engage in verification to stabilize a confrontational security relationship. They engage in oversight to prevent a confrontational situation from developing and to provide mutual protection against managerial errors or deliberate malfeasance at some subordinate level.

It is not evident that the cumulative pressure of sensitive experimentation against the background of a catastrophic threat will be sufficient to motivate the development of protective oversight for the more dangerous pathogens. Most of those involved in the very large enterprise of controlling infectious disease—scientists, doctors, public health officials, commercial entrepreneurs, and emergency response personnel—probably would agree that standards of responsible practice should be defined more precisely and that the flow of relevant information needs to be better organized in some sense. But the details involved in establishing systematic disclosure rules and in exercising international oversight are bound to be controversial. No one will welcome the formal obligations involved. Everyone will be worried about inappropriate intrusiveness and potential misuse of the information gathered. If disclosure rules are to be established, then the purposes have to be accepted, the provisions carefully specified, the limits well defined, and the requirements universally applied. Intense and lengthy discussions yet to be held clearly will be required to establish these conditions.

It is technically feasible to work out powerful forms of regulation using oversight techniques. The information technology that is driving the underlying process of globalization enables rapid and efficient forms of monitoring of dispersed activities. Pathogen inventories at research laboratories and medical facilities could be reported routinely by electronic means with minimal burden. If the capacity to handle very large flows of information is combined with specified standards and systematic disclosure rules, much more robust protection against any illegal activity can be achieved in principle. Continuous monitoring techniques based on automated reporting are used to regulate financial markets, for example; and, although operating with defined standards and disclosure provisions that are still well short of their full potential, they have made insider stock trading and drug money laundering much riskier activities than they used to be. Because these techniques are potentially so powerful, the risk of misapplication qualifies the benefit to be achieved in any given instance, but it is reasonable to expect that a balance between these considerations eventually will be worked out for those activities that pose large inherent dangers. That class of activities includes the handling of all the agents of mass destruction. The comprehensive accounting system for fissionable materials, discussed in chapter 2, would be an oversight arrangement. But their distinctive features make biological agents the leading instance for the development of advanced oversight practices. There is no other reliable means of exercising protective control.

CHAPTER SIX

Transforming Security Relationships

ON SEPTEMBER 11, 1990, the incumbent American president, George Bush, addressed a joint session of Congress to explain the mobilization of forces that would soon liberate Kuwait from Iraqi occupation. He spoke of oil. He spoke of tyranny and aggression. He cited the menace of weapons of mass destruction. He also introduced a broader theme reminiscent of the memorandum Henry Stimson had sent to President Truman on the same day forty-five years earlier. "A new world order," Bush declared, "is struggling to be born, a world quite different from the one we've known. A world where the rule of law supplants the rule of the jungle. A world in which nations recognize the shared responsibility for freedom and justice. A world where the strong respect the rights of the weak."[1] The president, not known for doing so, was projecting a vision.

His phrasing struck many resonant chords. In the months and years that followed, long after the Gulf war had been concluded, the idea of a new world order was rehearsed extensively in American political discussion, often with derision. Many rushed to declare the implicit infant of the image to have been stillborn, others to denounce it as a monster in the making. Most pointedly withheld judgment until it could demonstrate its robustness, presumably in rites of adult passage after a lengthy term of stern apprenticeship. Only a few embraced it as a child to be nurtured.

Whatever the judgment, it is fair to presume that virtually everyone at all attentive to world events absorbed the phrase and made some effort to ponder it. Under the circumstances of discontinuity, a new world order is not an idea to be dispatched lightly. It insinuates itself, however roughly it might be greeted.[2]

President Bush himself did not elaborate much beyond his initial phrasing and did not seek to develop the theme beyond its application to the Gulf war. But the statement has a formidable simplicity and relentless implications that may well be long remembered. It may be one of those utterances that distant generations will appreciate much more than the ones that originally heard it. It suggests impending transformation—the ascendancy of equity over power for reasons that are compelling and the subordination of divisive identities to universal standards. If such a transformation does occur, it undoubtedly will be the work of several generations and will be recognized only with the advantage of lengthy retrospect. In the meantime, some of its predictable elements will command attention and are likely to prompt significant adjustments in security policy.

Whatever else might be involved, the process of globalization is changing the nature of threat and forcing some adaptation of basic strategic principles and the pattern of allegiance associated with them. Each of these dimensions—threat, strategy, and affiliation—is understood most readily in terms of a sharp conceptual distinction: the difference between a deliberate opponent and a natural process, between strategies of prevention and strategies of reaction, and between cooperative and confrontational alignments. Although in reality much of life is lived at the fuzzy edges of such distinctions and policy usually blends them, awareness of the conceptual difference is important in determining the direction of appropriate adjustments.

Traditional security policy has been concerned primarily with deliberate threat. A calculating opponent is provisionally identified who, it is presumed, will exploit any major vulnerability that can be detected. That presumption cannot be adopted in unqualified form since doing so would impose impractical requirements for continuous preparation, but for a half century it clearly has been the dominant conceptual reference. It has been disaggregated since the end of the cold war and rendered less specific by the major military establishments. Global enmities are not discussed in the blunt manner that the Soviet Union and the United States discussed them, but the underlying logic has been preserved. The formulations of threat currently used—ranging from major regional contingencies to lesser rogue states and terrorists to the eventual emergence of peer competitors—refer to the deliberately aggressive actions of calculating enemies who are assumed to have conscious identity even if they are not mentioned explicitly. The threat emanating from distributed processes—the unforeseen interaction of deployed forces, the erosion of legal standards, the evolution of dangerous pathogens, or the tipping of vital environmental balances—has been very much in the background of security thinking and clearly subordinate to the logic of strategic confrontation.[3] It seems likely that the process of globalization will make unintentional, distributed threats a much more prominent concern, and perhaps they will become, by force of experience and accumulating evidence, the predominant concern.

To the extent that this occurs, the balance of strategy and affiliation will shift. Distributed processes consequential enough to pose a security concern, particularly those susceptible to contagion effects, are very difficult to handle using policies designed for contingent reaction. By the time the effects of a dispersed process are imminent and obvious enough to trigger a contingent response, the momentum developed is likely to overwhelm the reaction. By their very nature, dispersed processes require policies emphasizing systematic prevention rather than contingency reaction. If the processes are globally dispersed, moreover, they require inclusive arrangements for practicing systematic prevention. In the prototype instance of an advanced infectious pathogen, for example, whether deliberately created or naturally evolved, the initiating development could occur anywhere in the world, and by the time it is manifest as an epidemic disease in any location, much of the protective leverage would have been lost. In the more difficult instance of legal decay, where detection and diagnosis of even a very advanced problem is much less assured than it is for infectious disease, prevention would have to be the main aspiration, and effective policies would have to be cooperative in character and inclusive in scope. In general, globalization appears to be generating a new class of security problems in which dispersed processes pose dangers of large magnitude and incalculable probability. In reaction to those problems, it seems likely that the weight of policy will have to shift from contingency reaction to anticipatory prevention and that this will have to be done in global coalition. That would appear to be the defining core of an impending transformation of security policy.

That shift will be difficult to accomplish. Whether they are judged to be democratic or authoritarian, all governments depend on a working consensus in order to act coherently. There is never enough concentrated authority to rule by that means alone. As a consequence, all governments have considerable difficulty formulating what scholars of the subject like to term grand strategy—a definition of fundamental purpose and of the means to achieve it that combines the elements of threat, strategy, and affiliation into an overall security policy. Generally there is too much confusion and disagreement to get a clean result. Also as a consequence, governments are extremely reluctant to depart from whatever working consensus they have managed to establish on these subjects. The transition is profoundly unsettling, even if the ultimate outcome is unquestionably superior; rarely if ever has a redesigned security posture been accepted in advance as superior.[4] This is especially true for the United States, which has emerged from the cold war period in the best position to establish the terms of grand strategy. As discussed in preceding chapters, the United States has adjusted its political rhetoric and its military forces in response to the end of the cold war, but not its fundamental security posture. It remains committed to the basic deterrent operations and contingency reactions that were established over the course of half a century and to the alliance arrangements in which they were embedded. There is little indication that the prevailing political sentiment is willing to undertake a truly fundamental revision. Many documents have advanced the rhetoric of such a revision, but none with broad political standing has defined and embraced the content of it.[5] Nor should that be expected. There has been too little time for comprehensive revisions to have ripened and no catalytic event sufficiently consequential to have advanced the schedule.

How, then, might the drama play out? Where might an impending transformation manifest itself most prominently? How might it be promoted most effectively? Of the many speculative answers that could be given to these questions, the most plausible have to do with the issues of affiliation. If it is accepted that a process of globalization is driving a security transformation, then one of its most important features would be the spontaneous interpenetration of historically separate societies—the binding together of economic fortunes and the many aspects of interest that follow from that. Whatever the magnitude and probability of threat associated with that process, the potential is significant enough to require preventive management, and the practice can be expected to develop most rapidly where the problem is greatest—at the historical boundaries of separation. In the first instance, that means Russia—at once the major victim of globalization, the leading venue of its security implications, and the most dangerously isolated of the major societies. The internal crisis in Russia is likely to be the occasion for fundamental revisions of security posture or the source of massive grief if those revisions are not accomplished. It also means China and India. With some 40 percent of the total human population between them, these two countries are facing demanding problems of internal development, problems of a magnitude that will be the preoccupation of several decades. The momentum and potential consequence of greenhouse gas emissions alone make the internal development of these two societies a matter of major global interest, and that fact defines their strategic importance much more than the relative size of their economies or the capacity of their military forces. In all probability, it means North Korea as well. North Korea is in as great an internal economic crisis as Russia and is even more isolated. It is the focus of one of the principal regional contingencies and a critical venue for the international control of ballistic missile technology and fissionable materials. All of these countries are currently outside the predominant alliance system operated by the United States and, to varying degrees, are in confrontation with it. In each case, however, the press of circumstance already has forced historical relationships to be revisited. That process, one can assume, is where the leading edge of transformation is to be found.

Russia

Since the Russian Federation emerged from the wreckage of the Soviet Union bearing the burden of its historical legacy, it has been engulfed in an internal transformation that is extensive even though the ultimate result is not evident and probably not yet determined. The political mechanisms that the Communist party used to rule the Soviet Union and to direct its economy have been dismantled. It is considered unlikely they could ever be reconstituted, although not, of course, absolutely impossible. An election process that meets international standards of fairness has been established as the fundamental basis for legitimate political rule, and most careful observers concede that Russian society as a whole has embraced that process with an impressive degree of consensus and active participation. Voter turnout and attentiveness to political campaigns have been greater in Russia than in the United States, and the level of complaint about the various forms of manipulation and illicit advantage has not been strikingly different in the two countries. The corresponding transition to a market economy is much less advanced and much more in question, but the intention is clearly to move in that direction. And if globalization is indeed the inexorable and powerful process it appears to be, then eventually and in some manner Russia will have to complete the transition. The demise of the Soviet-era central planning mechanisms presumably constitute the initial stage. Although there are plenty of skeptics on both points and some scope for reversion, in broad outline the Russian Federation has been a democracy from its inception and has been attempting to become a market economy.

After a decade of experience, however, it is increasingly evident that the economic transition in Russia is a problem of monumental proportions, not yet fully measured, let alone mastered. The aggregate size of the economy was very small at the outset for a society of nearly 150 million people dispersed over the world's largest national territory, and it has declined in net terms over the history of the Russian Federation. In 1998 gross domestic product (GDP) was estimated to be the equivalent of $160 billion at the prevailing exchange rate—twenty-sixth in the world in absolute terms and seventy-third in per capita terms—and it was shrinking at the rate of 5 percent a year. Because of inherent uncertainties of measurement, both the absolute level and the rate of decline are difficult to establish with confidence, but the most respected estimates suggest that Russia has lost up to 50 percent of its already sparse economic product since 1991. To some extent, that decline can be seen as an inevitable and in fact healthy aspect of the initial transition. Products of low economic value are supposed to be abandoned under market discipline in favor of products that are profitable. But that substitution has not been occurring in Russia to the degree required to reverse the overall decline and establish sustained economic growth. Standard reform measures espoused by the industrial democracies and standard macroeconomic discipline enforced by the International Monetary Fund (IMF) have failed to induce it for reasons that are deeply embedded in the economic structure inherited from the Soviet Union.

As noted in previous chapters, a major portion of the manufacturing sector of the Soviet economy was devoted to the development of the military establishment in competition with the combined assets of the U.S. alliance system. That effort, conducted from a much smaller economic base, succeeded in matching the opposing standard in basic quality and exceeding it in overall quantity up through the first three or four generations of cold war weapons. It then fell progressively behind in the application of information technology, where the driving impulse came primarily from commercial markets. The degree of dedication to military production could not have been sustained by the Soviet Union and has not been sustained by Russia, but the historical effort has left a major problem of industrial misalignment. The size, location, and product lines of many Russian enterprises, not only the direct weapons producers, were determined by central planners for reasons so far from market logic that they have little hope of surviving the transition. There has been no assessment of the market viability of Russian enterprises comparable to what was done for the East German enterprises when they were absorbed into West Germany's market economy, but it is doubtful that the results of such an exercise would be less daunting. In the East German case, all the major manufacturing enterprises required large reductions in their labor forces, major infusions of capital, and extensive internal reorganization to have any hope of adapting successfully to the market economy. Even with the equivalent of hundreds of billions of dollars in financial commitments from West Germany—much greater than has been available to Russia for a society roughly one-tenth the size—a quarter of the industrial enterprises had to be closed immediately.[6] To compound the difficulty, vital communal functions including the basic safety net for families and individuals have been embedded in Russian manufacturing enterprises, making it socially ruinous to abandon them without replacing these functions. To compound the problem further, the same pattern of large enterprises was imposed on agriculture as well, leaving the overall economy with virtually no base for the modest-scale entrepreneurship that has been the major engine of growth for economic transition elsewhere, in China in particular.

In coping with these structural conditions, the Russians collectively have learned to operate what one of their government commissions graphically termed a virtual economy.[7] Basically this involves using the portion of the economy that is viable under international market conditions—largely oil and gas and a few other mineral extraction industries—to subsidize the large segments of the manufacturing sector that are not viable. Soviet-era enterprises, operated by their managers independent of central direction, have been sustained through barter arrangements whereby they obtain material inputs in trade for products they produce at attributed prices higher than what actual market prices would be. The attributed prices mask the fact that, in terms of actual market value, the enterprises are consuming more than they produce and thus are absorbing economic assets rather than producing them. The assets absorbed are used in part to preserve their communal functions and to sustain their work forces. That arrangement produces an economy in which some 80 percent or more of the GDP takes the form of barter trade. With heavy reliance on agricultural produce grown on private plots by a substantial portion of the population and on other forms of economic subsistence at the household level, the virtual economy has sustained Russian society through the first decade of the federation. But it also has prevented an overall transition to market-based operations by buffering major segments of the manufacturing sector from the competitive pressures that would induce it and the operating conditions that would sustain it. One cannot develop the tax policies and legal rules associated with normal commercial practice while operating a virtual economy. Economic policy in Russia has sacrificed market discipline to protect social welfare.

The result is a process of disinvestment that drains the base of natural resources and accumulated capital to preserve current consumption. This process is ruinous over the longer term and ultimately unsustainable. The longer the virtual economy operates, the more difficult it will be to assimilate Russia into the market economy. But no reform program has yet been devised in Russia or anywhere else that could break the pattern. The so-called shock therapy initially urged by leading theorists of reform would have subjected so many people to such enduring austerity that it is hardly surprising the Russian political system protected itself from the implications. Any democracy would do that, and any political system that did not do it would have to rely on authoritarian mechanisms. A politically and socially feasible form of transition in Russia is difficult to devise, and no one has done it yet.

The consequences for the Russian government and for the military establishment it operates have been devastating. With enterprises using barter arrangements to cover their tax obligations—a practice accounting for 40 percent of federal government receipts in 1997—both the real value and the fungibility of the tax base have been eroded.[8] As discussed in chapter 3, cash revenues net of borrowing have not been adequate at any point in the Russian Federation's history to support the military forces or to perform any of the other basic governmental functions. Up to August 1998 those revenues were supplemented with international borrowing, as the Russian government in the first six years of its existence accumulated some $70 billion in new debt in the international markets on top of the $95 billion it inherited from the Soviet Union. Virtually all of that was used to subsidize consumption. Virtually none of it was invested in a manner that would allow it to be repaid. This pattern could not be sustained indefinitely, and it effectively collapsed in August 1998 when accumulating economic pressures forced a sharp devaluation of the currency. At the resulting market exchange rates, the debt service on loans denominated in dollars and other international currencies became unmanageable, forcing an effective default on international debt obligations. The entire banking system became insolvent. At the beginning of 1999, annual cash tax receipts were running at the ruble equivalent of less than $10 billion at the new market exchange rate. Debt obligations alone for the same year exceeded $17 billion. It was evident that Russia could pay very little of that debt unless it obtained new international credit to do so, nor could it meet the conditions for new credit that the IMF was obliged by its general operating principles to impose. Although no one was eager to admit it, that was a moment of epiphany for many of those involved, a glimmering of recognition that the magnitude, scope, and duration of the Russian crisis might exceed anything yet experienced or yet imagined.

That, of course, is not a welcome thought and not one that can be proved beyond question. Under the fluid, loosely organized circumstances of transition, some portion of Russian economic activity does escape measurement, making it impossible to determine the base and the trend with confidence. Official figures are prone to major error. More refined measurement would have to be based on surveys at the household level much more systematic and reliable than are being conducted. It is evident that people are improvising their livelihood at the household level and possible that a process of economic regeneration might emerge from that activity well before its aggregate effects can be detected. It is also possible, however, that the process simply masks the effects of aggregate decline and that the trend at that level is one of progressive exhaustion. Impressionistic accounts are somewhat contradictory. The frequently noted bustle in Moscow and to a lesser extent in St. Petersburg is offset by an active discussion of social stress—wage arrears, homelessness, surging crime, hunger, and declining standards of health. Official figures for grain production in 1998 were sufficiently low—48.4 metric tons in 1998 as compared to 87.1 metric tons in 1997—to trigger substantial international commitments of food assistance, but observers within Russia did not detect mass starvation or even an aggregate food shortage.[9] The general decline in health standards summarized in chapter 5 is alarming but has not yet reached catastrophic proportions. Basically it has reversed the substantial improvements that were made between 1970 and 1990, the final two decades of the Soviet Union. In terms of practical politics, those who would acknowledge a massive crisis in Russia and would act on that basis still have to carry a burden of proof that cannot be met, but the debt crisis coming in the wake of the Asian financial crisis issued a strong hint that at some point the political burden might shift. Russia is flirting with social catastrophe that might be manifested in many forms and might suddenly become unmistakably obvious.

At any rate if it is admitted that the problem of economic transition in Russia is likely to be proportionately comparable to what it has proved to be in East Germany, then a new security arrangement becomes an urgent need. Market transition of that magnitude is not something that any Russian government of whatever character could be expected to accomplish with internally generated resources alone or with those it could plausibly attract from commercial markets in the initial stages. Even if Russia embraces the principles of market discipline with no greater scope for qualification than the citizens of East Germany had under the conditions of unification and even if it manages to generate a substantial rate of internal savings despite enduring austerity, its market transition is necessarily an international development project. It almost certainly would require complete forgiveness of Soviet-era debt and extended repayment terms for the Russian Federation's own debt. It also would require facilitated market access for those segments of Russian industry that have a realistic chance of making the transition—for example, a tailored exemption from steel-dumping suits in the United States. In all probability, it eventually would require hundreds of billions of dollars in new credit on more accessible terms than private capital markets would consider outside the context of a dedicated international development program.

In this situation the Russian military establishment cannot sustain its current size and cannot meet the performance requirements of its inherited missions. Without an international development project, it could not expect for several decades, if ever, to command the resources necessary to continue active deterrent operations at acceptable standards of safety or basic conventional force missions under standard assumptions of contingency planning. Within the context of a development project, those commitments are unlikely to be considered either necessary or legitimate. Therefore, for basic reasons of safety and efficiency, an international development project would have to be accompanied by credible security assurances to Russia—in effect a transformation of its relationship with the American alliance system. However it is presented conceptually or implemented institutionally, the inclusion of Russia in this system is a necessary step in establishing a new security order, and the underlying economic crisis in Russia is a prime motivation for doing so.

This could be an inherently better deal for all concerned regardless of the background crisis. The confrontational principles that still provide the foundation for the security relationship despite the overlay of political accommodation are more dangerous and less efficient than the practice of systematic reassurance would be. If that more refined principle could be developed with Germany and Japan, there is no reason why it could not be developed with Russia. It is more likely to be the sense of danger, however, than the lure of opportunity that moves the mountains of political attitude involved in such a transformation, as it was in the earlier cases, and there is ample danger in doing the work required. To be sure, the withering of the Russian military establishment under an eroding economic base effectively precludes the classic forms of deliberate aggression, but that is hardly the only consequence. The windfall security benefit to the rest of the world is more than offset by the potential effects of radical internal disintegration. The Russian military establishment must exercise custodial control over its large inventory of weapons and must provide the foundation for basic civil order on Russian territory. Any major failure in performing either function could produce distributed-process threats of major global significance—the inadvertent triggering of deterrent operations; the irresponsible dissemination of weapons, materials, and technology; the generation of civil violence. The key to preserving custodial control and civil order is the military personnel system, and that system is severely threatened under the financial pressures imposed by the economic situation. The skills and attitudes required to operate the military establishment responsibly require continuous training and replenishment of personnel, and this requires resources. If the people are not paid and their families are starving, they will be forced to scramble for subsistence, and they will not be able to perform their necessary functions. It is as simple and as ominous as that.

Sustained underfinancing will drive the Russian military establishment to eventual disintegration in the context of prevailing policy. Unless it is dramatically reduced in size and incorporated into a comprehensibly protective security arrangement, it will fall apart, and a great deal of violence could accompany that process. The deterrent operation being conducted by the Russian military forces poses by far the largest physical threat to the United States and members of its alliance system. That operation can-

Table 6-1. *Foreign Direct Investment as a Percentage of Gross Domestic Product in Select Countries, 1996*

Country	*Foreign direct investment*	*Country*	*Foreign direct investment*
Albania	10.8	Latvia	13.5
Armenia	2.1	Lithuania	8.3
Azerbaijan	57.3	Moldova	8.4
Belarus	0.5	Poland	9.7
Bosnia and Herzegovina	0.0	Romania	4.1
Bulgaria	4.5	Russian Federation	1.5
China	24.7	Slovakia	5.8
Croatia	5.0	Slovenia	10.8
Czech Republic	13.6	Tajikistan	2.0
Estonia	20.4	TFYR Macedonia	1.1
Georgia	5.4	Turkmenistan	5.7
Hungary	33.2	Ukraine	3.3
Kazakhstan	19.8	Uzbekistan	1.5
Kyrgyzstan	80.7		

Source: United Nations Conference on Trade and Development, *World Investment Report 1998: Trends and Determinants* (United Nations, 1998), pp. 406–10.

not be safely sustained under the circumstances of economic crisis, and it is not likely to be removed short of incorporating Russia into the alliance system.

As yet no international development project and no corresponding security arrangement have been officially espoused that are adequate to address either dimension of the problem, and there is a serious question whether the limited measures that have been advanced have done more good than harm. Other than the accumulation of sovereign debt, international economic engagement with Russia has been minimal, a fact that is attributable to the underlying structural problems but remains significant nonetheless. As reflected in table 6-1, foreign direct investment in Russia has been exceedingly low, lower as a proportion of GDP than in virtually all of the surrounding countries of the region.

A brief spurt of investment in 1997 was knocked back by the ensuing debt crisis. The IMF rescue package pledged in July 1998 amounted to $22.6 billion in new credit over an eighteen-month period, roughly comparable to the fiscal erosion of the government budget that had occurred over the previous six months.[10] That was not enough to motivate the austerity measures on which it was conditioned or to fend off the subsequent currency devaluation. The initial disbursement of $4.8 billion quickly disappeared in currency transactions associated with the ruble devaluation it was intended to prevent. The experience produced an extended impasse between the international financial institution, which was defending standards meant to be applied universally, and the government, which was defending the society on which it depends. A second package of $4.5 billion was nominally provided in July 1999 but was devoted entirely to repaying IMF debt obligations. That avoided a formal default to the IMF but did not resolve the impasse. It cannot realistically be resolved without changing the conception of the relationship and expanding the scope of economic engagement.

Similarly, as summarized in table 6-2, various forms of security cooperation have been developed with Russia, ranging from programs designed to assure secure custody over nuclear materials, to joint peacekeeping exercises, to a projected joint center for monitoring missile launches. Regular collegial visits have accompanied these activities and have produced a network of constructive personal relationships that probably provides a workable foundation for meaningful collaboration. The reassuring effects of this activity have been overwhelmed, however, by what most Russians consider to be a threatening combination of adverse circumstance and political betrayal. As they read the diplomatic record, when they acceded to German unification, they were promised that NATO would not expand eastward. Yet within less than a decade NATO had extended its jurisdiction to the eastern states of Germany and had formally incorporated Poland, Hungary, and the Czech Republic.[11] The expansion of the alliance was accompanied by soothing rhetoric and formal consultation with Russia, none of which obscured the discrimination involved. Although presiding officials on the NATO side were careful to hold open the possibility that Russia eventually might be eligible for inclusion in NATO, the underlying intent of the most assertive advocates was to extend an institutional bulwark against the possibility of renewed belligerence from a resurgent Russia. The disingenuous undertones of the rhetoric undermined the currency of reassurance. Moreover, the practical effect of NATO expansion intensified the increasing disparities in military capability, most notably in active deterrent force and advanced tactical air operations. NATO's capabilities could be extremely dangerous to Russia with only a few days' preparation, and no accommodation has been offered to alter that circumstance. The internal deterioration within the Russian military establishment will make the situation increasingly more serious over time.

Russia's sense of its own vulnerability and of NATO's disingenuousness was reinforced by the air campaign conducted against Yugoslavia in 1999 in the course of intervention in Kosovo.[12] In the process of negotiating the 1997 Founding Act whereby Russia formally accommodated to NATO expansion, NATO officials emphasized that the alliance was inherently defensive in character and would not attack unless it was itself attacked. The action taken against Yugoslavia two years later was seen in Russia as a repudiation of that assurance conducted outside of NATO's legal treaty area in response to circumstances that involved no direct attack on a NATO member. It was initiated without any attempt to secure UN Security Council authorization, in violation, as the Russians viewed it, of international legal procedure. And this was done against a traditional Russian ally in reaction to actions that most Russians did not consider to be more egregious than those undertaken by American allies. In their view, Serbian intimidation of Albanians was similar to what the Croatians in Bosnia had done to Serbs in the Krajina region with implicit approval and indirect participation of the United States.[13] The message received was that Russia itself is subject to assertive NATO intimidation and has no reliable international protection against it. This implication will be long remembered and will severely limit NATO's ability to provide credible reassurance.

The Kosovo episode also had indirect reverberations affecting NATO's inclination to provide reassurance. In August of 1999 and again in September, armed groups of insurgents invaded several villages in Dagestan from bases in Chechnya proclaiming an intention to establish Islamic rule. Both Dagestan and Chechnya were formally constituent republics of the Russian Federation, but Chechnya had been ceded effective independence in 1996 as a result of a two-year civil war in which the Russian military had suffered a series of bitter defeats. The insurgent actions coincided with three major terrorist explosions in Moscow and one in the Russian city of Volgodonsk, all of which were attributed to Islamic militants from Chechnya and Dagestan. The Russian military quickly reasserted control over the remote villages the insurgents had briefly occupied and then developed a military campaign against Chechnya itself evidently designed to reassert the sovereign control that had been abandoned in 1996. The operation initially featured extensive bombing of infrastructure targets such as the phone system and power grid in explicit emulation of the NATO campaign against Yugoslavia. It evolved into a lengthy and highly destructive ground invasion of Chechnya that was solidly supported by political opinion within Russia but was appalling to much of the outside world.

Table 6-2. *U.S. Security Collaboration with Russia, 1991–99*

Form of collaboration	*Responsible U.S. government agency*	*Date initiated*	*Purpose*	*Expenditures through early 1999 (millions of U.S. dollars)*	*Projected annual cost (millions of U.S. dollars)*
Cooperative Threat Reduction (CTR) program, known as Nunn-Lugar program	Department of Defense	1991	Provide assistance to help dismantle arsenal of weapons of mass destruction	1,700	243
Materials Protection, Control, and Accounting Program	Department of Energy	1993	Reduce the threat of nuclear proliferation and nuclear terrorism by rapidly improving the security of all weapons-usable nuclear material in forms other than nuclear weapons	378	97
International Science and Technology Center	Department of State (with international assistance)	1992	Engage scientists, engineers, and other technical personnel with skills relevant to nuclear, chemical, and biological weapons and missile-delivery systems in order to prevent brain drain to countries of concern	118[a]	21[b]
Initiatives for Proliferation Prevention	Department of Energy	1994	Engage weapons scientists and institutes in productive nonmilitary work in the short term and create jobs for former weapons scientists in the high-technology commercial marketplace in the long term	64	30
Nuclear Cities Initiative	Department of Energy	September 1998	Promote nonproliferation by redirecting the work of nuclear weapons scientists, engineers, and technicians in Russia's ten nuclear cities to alternative scientific or commercial activities	15–20	120

Nonsecurity programs (for example, trade and investment, business and economic development, training and exchange, democracy, partnership, energy and environmental, nuclear power safety, social sector and humanitarian)	Various (for example, U.S. Agency for International Development, U.S. Department of Agriculture, U.S. Trade and Development Agency, Peace Corps, U.S. Information Agency, Department of Treasury, Department of Commerce, Environmental Protection Agency, Department of Energy, National Research Council)	1992–97	Specific to the program	3,561	To be determined

Source: For the Cooperative Threat Reduction program, Department of Defense, Cooperative Threat Reduction program website, "Funding," www.ctr.osd.mil/07frame.htm [accessed November 1999]; Judith Miller, "U.S. and Russia Extend Deal Reducing Threat from Arms," *New York Times,* June 17, 1999, p. A7. Pavel Felgenhauer, "Defense Dossier: Some U.S. Ties Survive War," *Moscow Times,* May 20, 1999. For Materials Protection, Control, and Accounting, U.S. General Accounting Office, "Nuclear Nonproliferation: Concerns with DOE's Efforts to Reduce the Risks Posed by Russia's Unemployed Weapons Scientists," GAO/RCED-99-54, report to the Chairman of the Senate Committee on Foreign Relations, February 1999; Congressional Budget Office, "Cooperative Approaches to Halt Russian Nuclear Proliferation and Improve the Openness of Nuclear Disarmament," CBO Report (May 1999); Nonproliferation Project, Carnegie Endowment for International Peace, "U.S.-Russia Programs Survive Kosovo, but Now Face Congressional Threat," *Proliferation Brief*, vol. 2 (May 5, 1999); and Materials Protection, Control, and Accounting program homepage: www.nn.doe.gov/mpca/frame01.htm [accessed November 1999]. For International Science and Technology Center, Congressional Budget Office, "Cooperative Approaches"; Non-Proliferation Project, "U.S.-Russia Programs"; and Carnegie Endowment for International Peace, "U.S.-Russia Programs Survive Kosovo." For Initiatives for Proliferation Prevention, U.S. General Accounting Office, "Nuclear Nonproliferation," p. 5; Congressional Budget Office, "Cooperative Approaches." For Nuclear Cities Initiative, U.S. General Accounting Office, "Nuclear Nonproliferation," pp. 50, 54. For nonsecurity programs, Office of the Coordinator of U.S. Assistance to the New Independent States, U.S. Department of State, "U.S. Government Assistance to and Cooperative Activities with the New Independent States of the Former Soviet Union, FY 1994–1998 Annual Reports," submitted to the Congress pursuant to Section 104 of the Freedom Support Act, Public Law 102-511, www.state.gov/www/regions/nis/nis_assist_index.html [accessed November 1999].

a. Approximately $71 million from non-U.S. sources.

b. $14 million from non-U.S. sources.

The intensity of resistance within Chechnya made it doubtful that Russia could ever establish stable legal rule, but it was also evident that the international community generally and NATO in particular had nothing but criticism to offer—a situation that promised to be indefinitely divisive.

Compounding the divisiveness, moreover, the United States simultaneously put into question one of the primary load-carrying pillars of bilateral reassurance—the 1972 antiballistic missile (ABM) treaty that the Russians consider to be essential for all the formalized restrictions on nuclear weapons deployments. In July 1999 President Clinton signed legislation proclaiming that the policy of the United States was to deploy a national missile defense system "as soon as technologically possible."[14] That legislation did not authorize or finance an actual deployment program, and it had been discussed in advance with President Yeltsin. Nonetheless, it issued a sharp political warning that could not be ignored. It suggested that intense proponents of missile defense in the United States might be capable of forcing an active deployment under terms that Russia could not accept. In the course of prior consultations, President Yeltsin had agreed in principle to discuss modifications of the ABM treaty, implying that a suitably limited American program might be accommodated, but that almost certainly reflected a political tactic rather than a strategic security judgment.[15] As Russian defense planners are acutely aware, even the most limited national defense system would create most of the sensing and information management infrastructure required for a more extensive system, and the level of deployment that Russia would have to consider extensive is actually very small. Under pessimistic rules of assessment, Russian deterrent forces cannot count on having more than a few tens of missile launchers surviving a systematic first strike. Given that circumstance, any U.S. missile defense deployment of whatever size would constitute a threat to the viability of the Russian deterrent force and would make credible strategic reassurance virtually impossible to achieve.

Extending back through the Soviet period, the Russian political system has been extremely reluctant to admit any security deficiency, a characteristic that is hardly unique but is unusually strong. In distinct contrast to the United States, the Soviet Union generally proclaimed greater military power than it possessed, and it did not discuss its inner security concerns with sufficient candor to make them comprehensible to anyone else. That practice was adjusted during the Gorbachev period and even more under the Yeltsin government, but it was not entirely reversed. The instinct to compensate for weakness by projecting resolve assuredly will make it very difficult to work out an adequate program of reassurance and probably will drive some renewed attempt within Russia to sustain the requirements of deterrent confrontation. That reaction was evident during NATO's bombardment of Yugoslavia. On April 29, 1999, Yeltsin chaired a secret session of the Russian Security Council that was reported to have ordered an enhancement of its nuclear forces, including the development of a new weapons design for tactical application and the strengthening of alert procedures.[16] In late June, just after air operations against Yugoslavia had been terminated, the Russian military conducted its largest field exercise since the founding of the federation in which it practiced initiating the use of nuclear weapons against a hypothesized conventional air assault from the West directed at Belarus and Kaliningrad.[17] With 50,000 troops participating in the exercise and conducting live missile firings into Russian test ranges, it was evident that the exercise must have been planned well before NATO's action against Yugoslavia began. But it also was evident that the fortuitous timing was a welcome opportunity to demonstrate both the capacity and the intent to defend Russia by all means available.

That demonstration of resolve might well be reinforced by a higher level of weapons production—a provision that would be seen both as necessary compensation for the precipitous decline in weapons production that followed the dismemberment of the Soviet Union and as a policy of industrial renewal. Since large segments of the old industrial structure were devoted to weapons production and since increased weapons production could be accomplished through barter mechanisms, any Russian political figure would be sorely tempted to conclude that immediate security and economic imperative align in compelling fashion. And indeed, in suitably modest form, increased investment in defense might well be necessary in Russia to fend off more extremist reactions to security pressures and economic decline. Over the longer term, however, such a policy involves two major dangers. Russia is even less able than was the Soviet Union to support active military confrontation with the rest of the world. A sustained effort to do so could preempt the extensive form of economic engagement that clearly will be necessary to extract the country from its deep and enduring economic crisis. In addition and yet more ominously, a military investment program operating under severe financial restriction can be expected to rely heavily on nuclear weapons to cover not only core deterrent functions but also the major missions normally assigned to conventional forces. That, in turn, would further entrench the unsafe operational practice of depending on rapid reaction to a warning of attack in order to compensate for physical vulnerability of the deterrent force. Those developments would make global security conditions a great deal less benign than has been assumed over the past decade—not because either country has an impulse for aggression, but rather because one side does not comprehend the desperation of the other.

Limited measures of reassurance grafted onto a traditional policy of confrontation will not master this situation and might well intensify its dangers by breeding belligerent resentment. The only feasible escape would require not merely a conveniently modest adjustment of the traditional security relationship with Russia but also a fundamental transformation sufficient to establish the principle of reassurance as its primary basis. A conceptual shift of that magnitude is admittedly very difficult to accomplish, and the detailed implications would take a decade or more to work out. In particular the obvious priority item—the termination of active deterrent operations and their replacement with an inherently safer configuration of nuclear arsenals—involves an elaborate agenda that would have to be arranged between Russia and the United States and, in its advanced stages, would have to involve all the other deployed nuclear forces. That, in turn, would require corresponding measures to assure the major conventional missions—continuous surveillance and active defense of Russian air space and protection of Siberia and of the home waters of the Russian navy. These purposes can be more efficiently and more reliably accomplished by methods of reassurance than they can be through independent confrontation. The primacy of that principle would have to be prominently acknowledged before an extensive effort to develop the intricate details would be undertaken. One cannot predict with any confidence that a conceptual shift from deterrence to reassurance will occur and that the core security relationship between the United States and Russia will be redesigned. But neither can one dismiss that possibility on the basis of historical experience. The relentless fact is that Russia cannot live with the inherited situation and neither, therefore, can anyone else.

China

China presents a variation of the same problem—one that is less apparent, or urgent, but ultimately of comparable significance. China's aggregate economic performance has been substantially more successful than Russia's, generating an average annual rate of growth of more than 10 percent since its economic reform effort was initiated in 1979. While

Russia's economy was decreasing 50 percent, China's grew more than 90 percent. That strong performance was based on the transformation of subsistence agriculture into commodity trade and light consumer product manufacturing, a process that produced a progressive monetization of the domestic economy and was accompanied by a surge of export trade and direct foreign investment. In 1997, the year of the Asian financial crisis, China's exports grew 20 percent, producing a $40 billion trade surplus, and its accumulation of foreign exchange reserves reached $140 billion, second only to Japan's.[18] Direct foreign investment was $41.5 billion in 1997—second only to the United States in absolute terms. By virtue of its strict controls over currency transactions, China was not embroiled in the Asian financial firestorm, and its willingness and ability to avoid a currency devaluation provided an immediate bulwark for the international financial system. China's internal accumulation of public debt clearly is unsustainable, however, and its banking system is at least as fragile as the banking systems that triggered the Asian crisis.[19] At the core of both conditions is the same problem that burdens Russia. Very few of the large state-owned enterprises in China that were generated over the decades of central planning are viable under international market conditions, and most have been preserved through state subsidization for the same reasons that they have been in Russia. They provide both employment and communal services for well over half of the urban labor force—a segment of the population that in China, unlike in Russia, is expected to grow substantially over the next two decades. Impressive as it has been so far, China's economic transition is not complete, and its ultimate success is not assured. The more difficult passages of uncertain but probably lengthy duration have been scheduled for the third decade of China's reform effort. The successful navigation of those passages, it is prudent to assume, also is likely to be a major international development project.

China's military establishment has not yet imposed a major burden on the reform process. Over the course of the cold war, it did not engage in active military confrontation to the extent that the Soviet Union did and did not claim as extensive a resource commitment. In the strategic conceptions of the political leadership, military investment has been explicitly subordinated to economic development and is expected to remain so for the indefinite future:

> China being at the primary stage of socialism, the fundamental task of the state is to concentrate its strength on the socialist moderniza-

> tion program. The situation in which China has a large population, a poor foundation, uneven regional development, and underdeveloped productive forces will continue for a comparatively long period of time to come. China is now confronted with the extremely heavy task of economic construction, so the work in defense must be subordinate to and in service of the nation's overall economic construction.[20]

By China's own accounting, military investment declined slightly in real terms from 1979 to 1994, and even with annual increases thereafter the defense budget remained below $10 billion in 1998.[21] Although most American assessments contend that total support for China's military establishment is three or four times that amount, everyone concedes that China's existing military capacity is modest by international standards.[22] Its nuclear deterrent forces are acknowledged to be much smaller than their American and Russian counterparts—on the order of 400 total warhead launcher positions, only about twenty of which are capable of reaching the continental United States. Chinese forces are also much more quiescent.[23] They are not maintained on ready alert status on a daily basis and rely for protection largely on dispersion and physical protection rather than on rapid reaction. They are not configured to attempt preemptive destruction of either of the larger nuclear forces, and their residual deterrent functions therefore have been conceded much more readily. There is no indication that China ever has encountered a situation in which it considered the use of nuclear weapons to have been an imminent possibility, and its forces are not continuously poised for such a situation in the manner that those of the United States and Russia are. Similarly, its conventional forces have not been prepared for a rapidly executed offensive of the sort that the Soviet Union contemplated against Western Europe or even for a large, rapidly developing contingency on its own territory. On the whole, China was not a frontline participant in the cold war and did not become deeply entangled in the volatile operational interactions that result from advanced contingency preparations.

The future burden of China's military establishment is a much more serious question, however. China is intimately involved in the single most serious jurisdictional issue to survive the cold war—the question of Taiwan's affiliation—and in its own assessment that situation imposes a potential military requirement that existing and currently projected Chinese military forces could not meet. China has vowed to protect its jurisdictional claim to Taiwan with force if necessary, as distinct from enforcing it that way. But in the very conceivable event that Taiwan proclaims independence by majority vote, China does not have the basic capability that would be required to occupy the island and has no immediate prospect of doing so if the United States chooses to defend it. In order to give some credible effect to its commitment, China has deployed ballistic missiles with conventional warheads in range of the island and has implicitly threatened a bombardment consequential enough to be highly disruptive to normal financial and commercial transactions.[24] That expediency is not something that any military planning system would accept as an enduring policy. The threat is hardly decisive and could readily backfire. There is a significant chance that the United States will use it to justify the deployment of theater ballistic missile defenses for the region. There is an outside chance that a particularly willful leadership in Taiwan might deliberately seek to provoke it as a means of forcing the defensive commitment that the United States in deference to China's sensitivities has been reluctant to provide. In this situation, China has plausible grounds for believing that it must develop sufficient capability to project power to defend its jurisdictional claim to Taiwan in more credible fashion and must do so in potential confrontation with the United States.

The practical implications of that conclusion, however, are daunting to the point of being unmanageable. An appeal to nuclear weapons is out of the question. It is not credible to suggest that the use of nuclear weapons would be initiated against Taiwan directly as an assertion of sovereign authority over it, and even the barest hint of that would corrode the legitimacy of China's claim. When speculation about such a threat arose in the international press in the summer of 1999, China quickly reacted with a statement that imposed additional restriction on its declaratory nuclear doctrine—already the most restrained of all the nuclear weapons states. In a press conference in Beijing on September 3, a spokesman for China's Foreign Ministry stated, "We will not be the first to use nuclear weapons and will not use nuclear weapons against non-nuclear weapons countries and regions, let alone against our Taiwan compatriots."[25] Nor could China evoke the threat of nuclear weapons in an attempt to fend off U.S. conventional forces without subjecting China's nuclear forces to a degree of active operational engagement for which they are not prepared. The more credible forms of applicable force—an imposing capacity to seize the island or to blockade it effectively—would have to be supported by tactical air operations that are at least locally commensurate with the capabilities that Taiwan and the United States together could bring to bear. That would require an extensive development effort likely to be identified well before it reaches maturity and likely to trigger aggressively competitive reactions. The United States would predictably focus its own larger and more advanced weapons development process to stay ahead of what it would perceive to be an emerging threat, would attempt to interdict China's access to relevant technology, and very likely would expand the scope of military cooperation with Taiwan. Such an interaction would seriously damage China's economic reform effort at a critical stage and would violate the subordination of military investment to economic development, but it is likely to be perceived as mandatory for state security if principles of confrontation are used to derive the requirements. The need to escape the dilemma is not as urgent for China as it is for Russia, but it is of similar character. China also has substantial need for a different security arrangement based on the less volatile and more efficient principle of reassurance.

With a less elaborately developed engagement of military forces than in Russia and with a more extreme form of political estrangement to use as historical backdrop, China and the United States have been better able to overcome cold war antagonism by means of executive declarations. In three joint communiqués issued on February 28, 1972, December 15, 1978, and August 17, 1982, the two countries established the foundations for normalizing their relationship with more authority than unratified statements usually have.[26] Although the terms used in those declarations imply the absence of direct military confrontation, they do not establish the presence of active reassurance, and they have not been accompanied by the institutional arrangements—scheduled consultations, operational exercises, formal exchange of information, and so forth—necessary to give the basic principle of reassurance serious practical effect. The security relationship between China and the United States resides somewhere in between the systematic jurisdiction of either of the contending principles—confrontation on one hand and reassurance on the other.

The resulting ambiguity affects all major issues, but it is especially evident with regard to Taiwan, the most serious matter of potential contention. The United States severed official ties with Taiwan in 1978 in order to establish diplomatic relations with the People's Republic of China and accepted at that time that "there is but one China, and Taiwan is part of China," a phrase that appears in all three of the foundation communiqués.[27] That formulation precludes a binding commitment by the United States to defend the island against occupation by China, but it was accompanied by a less formalized understanding that China would not attempt such a venture. Were China nonetheless to do so in a manner that was judged in the United States not to have been justly provoked, then direct resistance from the United States would be quite probable. Certainly China would have to assume as much, given the American capacity and inclination to intervene and the strong economic and political ties that Taiwan has retained with U.S. society as a whole.

As far as the process of security transformation is concerned, the political evolution of Taiwan clearly will be affected and quite possibly determined by distributed processes that no one can reliably control. The government of Taiwan is becoming a robust democracy, and that legitimate and fundamentally healthy process is giving expression to separatist sentiment with extensive historical roots. As required by the joint communiqués, the United States has sincerely opposed a unilateral declaration of independence by Taiwan and has made a reasonably attentive effort to balance its encouragement of the democratization process and its commercial interactions with an increasingly vibrant economy against the protocol requirements of respect for Chinese sovereignty. There have been incidents of sharp collision between American and Chinese policy, however, with consequences significant enough to constitute a general warning. In 1992 the Bush administration authorized the sale of F-16 fighters to Taiwan in what China considered to be a direct violation of the 1982 communiqué whose primary purpose was to regulate such sales. Although the connection was never made explicit, China's sales of M-11 ballistic missiles to Pakistan seem to have been undertaken in pointed retaliation, an event that generated a set of legislated sanctions against China in the United States that have threatened trade relations ever since. In 1995 the Clinton administration issued a visa to the president of Taiwan, Lee Teng-Hui, allowing him to give a speech at Cornell University's commencement exercises. Although the visit was unofficial, it broke diplomatic precedent in that it was the first time an incumbent president of Taiwan was allowed to visit the United States, and the event had political overtones that China interpreted to be a violation of the normalization documents. Lee Teng-Hui was attempting to upgrade Taiwan's international standing as an independent entity and was presenting that effort as a basis for his ultimately successful campaign to become the first directly elected president of Taiwan. In protest against the action, China canceled a scheduled visit to the United States of its defense minister and a series of high-level meetings that were meant to define the security relationship in more detail. That disruption of the normalization process created the background for an incident in March 1996, just prior to the Taiwanese presidential election, in which China conducted missile tests in the Taiwan strait and the United States maneuvered two aircraft carriers in reaction. Although it was evident that both sides were displaying resolve rather than priming their forces for imminent combat, the perceived need for such an exercise revealed the dangers of ambiguity. China and the United States have not established the organizing principle of their security relationship and are hostage to the internal politics of Taiwan. The situation is a major strategic accident waiting to happen and promising to do so.

In the wake of the 1996 incident, China and Taiwan held occasional, rudimentary discussions designed to deflect military confrontation, and in the course of an official visit to China in 1998 President Clinton appeared to have restored the process of normalization to its previous indeterminate state. Both developments were quickly overshadowed, however, by several prominent incidents that provoked a public sense of confrontation—a widely publicized failure during President Jiang Zemin's return visit to the United States in 1999 to reach agreement on China's membership in the World Trade Organization, an inflammatory series of reports in the United States alleging that China stole nuclear weapons design information and violated ballistic missile export controls, and a provocatively ambiguous series of statements by Lee Teng-Hui challenging the traditional formulation of Taiwan's connection to China.[28] The largely contentious public discussion of these incidents clearly demonstrated that the term officially derived to summarize the relationship between China and the United States—constructive strategic partnership—does not yet provide an organizing conception authoritative enough to contain the direct military interactions and regional reverberations of the Taiwan situation. It remains, nonetheless, a significant aspiration with a credible basis in strong mutual interest. Not only is it regionally important to avoid a collision over Taiwan, but it is globally important to engage China in the process of transformation. China would have to be intimately involved, for example, in any arrangement that relieves the Russian military of its unmanageable burdens, in particular in the termination of active deterrent operations and in the conditions for security in Siberia. The combination of circumstances means that China's own fundamental security requirements would have to be part of a viable formula. Again it would require an extensive series of official discussions to work out the details of these requirements, and again that will not even be attempted without a more developed conception of purpose based on the principle of reassurance. China is a central participant in the process of transformation and provides a substantial part both of the motive and of the venue for undertaking it.

North Korea

Judged in terms of its normally attributed characteristics, North Korea would seem to be a necessary exception to the process of transformation rather than an integral participant. It is among the poorest, most isolated, and most demonized of all societies, and, in the assessment of much of the world, it has done a great deal to deserve that fate. Despite the fact that its economy is clearly in shambles and its people are starving by the millions, North Korea has made virtually no internationally credited effort to undergo internal economic reform or political transformation. Nor has it escaped the burden of its unusually belligerent history. Kim Il Sung, considered to be the person primarily responsible for the Korean war, ruled the country for forty-six years in a highly repressive manner until his death in 1994 and relentlessly imposed an ideology of extreme self-reliance. Formal authority was then passed directly to his son, Kim Jong Il, with no substantial alteration of the political system and no obvious revision of the long-established ideology. That provides apparent continuity of responsibility for a long series of violent episodes on the peninsula and alleged criminal activities elsewhere. Whenever the term *rogue state* is accompanied by examples, North Korea nearly always makes the list.

Judged by its surrounding circumstances, however, North Korea is in position to play an important catalytic role in a process of transformation. The unification of Korea is one of the major events that naturally would be expected to accompany such a process and would provide an occasion for determining its implications. The division of Korea was as much an artifact of the cold war as the division of Germany, and there is a strong presumption that a valid expression of social consensus within Korea would overturn the division. Moreover, the fortified border that preserves the division is now the principal instance of military confrontation in the entire world. There are other places where hostile ground forces are continuously deployed in close proximity, but none of them involves the United States and thus none of them has comparable global resonance. Should North Korea choose to promote the process of unification on reasonable terms and to dissolve the military confrontation in the course of that process, such an initiative would be irresistible. It generally is assumed that

North Korea's political leadership is compelled to reject any such effort because it would expose the stark disparities in standards of living and in military capability and inevitably would destroy their authoritarian form of rule. But the reverse strategy is probably the only plausible route to economic salvation, and it offers substantial leverage to political figures who are capable of grasping that fact and are willing to broker a graceful transition. A chaotic internal collapse in North Korea is a sufficiently serious and sufficiently appalling possibility that a reasonable opportunity to prevent it would command responsiveness from South Korea and from the international community as a whole, including a substantial commitment of resources.

In addition to its ability to affect the process of unification, North Korea has acquired substantial leverage over the process of controlling weapons proliferation as a result of two technical investments made in the course of pursuing its strategy of self-reliance. North Korea is the major independent source of ballistic missile technology not included in the informal Missile Technology Control Regime that was initiated by the United States in 1987 to control the proliferation of those weapons. It has copied and produced two of its own versions of the 300–500-kilometer-range Soviet Scud-B missile, retaining several hundred for its own forces and selling 300 to 400 more on the international market—primarily to Iran and Syria—for export earnings estimated to be on the order of $1 billion.[29] It also has developed a 1,000-kilometer-range missile, tested once in 1993; in August 1998 it used the first stage of that missile together with a Scud second stage and an unknown third stage to attempt a satellite launch. The attempt failed, but the missile created a political sensation by flying over Japan, indicating that its indigenous capabilities have regional significance. Moreover, the missile programs that India and Pakistan are pursuing at ranges of 1,000 kilometers and above are believed to be based on North Korean technology, indicating that its export capacities have global significance.

North Korea also has developed a substantial potential to produce weapons-grade fissionable material. In 1986 it began operating a small nuclear reactor of the graphite-moderated design historically used by France and Great Britain to produce weapons-grade plutonium. It subsequently began constructing two larger reactors of the same design and expanding the reprocessing facility located near the small reactor. Completion of all the facilities with a combined thermal output approaching 1,000 megawatts would provide the theoretical capacity to produce as much as 250 kilograms of weapons-grade plutonium each year of operation, enough material for fifty nuclear weapons.[30] North Korea signed the nuclear nonproliferation treaty (NPT) in 1985 but did not allow the required IAEA (International Atomic Energy Agency) inspection of its facilities to occur until 1992. In their initial observations, the IAEA inspectors found major accounting discrepancies associated with the operating reactor, and their attempts to resolve them generated a series of disputes resulting in North Korea's announcement in 1993 that it would withdraw from the treaty. At that point the implication that North Korea intended both to deploy nuclear weapons itself and to export weapons-grade fissionable material was recognized to be a severe threat to the entire NPT regime—a development that might trigger nuclear weapons programs in the societies inherently capable of undertaking them (Japan, South Korea, Taiwan) and might provide Iran, Iraq, and Syria with fissionable material they themselves could not produce.

That situation broke open the implacable but largely dormant confrontation between North Korea and the United States that had been maintained since the Korean war armistice. The United States was sufficiently alarmed that it considered a preemptive attack on the North Korean facilities and signaled that possibility in a series of subtle military maneuvers designed to avoid a major public display while being convincingly ominous to North Korea.[31] The United States was sufficiently aware of the danger of such an exercise, however, to explore accommodation as well and in doing so initiated the first bilateral negotiations with North Korea since the armistice. The ensuing process was contentious but in the end produced substantial terms of accommodation. In a document entitled the Agreed Framework signed in October 1994, North Korea agreed to halt its incipient nuclear weapons program by shutting down the small reactor and reprocessing plant, ending construction on the new reactors, and ultimately dismantling the entire complex. In return, the United States agreed not only to replace but also to expand the power-generating capacity that would be lost. Specifically, the United States agreed to organize and arrange financing for the construction of two new light water reactors with a combined electrical power output of 2,000 megawatts—nearly eight times greater than the electricity-generating capacity of the reactors to be dismantled—but of a design much less suitable for producing plutonium.[32]

In agreeing to that arrangement, North Korea not only terminated what probably had been its highest-priority national development project but did so in a manner that would prejudice any attempt to regenerate it. The

Agreed Framework is a more advanced regime of control than the NPT in that it effectively internationalizes physical custody of and administrative responsibility for the reactor fuel. The construction and eventual operation of the new reactors will involve much more extensive international oversight of its nuclear activities than the IAEA inspections it had been resisting, and any failure to comply with the associated provisions would constitute more credible justification for sanctions or military coercion than the NPT alone provided. For its part the United States established an explicit presumption of eventual normalization. The Agreed Framework includes specific provisions for establishing diplomatic representation and for removing the economic sanctions that the United States has maintained since the Korean war. At any rate it would not be possible to construct two nuclear reactors and to manage the provision and disposition of their fuel elements without establishing a robust and fairly extensive basis for collaboration. The reactor project is not something that occurs between countries that expect to go to war with one another on short notice.

Within the United States, however, the deal was not conceived and not presented as the initial item in a full program to transform the relationship with North Korea, and its evident inconsistency with the presumed continuation of military confrontation inspired sharp partisan critique. Congressional Republicans interpreted its timing as an attempt to influence the 1994 elections, and they reacted with blistering objection, arguing that North Korea could not be trusted to implement the deal and at any rate should not be rewarded for adhering to obligations already incurred under the NPT. The Clinton administration blunted that reaction by arguing that compensation was better than war but did not conduct a prominent public defense of the deal and did not establish a base of congressional support. Budget appropriations over the first four years provided less than half of the modest annual amount, about $65 million, required to purchase the fuel oil the United States was obligated to deliver, and that small but telling fact impeded the attempt to induce commitments from regional allies of the several billion dollars required to construct the reactors. By 1998 the promised oil deliveries were running late, the reactor project was well behind the schedule required to meet its target date for completion in 2003, diplomatic normalization had not progressed, economic sanctions had not been removed, and the overall record of U.S. compliance with the Agreed Framework was hardly reassuring to North Korea.

The political process in North Korea is too opaque to allow any solid reading of how the government conceptualized the Agreed Framework. North Korea has established a record of compliance that presumably would pass an objective review. The small reactor has been shut down, and under direct supervision of U.S. technicians, all of its fuel elements have been placed in storage containers. The reprocessing facility also has been shut and sealed, and construction has been terminated at the two larger reactor sites. Access to construction sites for the new reactors has been provided for the international consortium responsible for the project, including South Korean nationals, and the individuals have been well treated. The United States, however, has not been entirely reassured. In 1998 it announced the discovery of a large underground construction project, which it claimed on the basis of undivulged intelligence information to be associated with the nuclear program. It suggested that the project was intended to be a clandestine replacement of the facilities to be dismantled and hence a direct violation of the Agreed Framework. It nonetheless conceded that the large excavation did not appear to have any machinery in it, leaving considerable room for ambiguity about the purpose and ultimate disposition of the site. North Korea deliberately has raised issues of its own compliance by interrupting disposition of the small reactor's fuel just short of completion and by unsealing the reprocessing plant to conduct an inspection. But those actions clearly were designed to pressure the United States to meet its obligations without involving any irreversible violation on North Korea's part.

A detailed assessment of North Korea's public statements and policy actions over the course of negotiating and implementing the Agreed Framework suggests a systematic determination not only to comply with the terms of the agreement but also to use it as the basis for working out a general security arrangement and a process of economic rehabilitation in which North Korea is protected and assisted by the United States rather than threatened and sanctioned.[33] The assessment suggests further that this broad objective is being pursued with a classic tit-for-tat strategy in which North Korea deliberately reacts to threat with a counterthreat and to accommodation with accommodation. Although that is an interpretative account that does not fit the traditional image of North Korea, it does fit the circumstances. There are few options for a small, inherently vulnerable, and exceedingly poor country that has lost its external military and ideological protection. Attempting to attach oneself to the patron of the dominant alliance and the representative of the largest economy is one of the few serious possibilities.

There was at least a tentative display of that logic following the long-range missile test and public revelation of the underground excavation in August 1998. In combination the two events produced political reactions in the United States and Japan virulent enough to put continuation of the Agreed Framework into question. In an effort to rescue the agreement, former secretary of defense, William Perry, who had presided over the 1994 confrontation, was appointed as a special envoy, and he traveled to Pyongyang in May 1999 to present terms of accommodation designed to test North Korean intentions. Just before his visit and clearly related to it, American officials were allowed to visit the underground excavation to determine that indeed it did not contain any suspicious equipment. And as an apparent result of the mission, after formal talks in September, North Korea announced an indefinite moratorium on ballistic missile tests, while the United States lifted four specific economic sanctions. That appeared sufficient to avoid a breakdown in the process of accommodation and even to give it some sense of renewal.

One can plausibly imagine, then, that North Korea might gradually learn to use the leverage at its disposal to broaden the accommodation with the United States, South Korea, and Japan and that the Agreed Framework is the initial stage of that process. It is extremely doubtful that the terms of that agreement can be completed without substantially expanding the scope of accommodation, and at some fairly early stage in that process there would have to be an explicitly formulated shift in the prevailing conception of the relationship. Without being aware of it, or at any rate without acknowledging whatever awareness they actually have, all the parties principally engaged in the North Korean situation—the two Korean governments, the United States, China, Japan, and ultimately Russia as well—are being transformed by circumstances they cannot avoid and implications they cannot deflect. The ultimate outcome is not yet apparent, but it is evident that some change of regional and global consequence will occur there.

The United States

If a global transformation of security relationships is to occur, then the United States would have to enable the process and, in principle, should lead it. It wields the most capable military forces. It is the patron of the dominant alliance. It presides over the largest economy and the one that has generated much of the technical impulse underlying the process of globalization. In practical terms a basic shift in organizing principles from confrontation to reassurance and from contingency reaction to anticipatory prevention cannot occur unless the United States ratifies the outcome and is unlikely to occur unless the United States assertively promotes it. In ethical terms it is natural to expect the predominant military establishment to bear the preponderant burden for initiating accommodation with the others.

Those precepts would require fundamental adjustments of attitude of the sort that historically have been difficult to accomplish. Germany and Japan have been transformed from enemies to intimate collaborators; but, as dedicated realists would hasten to point out, that transformation was initiated by their unconditional surrender at the end of a massively destructive war and was consolidated by their constructive reaction to a subsequent period of military occupation and direct political tutelage—not a generally applicable formula. Those transitions occurred, moreover, in the context of a common confrontation with the Soviet Union. The United States has yet to demonstrate that it can conduct an active security policy without the organizing focus of a designated enemy defined in the traditional terms of deliberate aggression. Within the United States, of course, predominant responsibility for confrontational relationships has been attributed to the opposing countries. In human affairs of any sort there are always plenty of reasons to assign blame. Were there a truly objective observer to judge the matter, however—the equivalent of the chorus through which the ancient Greek tragedians conveyed much of their wisdom—the United States would presumably not be entirely exonerated. Indeed the view from the chorus would very likely warn of a potentially fatal flaw. The champion of democracy, of market discipline, and of respect for cultural diversity appears to need a designated enemy to justify its actions. Much of the established American thinking about security assumes the immediate presence or eventual emergence of such enemies as a fundamental axiom and does so with an emotional intensity that extends well beyond any immediate threat. Active confrontation is an ingrained American inclination that significantly compounds the corresponding difficulties that Russia, China, and North Korea have in realigning their own attitudes.

As discussed in previous chapters, there are strong reasons for the United States to revise its confrontational attitudes, however entrenched they might be. The practice of deterrence will not be adequately safe or even reliably effective until the dangerous operational commitments to continuous alert, rapid reaction, and mass targeting are eliminated. That will require a pattern of residual deployment that is considered to be broadly equitable, especially to Russia and to China. Since the possible breakdown of active deterrent force operations represents the gravest physical threat to the United States and to the rest of the world as well, that particular element of transformation is especially compelling. It seems evident that it could not be accomplished without a corresponding transformation of the underlying security relationships. Nor could it be accomplished without commensurate rules for conventional force operations. The advanced capacity for intrusive bombardment that the United States has assertively displayed creates a substantial problem of reassurance that will have to be addressed systematically not only to set conditions for more secure management of nuclear weapons but also to contain provocative conventional reactions. The United States will damage its own security over the longer term and everyone else's as well unless it develops a more refined and more generally acceptable set of principles to regulate the application of its advanced conventional capabilities. In addition, the problems of communal violence and the related problem of clandestine mass destruction could become overwhelming unless more effective measures of prevention, enabled by direct collaboration, are developed. The emerging doctrine of sovereign responsibility that provides the basis for assertive prevention must be backed by a global coalition if it ever is to have the standing required to be effective. Neither the United States nor its traditional allies ever will have sufficient military capacity to contain diffuse violence exclusively by means of a deterrent threat or contingency reaction. For all of these matters, principles of equity on which reassurance is based are likely to be more important determinants of security than the intimidating capacity for massive or precise destruction. At any rate the latter is useless or worse without solid connection to the former. That promises to be a relentless lesson of the emerging era—one that is conveyed repeatedly and powerfully enough to reshape historical attitudes and patterns of affiliation.

It is evident, however, that very little reshaping has occurred within the United States. A decade after the end of the cold war, American security policy remains predominantly confrontational in character. That character has been set by the continuation of large-scale active deterrent operations and by the concentration of conventional forces on major combined-arms contingencies arising on short notice. It has been reinforced by the principal initiatives of recent policy—the projected deployment of a national missile defense system, the closely associated development of broad-area missile defense systems for theater application, the diffuse but technically consequential pursuit of a "revolution in military affairs," and the political program for selective expansion of NATO. The various initiatives designed to convey reassurance beyond the alliance system—primarily the Nunn-Lugar program for Russia and NATO's partnership for peace program—have been far too modest to mitigate the pattern of confrontation to any substantial extent. American missile defense advocates claim that it represents a morally superior and inherently less threatening development of policy. This is simply not credible to potential opponents and in fact has been received as evidence of ominous disingenuousness. The projected missile defense systems are too readily penetrated and circumvented to be operated in the exclusively reactive fashion advertised. In any opposing assessment, it is a great deal more believable that the United States would undertake a missile defense deployment as a supplement to offensive operations it initiates. That assessment readily translates into the inference that America's real intention is to acquire a decisive preemptive capability against the Russian and Chinese strategic forces and to preserve the overwhelming capacity it already possesses against North Korea and other countries designated as rogue states. No amount of rhetorical reassurance could override that implication. No systematic policy that might do so has yet been generated within the American political system.

A dedicated U.S. policy to achieve transformation would necessarily focus on Russia as the most urgent and most consequential application. Such a policy would have to be based on a combined program of economic engagement and security reassurance commensurate with requirements in both areas. In broad outline that would involve offering debt relief, improved market access, infrastructure investment, and new commercial credit conditioned primarily on the acceptance of accounting transparency throughout the Russian economy and a judiciously scheduled program of industrial restructuring. It would involve credible assurance for legitimate security missions so that the size and financial requirements of the Russian military could be set at sustainable levels and the currently unmanageable operational burdens could be relieved. In order to establish the basis for a comprehensive transformation of security relationships, moreover, corresponding programs would have to be devised for China and North Korea as well.

In principle a sweeping initiative of this sort might emerge through some feat of political leadership in the United States, but that expectation is not immediately plausible. The American political system does not readily produce dramatic excursions of policy on any topic, particularly not against the inclinations of prevailing opinion. A major adjustment might be precipitated by just the right catalytic event. Short of a fortuitous bolt of fate, however—one miraculously designed to enlighten at tolerable cost—whatever process of transformation does occur is likely to come in incremental stages and is likely to be embodied at a level of detail too intricate and too protected by security classification to be broadly visible. Nonetheless some leading elements of the process undoubtedly will be apparent.

Debt relief is one of them. It is fairly obvious that the Russian Federation cannot repay its accumulated debt anytime soon. By any rule of prudence, at least the Soviet-era portion of that debt, some $95 billion, should already have been written off in the accounting systems of those who hold it. At some point the inexorable fact that Russia cannot repay that debt will have to be explicitly acknowledged. If that mutual admission is combined with an agreed extension of Russian-era debt to relieve the government's fiscal burdens, that might be taken as a relevant sign of incremental transformation. That will be difficult to accomplish because many other countries—some yet more destitute than Russia—have pressing claims for debt relief. It is feasible, however, and eventually probable given the extraordinary dangers Russia poses.

With regard to direct security matters, the most significant sign of incremental transformation would be meaningful implementation of the joint missile warning activity that was announced at the September 1998 summit meeting but suspended in reaction to the Kosovo bombing campaign. Surveillance of threatening ballistic missile trajectories is one of the most glaring deficiencies of Russian deterrent forces. On the one hand, if the United States were to provide comprehensive data in timely detail and if Russian forces were to rely on that information for managing their deterrent operations, that would constitute a truly significant watershed of collaboration—the direct practice of mutual reassurance on a vital matter. On the other hand, if the scope of collaboration on missile surveillance were too constrained, it could become a breeding ground for suspicion. Achieving a constructive result in this instance is likely to be more difficult than debt relief. In order to reassure Russia, the United States would have to provide direct access to the raw data generated by its various sensing systems and to the algorithms necessary to interpret the data. Since that information always has been protected by elaborate security classification, improbably willful decisions would be necessary to breach those barriers. By its very nature, however, the exercise of sharing warning information presents a major test of intent, and the outcome can be taken as a significant measure of incremental transformation.

The circumstances most likely to make the question of transformation more than incremental are those surrounding the possible deployment of national missile defense by the United States. Because of the threat to the integrity of their deterrent operations, both Russia and China would feel compelled to react assertively to an American deployment program. They would have to consider increasing the size and technical sophistication of their offensive forces, increasing their reliance on rapid reaction for protection—in the case of China, initiating such reliance—and developing methods for negating the American missile defense system, most probably by attacking its space assets. As long as the underlying security relationships remain confrontational, no bargain would preclude these reactions. That sequence of deployment and reaction would make the practice of active deterrence more dangerous than it already is, but the intense advocates of missile defense in the United States certainly will not admit that implication. Initially at least, they are unlikely to be disciplined on that point by majority opinion. No one is eager to acknowledge the perverse effects of what is believed to be a morally superior principle. Nonetheless, since the process of designing, testing, and completing a national missile defense system would extend for a decade or more and since the predictable reactions can occur more rapidly than that, the American political system is likely to experience the international implications before it completes the legislated intention. That might be the occasion for recognizing the merits of transformation. The antagonistic reaction of Russia and China presumably could be prevented if both were covered in a meaningful way by the American missile defense system. If the advertised purpose of the system—to protect against limited rogue actions—is in fact the real and exclusive intent, then there is no reason why Russia and China could not be included. Doing so would provide both countries with the comprehensive, reassuring surveillance capability they are unlikely to acquire with their own resources and would be a major element of transformation. Judged by past experience, of course, it is quite a stretch to imagine that this might be achieved, but short of such comprehensive inclusion the United States cannot undertake a national defense deployment without seriously damaging its own net security. One way or the other, the emotional energy generated by the vision of missile defense might eventually have a constructive result precisely because its perverse potential is too large to be ignored.

In the summer of 1999, the Aspen Strategy Group held a week-long review of the relationship between Russia and the United States involving several people who had been officially responsible for managing it. None of the participants believed that an adequate result had been achieved, and all of them were acutely concerned about the implications of that fact for the management of nuclear weapons. Although the participants shared these concerns, there was no consensus on a program of transformation and not even a common judgment that such an outcome was feasible. But it was evident that at least one of the prominent Americans had been personally transformed in the course of a decade. As co-chair of the meeting, Sam Nunn delivered a summary judgment with his 1991 question directly in mind. "We must reverse the course of history," he declared. And soon, one might add.

Notes

Chapter One

1. As with any extensively developed school of thought, there are many proponents with many variations of perspective. Hans J. Morgenthau, *Politics among Nations: The Struggle for Power and Peace,* 5th ed. (Knopf, 1976); Kenneth N. Waltz, *Theory of International Politics* (Reading, Mass.: Addison-Wesley Publishing Co., 1979); and Robert Gilpin, *War and Change in World Politics* (Cambridge University Press, 1981), are considered to be pillars of the realist school. Michael Mastanduno, "Preserving the Unipolar Moment: Realist Theories and U.S. Grand Strategy after the Cold War," *International Security,* vol. 21 (1997), pp. 49–88, discusses realist reactions to the ending of the cold war. Barry R. Posen and Andrew L. Ross, "Competing Visions of U.S. Grand Strategy," *International Security*, vol. 21 (1996/97), pp. 5–53, review contemporary variations.

2. John Mearsheimer, "The False Promise of International Institutions," *International Security*, vol. 19 (1994/95), pp. 5–49.

3. Passages of the following discussion are derived in part from John D. Steinbruner, "Can the United States Lead the World?" in Ken Booth, ed., *Statecraft and Security: The Cold War and Beyond* (Cambridge University Press, 1998), pp. 135–48, and "The Strategic Implications of Emerging International Security Conditions," in Gabriel Sheffer, ed., *U.S.-Israeli Relations at the Crossroads* (London: Frank Cass, 1997), pp. 17–26.

4. There is no single official source for the exact number. One of the most

carefully constructed compendia is provided by Ruth Leger Sivard, *World Military and Social Expenditures 1996* (Washington, D.C.: World Priorities, 1996), p. 7, which states that there have been "109,746,000 war-related deaths" in this century, "six times as many deaths per war in the 20th century as in the 19th."

5. Henry L. Stimson, *On Active Service in Peace and War* (New York: Harper, 1948), p. 644.

6. Alice Calaprice, ed., *The Quotable Einstein* (Princeton University Press, 1996), p. 131.

7. The speed of Minuteman III is approximately 15,000 miles per hour, while the maximum speed of the B-29 was 357 miles per hour.

8. See Kenneth W. Dam and Herbert S. Lin, eds., *Cryptography's Role in Securing the Information Society*, Report of the Committee to Study National Cryptography Policy, National Research Council (Washington, D.C. : National Academy Press, 1996), pp. 384. The factor of 100 million is based on an assessment of the cost of performing a standard cryptographic calculation in 1945 and 1995. That comparison provides a reasonable estimate of the general improvement that has occurred in storing and processing information at a given location. Efficiency gains in long-range transmission were somewhat less over this period—improvements by a factor of a million or so—but technical progress in this area is expected to be rapid over the next several decades.

9. The question, of course, has been actively discussed. See Thomas L. Friedman, *The Lexus and the Olive Tree* (Farrar, Straus, and Giroux, 1999), for a journalist's account, and David Held, Anthony McGrew, David Goldblatt, and Jonathon Perraton, *Global Transformations: Politics, Economics, and Culture* (Stanford University Press, 1999), for a synthesis of the academic literature, including arguments of the skeptics.

10. The most recent UN estimates indicate that the world's population reached 1 billion in 1804, 2 billion in 1927, 3 billion in 1960, 4 billion in 1974, and 5 billion in 1987. UN Population Division, Department of Economic and Social Affairs, "World Population Nearing 6 Billion, Projected Close to 9 Billion by 2050," www.popin.org/pop1998/1.htm [accessed November 1999].

11. Murray Gell-Mann, *The Quark and the Jaguar: Adventures in the Simple and the Complex* (W. H. Freeman and Company, 1994), p. 349.

12. Current UN estimates indicate that the world's population will reach 8 billion in 2028. See UN Population Division, "World Population Nearing 6 Billion," table 1 and fig. 1.

13. UN Population Division, "World Population Projects to 2150" (New York: United Nations, February 1998).

14. UN Population Division, "World Population Nearing 6 Billion."

15. A given population segment will just replace itself when the women included in it on average produce only one daughter during their lifetime. For the total fertility rate—the average number of all children produced by the women of

a population segment—the replacement level is considered to be 2.1. UN Population Division, "Below-Replacement Fertility," www.popin.org/pop1998/7.htm [accessed November 1999].

16. See UN Population Division, "Aging," www.popin.org/pop1998/8.htm [accessed November 1999], fig. 2.

17. Gary Burtless, "Worsening American Income Inequality: Is World Trade to Blame?" *Brookings Review*, vol. 14 (Spring 1996), p. 28; Gary Burtless, "Effects of Growing Wage Disparities and Changing Family Composition on the U.S. Income Distribution," Working Paper 4 (Brookings, Center on Social and Economic Dynamics, July 1999), p. 1.

18. Burtless, "Effects of Growing Wage Disparities," table 2, p. 16.

19. Clifford G. Gaddy, *The Price of the Past: Russia's Struggle with the Legacy of a Militarized Economy* (Brookings Institution, 1996).

20. John D. Steinbruner and William W. Kaufmann, "International Security Reconsidered," in Robert D. Reischauer, ed., *Setting National Priorities: Budget Choices for the Next Century* (Brookings Institution, 1997), pp. 155–96.

21. William S. Cohen, *Report of the Quadrennial Defense Review* (Department of Defense, May 1997).

22. In justifying bombing missions carried out against Libya on April 15–16, 1986, President Ronald Reagan claimed that the U.S. government had "irrefutable proof" that Libya had directed the terrorist bombing of a West Berlin discotheque that had killed two Americans and injured 200 others earlier in the month. Cruise missile attacks in August 1998 were directed against targets in the Sudan and Afghanistan said to have been used by individuals responsible for terrorist attacks on U.S. embassies in Kenya and Tanzania.

23. On June 26, 1993, President William Clinton ordered the launch of cruise missiles against Iraq in retaliation for the alleged assassination plot against former president George Bush. Beginning on December 16, 1998, the U.S. and British forces initiated sea-launched cruise missile and fighter aircraft attacks against a variety of Iraqi targets in response to Iraq's refusal to comply with United Nations Security Council resolutions as well as their interference with United Nations Special Commission (UNSCOM) inspectors.

24. The basic security principles involved in such a shift were originally outlined in Ashton B. Carter, William J. Perry, and John D. Steinbruner, *A New Concept of Cooperative Security*, Brookings Occasional Papers (Brookings Institution, 1992). Subsequent elaboration and variations are provided by Paul Stares and John Steinbruner, "Cooperative Security in the New Europe," in Paul Stares, ed., *The New Germany and the New Europe* (Brookings Institution, 1992); Janne Nolan, ed., *Global Engagement: Cooperation and Security in the 21st Century* (Brookings Institution, 1994); and Ashton B. Carter and William J. Perry, *Preventive Defense: A New Security Strategy for America* (Brookings Institution, 1999).

25. Eric J. Barron, "Climate Models: How Reliable Are Their Predictions?"

Consequences, vol. 1 (1995), gcrio.ciesin.org/cgi-bin/showcase?/CONSE-QUENCES/introCON.html [accessed October 1999].

26. Intergovernmental Panel on Climate Change, *Climate Change 1995—The Science of Climate Change. Summary for Policymakers, and Technical Summary of the Working Group I Report* (Intergovernmental Panel on Climate Change, 1996); Barron, "Climate Models."

27. Allen Hammond, *Which World? Scenarios for the 21st Century* (Washington, D.C.: Island Press, 1998).

28. See Ted Robert Gurr, "On the Political Consequences of Scarcity and Economic Decline," *International Studies Quarterly*, vol. 29 (March 1985), pp. 51–75; Thomas Homer-Dixon, "On the Threshold: Environmental Change as Causes of Acute Conflict," *International Security*, vol. 16 (Fall 1991), pp. 76–116; Donald Kennedy and others, *Environmental Quality and Regional Conflict*, report to the Carnegie Commission on Preventing Deadly Conflict (Carnegie Corporation of New York, December 1998).

Chapter Two

1. William Clinton, "U.S., Russia Will De-Target Strategic Nuclear Missiles" (Moscow: White House, Office of the Press Secretary, January 14, 1994).

2. Clinton, "Radio Address by the President to the Nation" (Minsk, Belarus: White House, Office of the Press Secretary, January 15, 1994).

3. White House, "A National Security Strategy for a New Century" (National Security Council, May 1997).

4. Official assessments of the damage that strategic forces might inflict attempt to reflect all that is known about the effects of nuclear explosions, the operating characteristics of their delivery systems, and the expected pattern of the attack plans, including the statistical uncertainties involved. The much simpler account presented in tables 2-1 through 2-4 provides a less refined but fundamentally accurate assessment of lethal potential. It indicates what the immediate blast effects of the deployed weapons would be capable of doing if they were directed in an efficient manner against major concentrations of population. This leaves out the more extended consequences of other weapons effects, such as radioactive fallout, but also the mitigating results of whatever attrition the warring forces might inflict on each other. Most official analysts probably would consider the latter effect to be greater than the former and therefore would judge the simple account to be on the high end of what an actual strategic force engagement might produce. The lethal potential indicated in tables 2-1 through 2-4 certainly is conceivable, however, in physical terms.

5. John D. Steinbruner, "Revising the Practice of Deterrence," in Naval Studies Board and Research Council, *Post-Cold War Conflict Deterrence* (Washington, D.C.: National Academy Press, 1997), pp. 64–74; Alexander L. George and

Richard Smoke, *Deterrence in American Foreign Policy: Theory and Practice* (Columbia University Press, 1974).

6. Desmond Ball, *Politics and Force Levels: The Strategic Missile Program of the Kennedy Administration* (University of California Press, 1980).

7. See Thomas C. Schelling, *The Strategy of Conflict* (Harvard University Press, 1960); George and Smoke, *Deterrence in American Foreign Policy*; Lawrence Freedman, *The Evolution of Nuclear Strategy*, 2d ed. (St. Martin's Press, 1990).

8. Implacable as it has proved to be, this feature of weapons technology has been a major point of political dispute. In principle, of course, it would be strategically and morally preferable if the technical advantage could be made to favor defense over offense, and an intense body of opinion argues that with sufficient effort this could be achieved. The unrelenting fact, however, is that offensive application has sustained a decisive technical advantage over defensive application. No technical basis has been identified for a defensive system that could defeat an unrestrained offense so reliably that the deterrent effect could be abandoned. Practical arguments about defensive deployments have to do with the desirable mix of forces to preserve the deterrent effect rather than to replace it.

9. See Ronald H. Spector, *Advice and Support: The Early Years, 1941–1960, United States Army in Vietnam* (Government Printing Office, 1983), for discussion of the consideration of whether to use nuclear weapons in Vietnam in 1954. See McGeorge Bundy, *Danger and Survival: Choices about the Bomb in the First Fifty Years* (Random House, 1988), regarding President Truman's comments about the possibility of using the bomb in Korea (pp. 237–38) and regarding the Eisenhower administration's deliberations over whether to use nuclear weapons after China bombarded Quemoy and Matsu (pp. 273–87).

10. There is a clear logical distinction between extending the deterrent effect to cover a nuclear assault on allies and extending it to cover threats of conventional attack. In use of the term "extended deterrence," however, the two notions usually have been blended, particularly in discussions relating to Europe. For the United States itself, there has been no need to evoke nuclear weapons to defend national territory against conventional attack. No country has been in a position to mount such an attack that could not be defended by conventional means. For allies in Europe and Asia, however, a massive conventional assault was more imaginable during the cold war period and the misery it would involve was closer to the anticipated consequences of nuclear war than it was for the United States.

11. U.S. nuclear weapons were also deployed in the U.S. territories of Guam, Johnston Island, and Puerto Rico. William M. Arkin, Robert S. Norris, and Joshua Handler, *Taking Stock: Worldwide Nuclear Deployments 1998* (Washington, D.C.: National Resources Defense Council, March 1998), p. 18. A 1999 article asserted that nuclear weapons were also based in Cuba, Iceland, Johnston Island, Kwajalein Atoll, Midway Island, and Morocco. See Robert S. Norris, William M. Arkin, and William Burr, "Where They Were," *Bulletin of Atomic Scientists*, vol. 55 (November/December 1999), pp. 26–35.

12. The commitment has been made most prominently as a "negative" security guarantee associated with the nuclear nonproliferation treaty (NPT). In an oft-repeated statement considered to be a politically binding part of the diplomatic record, the United States has stated, "The United States will not use nuclear weapons against any non-nuclear weapon state party to the NPT or any comparable internationally binding commitment not to acquire nuclear explosive devices, except in the case of an attack on the United States, its territories or armed forces, or its allies, by such a state allied to a nuclear weapon state, or associated with a nuclear weapon state in carrying out or sustaining the attack." See Treaty on the Non-Proliferation of Nuclear Weapons, "Narrative," www.acda.gov/treaties/npt1.htm [accessed October 1999].

13. The considerations involved in making this judgment are discussed in Michael M. May, George F. Bing, and John D. Steinbruner, *Strategic Arms Reductions* (Brookings Institution, 1988), pp. 30–59.

14. Arthur Katz, *Economic and Social Consequences of Nuclear Attacks on the United States: A Study Prepared for the Joint Committee on Defense Production* (Senate Committee on Banking, Housing, and Urban Affairs, U.S. Government Printing Office, 1979), p. 9.

15. Officially it was claimed that the targeting of missile installations was designed to prevent their reuse, and the initial configuration for some of the ballistic missile systems did appear to provide for the possibility of multiple firings from the same location. As surveillance and guidance system technology evolved, however, operations of that sort became wildly impractical and were not seriously developed.

16. Nuclear Age Peace Foundation, "The Nuclear Files, 1961" www.nuclearfiles.org/chron/60/1961.html [accessed October 1999]; Allen H. Lutins, "U.S. Nuclear Accidents," www.nitehawk.com/alleycat/nukes.html [accessed October 1999].

17. See John Steinbruner, "An Assessment of Nuclear Crises," in Franklyn Griffiths and John C. Polanyi, eds., *The Dangers of Nuclear War* (University of Toronto Press, 1979), pp. 34–49; Ernest R. May, John D. Steinbruner, and Thomas W. Wolfe, *History of the Strategic Arms Competition, 1945–1972* (Office of the Secretary of Defense, Historical Office, March 1981), chaps. 9 and 10.

18. Some would perceive a positive ratio and defend active deterrent practices even if the latter term were not so small, but broad acceptance of the practice clearly depends on a common judgment that it is.

19. Bruce G. Blair and John D. Steinbruner, *The Effects of Warning on Strategic Stability,* Brookings Occasional Papers (Brookings Institution, 1991).

20. David Hoffman, "Cold-War Doctrines Refuse to Die," *Washington Post,* March 15, 1998, p. A1; Lachlan Forrow and others, "Accidental Nuclear War—A Post–Cold War Assessment," *New England Journal of Medicine,* vol. 338 (April 30, 1998), pp. 1326–31.

21. President's Commission on the Accident at Three Mile Island, *The Need for Change: The Legacy of TMI* (U.S. Government Printing Office, 1979).

22. A serious coolant leak in a pressurized water reactor of the Three Mile Island type can damage the core within a few minutes. It is now recognized that a graphite moderated reactor of the Chernobyl type cannot be operated safely at low levels of power as the operators were attempting to do during the incident in question. Below a certain threshold of power output, corresponding to about 700 megawatts thermal in the Chernobyl case, the reactor must be shut down completely because a property known as a positive void coefficient makes it susceptible to sudden power excursions. See William Sweet, "Chernobyl: What Really Happened," *Technology Review,* vol. 92 (July 1989), p. 43; IAEA "Ten Years after Chernobyl," www.iaea.at/worldatom/inforesource/other/chernoten/facts.html [accessed November 1999].

23. Dorn Crawford, *Conventional Armed Forces in Europe (CFE): A Review and Update of Key Treaty Elements* (U.S. Arms Control and Disarmament Agency, January 1998).

24. International Institute for Strategic Studies, *The Military Balance, 1989–1990* (London: Brassey's, 1989), pp. 45–51.

25. International Bank for Reconstruction and Development/World Bank, "Table: Total GDP 1997," *1999 World Development Indicators,* CD-ROM (Washington, D.C., 1999). The author estimates current Russian gross domestic product to be $160 billion.

26. Aircraft also carry nuclear weapons and generally have longer flight times to their targets, but, because they are continuously controlled by their pilots, their flight paths cannot be predicted reliably from early observation. Since ballistic missile trajectories can be projected on the basis of initial observation, missile launches were accepted as a valid basis for authorizing strategic retaliation.

27. John D. Steinbruner and William W. Kaufmann, "International Security Reconsidered," in Robert D. Reischauer, ed., *Setting National Priorities: Budget Choices for the Next Century* (Brookings Institution, 1997), pp. 155–96.

28. An authoritative discussion of the financial and operational burdens imposed on Russian military planners and of the military doctrine evolved in reaction is provided by Alexei G. Arbatov, "Military Reform in Russia: Dilemmas, Obstacles, and Prospects," *International Security,* vol. 22 (Spring 1998), pp. 83–134. Arbatov is both a noted scholar and a member of the Russian State Duma, where he serves on the defense committee. A revised version of the military doctrine Arbatov discusses was subsequently approved and published. See "Russia's National Security Concept," *Nezavisimoye Voennoye Obozreniye,* January 14, 2000.

29. In working out the theory of deterrence, it was recognized that executing a massive deterrent threat might not be rational. If a massive threat did not succeed in preventing war, then the real interest after the fact would be to contain the

scope of retaliation in order to limit the consequent damage, and that realization could undermine the credibility of deterrence in the first place. The main argument advanced to deal with this conundrum was the idea of a threat "that left something to chance"—basically the notion that any finely calculating aggressor would have to consider the organizational inertia embodied in the programmed commitment to massive retaliation combined with the emotional provocation of the initial attack probabilistically sufficient to override the narrower rational incentive to limit or even completely renege on the massive threat. Introducing higher standards of operational safety would undermine this argument to some degree.

30. General Lee Butler and General Andrew Goodpaster, "Joint Statement on Reduction of Nuclear Weapons Arsenals: Declining Utility, Continuing Risks," speech before the National Press Club Newsmakers Luncheon, December 4, 1996.

31. National Resources Defense Council, "U.S. Nuclear Warheads, 1945–1996," www.nrdc.org/nrdcpro/nudb/datab9.html [accessed October 1999].

32. Bruce G. Blair, John Pike, and Stephen I. Schwartz, "Targeting and Controlling the Bomb," in Stephen I. Schwartz, ed., *Atomic Audit* (Brookings Institution, 1998), pp. 198, 201. "Strategic war planning from 1960 to 1992 was carried out by the Joint Strategic Target Planning Staff, formed in 1960 at Strategic Air Command headquarters near Omaha, Nebraska. . . . The first NSTL [National Strategic Target List] and SIOP [Single Integrated Operational Plan] were completed by November 1960."

33. In 1961 the operational planning system began setting aside a relatively small portion of the deployed weapons—reported to be about 150—for adaptive application to unanticipated circumstances. This reserve force was not committed to the basic plan. Peter Pringle and William Arkin, *SIOP: The Secret U.S. Plan for Nuclear War* (W.W. Norton, 1983), pp. 121–22.

34. It is said that the president has codes that would have to accompany any authorized instruction to use nuclear weapons and that the military chain of command has a separate set of codes that enable the weapons to work as intended. The ambiguity has to do with how the process of validating authority and enabling the weapons is combined and how many people are able to establish the required combination.

35. Robert A. Dahl, *Controlling Nuclear Weapons: Democracy versus Guardianship* (Syracuse University Press, 1985).

36. For the development of nuclear war fighting plans from the SIOP-62 in 1961 to SIOP-4, Revision K, in 1972, see Ernest R. May, John D. Steinbruner, and Thomas W. Wolfe, *History of the Strategic Arms Competition, 1945–1972* (Office of the Secretary of Defense, Historical Office, March 1981), pp. 592–612. For a discussion of Secretary Schlesinger's instructions, see Pringle and Arkin, *SIOP,* pp. 177–79. For a discussion of changes during the Carter administration, see Pringle and Arkin, *SIOP,* pp. 185, 191–97. For the Reagan administration's plans to fight a protracted nuclear war, see Robert Scheer, *With Enough Shovels: Reagan, Bush, and Nuclear War* (Random House, 1982), as cited in Desmond

Ball, "Development of the SIOP 1960–1983," in Desmond Ball and Jeffrey Richelson, eds., *Strategic Nuclear Targeting* (Cornell University Press, 1986), pp. 79–81. For the 1997 change in directive, see R. Jeffrey Smith, "Clinton Directive Changes Strategy on Nuclear Arms; Centering on Deterrence, Officials Drop Terms for Long Atomic War," *Washington Post,* December 7, 1997, p. A1; William Arkin, "The Last Word: Crossed Ts, Dotted Is," *Bulletin of the Atomic Scientists*, vol. 54 (March/April 1998), p. 72; and Robert Bell, "Strategic Agreements and the CTB Treaty: Striking the Right Balance," *Arms Control Today*, vol. 28 (January/February 1998), pp. 3–10.

37. Raymond L. Garthoff, *The Great Transition: American-Soviet Relations and the End of the Cold War* (Brookings Institution, 1994), pp. 242, 521.

38. Graham T. Allison and others, *Avoiding Nuclear Anarchy: Containing the Threat of Loose Russian Nuclear Weapons and Fissile Material* (MIT Press, 1996).

39. George H. W. Bush, "Address to the Nation on United States Nuclear Weapons Reduction," *Public Papers of the Presidents of the United States: George Bush, 1991,* book 2 (U.S. Government Printing Office, 1992), p. 1220. Bush's announcement reversed the standing orders for the forty nuclear-armed B-52 bombers that stood on twenty-four-hour ground alert, prepared to go aloft at a moment's notice. From 1961 to 1968, nuclear-armed B-52s operated on continuous airborne alert. This practice was discontinued, in part, after one nuclear-armed B-52 crashed in January 1966 and another in January 1968. Patrick E. Tyler, "And for the B-52s, the Alert Is Finally Over," *New York Times*, September 29, 1991, p. A11; Robert S. Norris, Steven M. Kosiak, and Stephen I. Schwartz, "Deploying the Bomb," in Schwartz, ed., *Atomic Audit*, p. 180.

40. Bruce G. Blair, *Global Zero Alert for Nuclear Forces* (Brookings Institution, 1995).

41. Virtually all states could claim a legitimate interest in receiving verification, and some have treaty commitments that arguably confer a right to it. Very few have any independent means of verification, and none can match the capacities of the United States and Russia.

42. National Academy of Sciences, Committee on International Security and Arms Control, *The Future of U.S. Nuclear Weapons Policy* (National Academy Press, 1997), p. 2; Canberra Commission on the Elimination of Nuclear Weapons, *Report of the Canberra Commission on the Elimination of Nuclear Weapons* (Canberra, Australia, August 1996); Henry L. Stimson Center, *An American Legacy: Building a Nuclear-Weapon-Free World*, final report of the steering committee project on eliminating weapons of mass destruction chaired by General Andrew Goodpaster, Report 22 (March 1997); "Statement on Nuclear Weapons by International Generals and Admirals," released on December 5, 1996, www.stimson.org/zeronuke/generals/internat.htm [accessed October 1999]; State of the World Forum, "Statement on Nuclear Weapons by International Civilian Leaders," released at the National Press Club on February 2, 1998, www.stimson.org/policy/intl-civ.htm [accessed October 1999].

43. Only four states—India, Pakistan, Israel, and Cuba—have not signed the nonproliferation treaty; see Strobe Talbott, "Dealing with the Bomb in South Asia," *Foreign Affairs,* vol. 78 (March/April 1999), pp. 110–22.

44. Treaty on the Non-Proliferation of Nuclear Weapons, "Narrative."

45. Paul Podvig, "The Russian Strategic Forces: Uncertain Future," *Breakthroughs,* vol. 7 (Spring 1998), pp. 11–21.

46. National Academy of Sciences, *Future of U.S. Nuclear Weapons Policy;* Committee on Nuclear Policy, "Jump—START: Retaking the Initiative to Reduce Post–Cold War Nuclear Dangers" (Henry L. Stimson Center, February 1999).

47. Butler and Goodpaster, "Joint Statement on Reduction of Nuclear Weapons Arsenals."

48. National Academy of Sciences, *Future of U.S. Nuclear Weapons Policy.*

49. *Weekly Compilation of Presidential Documents,* vol. 19 (Office of the Federal Register, March 1983), pp. 423–24. The logic would require defenses against all other potential forms of attack as well, but the predominant focus has been on defense against ballistic missiles.

50. A strategic force committed to offensive retaliation as the basis for deterrence facing an opponent dedicated to defensive reaction has the problem of assuring credible offensive penetration. With deployments limited, that presumably could not be done by brute force—that is, saturation of the opposing system—and would have to depend on carefully coordinated details of offensive operations and hence on command system functions. As long as any offensive weapons were arrayed against such a force, there would be a threat of disruption to the command system and a corresponding incentive to react rapidly to any perceived threat of attack.

51. The ABM treaty originally was negotiated to limit defensive deployments in order to assure that simultaneously limited offensive deployments would be able to perform the massive retaliatory missions that were considered to be the necessary basis for deterrence. The advocates of a defensive arrangement object to that formula and hence to the treaty. They have not acknowledged that the procedural rule—no defense except by mutual agreement—is also necessary for the opposite formula, namely, a limitation of offensive deployments in order to assure performance of the defensive system. Defensive systems have no reasonable chance of providing reliable security against an unrestrained offense.

52. This cumulative discrepancy between accounting records and physical inventory is understood to be largely due to statistical measurement errors concentrated in the earlier years of the plutonium production program, but it allows for the possibility of diverted material. See U.S. Department of Energy, "Plutonium: The First 50 Years. United States Plutonium Production, Acquisition, and Utilization from 1944 through 1994," apollo.osti.gov/html/osti/opennet/document/pu50yrs/pu50y.html [accessed November 1999].

53. The Nunn-Lugar program is formally known as the cooperative threat

reduction program. The $1.5 billion figure does not capture all monies spent on Nunn-Lugar activities, as $197.1 million has been spent on biological and chemical weapon activities. See Department of Defense, "Cooperative Threat Reduction Program Funding" www.ctr.osd.mil/07frame.htm [accessed November 1999]; Judith Miller, "U.S. and Russia Extend Deal to Cut Threats from Old Weapons," *New York Times*, June 17, 1999. Other initiatives designed to reduce the likelihood of nuclear materials or knowledge leaking out of Russia include the materials protection, control, and accounting program run by the U.S. Department of Energy; the International Science and Technology Center, administered primarily by the U.S. Department of State; initiatives for proliferation prevention run by the Department of Energy; and the nuclear cities initiative also run by the Department of Energy. See Toby F. Dalton and Denis Dragovic, "U.S. Programs Face Growing Russian Threat," Carnegie Endowment for International Peace Proliferation Brief, vol. 2 (March 4, 1999), www.ceip.org/programs/npp/brief24.htm [accessed November 1999].

54. Dunbar Lockwood, "Presidents Place New Limits on Fissile Material Use," *Arms Control Today*, vol. 25 (June 1995), p. 21.

55. The two principal materials used to generate nuclear explosions are the uranium isotope, U235, and plutonium isotope, PU239. The radioactive decay rate of both materials is extremely slow by human standards of time. It requires more than 700 million years for radioactive decay to reduce a given amount of uranium by half and more than 24,000 years in the case of plutonium. Natural uranium contains less that 1 percent of the isotope 235, however, and that concentration is normally increased to more than 90 percent to create material suitable for use in a nuclear weapon. All the known processes for increasing that concentration are laborious and expensive, but they can be readily reversed by mixing the product with natural uranium. Below concentrations of about 20 percent U235, uranium cannot be used to generate a nuclear explosion, although it can be used to run standard power reactors. That situation provides a natural way to dispose of weapons-grade uranium, but there is no comparably decisive method for disposing of plutonium. If blended with other isotopes, plutonium becomes less efficient and less convenient but is still a feasible explosive material. If burned in a reactor as a mixed oxide fuel, it generates more plutonium embedded in the spent fuel. U.S. Congress, Office of Technology Assessment, *Technologies Underlying Weapons of Mass Destruction*, OTA-BP-ISC-115 (U.S. Government Printing Office, December 1993), p. 121; National Academy of Sciences, *Future of U.S. Nuclear Weapons Policy*.

56. Deployment counts have been assisted by legal rules and data exchanges embodied in formal arms control agreements, but the details were known independently to very close approximation before they were specified in formal negotiations.

57. Seymour Hersh, *"The Target Is Destroyed": What Really Happened to Flight 007 and What America Knew about It* (Random House, 1986).

Chapter Three

1. Arms Control and Disarmament Agency, *World Wide Military Expenditures and Arms Transfers* (various years, 1963–90). Data are available on worldwide military spending for the period 1963–90.

2. In both cases these formal expectations serve broad political purposes and are connected only loosely to force operations. Under the cold war formulation, nuclear weapons associated with the deployment of conventional forces in Europe and in Korea were prepared to operate more rapidly than conventional units and probably would have done so had they been used at all. Moreover, the official assessment of threat was biased heavily toward overestimating the opponent and underestimating indigenous capability. In retrospect it is evident that NATO's capacity to defend Western Europe in conventional terms alone was much greater than the official expectation stated, and force commanders at the time appreciated that fact. A more candid assessment was not politically acceptable within the alliance, however, because of fears that it would undermine the deterrent effect of nuclear weapons and thereby encourage a large conventional battle in Europe. Similarly the revised formulation ignores the fact that any competent operation directed against Iraqi or North Korean aggression would not wait until the attack succeeded before conducting the counterattack. The first time that this situation occurs it can be excused, but one can hardly make the contingency the central focus of defense planning and still tolerate that degree of surprise. It is politically awkward to admit, however, that U.S. forces would be used preemptively if these contingencies were to arise again and that their capacities exceed those of the opposition by so much that it is difficult to justify the level of forces on those grounds.

3. Executive Office of the President of the United States, Office of Management and Budget, "Historical Tables: Section 3—Federal Government Outlays by Function; Table 3.2—Outlays by Function and Subfunction: 1962–2004," in *Budget of the United States Government, Fiscal Year 2000*, www.access.gpo.gov/usbudget/fy2000/hist.html [accessed November 1999].

4. This interpretation was advanced most systematically by Michael MccGwire, *Military Objectives in Soviet Foreign Policy* (Brookings Institution, 1987). Most of those who disputed it did so on grounds that there was a stronger element of aggression in Soviet intentions. Very few disputed that Soviet forces in Central Europe were configured primarily for offensive operations.

5. John D. Steinbruner and William W. Kaufmann, "International Security Reconsidered," in Robert D. Reischauer, ed., *Setting National Priorities: Budget Choices for the Next Century* (Brookings Institution, 1997), pp. 155–96; Michael E. O'Hanlon, "Stopping a North Korean Invasion: Why Defending South Korea Is Easier Than the Pentagon Thinks," *International Security*, vol. 22 (Spring 1998), pp. 135–70; Nick Beldecos and Eric Heginbotham, "The Conventional Military Balance in Korea," *Breakthroughs*, vol. 4 (Spring 1995), pp. 1–8.

6. William J. Perry, "Desert Storm and Deterrence," *Foreign Affairs,* vol. 70 (Fall 1991), pp. 66–82.

7. Vernon Loeb and Walter Pincus, "Bomb Suspect Has Been a Target; Aides Say Bin Laden Had Motive, Means to Attack Embassies," *Washington Post*, August 13, 1998, p. A1.

8. Federation of American Scientists, "Infinite Reach: Striking Back against Terrorists, August 20, 1998," www.fas.org/man/dod-101/ops/strike_back_n.htm [accessed November 1999].

9. His various doctrinal writings and those of his Soviet military colleagues are summarized in Mary C. Fitzgerald, "Marshal Ogarkov and the New Revolution in Soviet Military Affairs," Research Memorandum CRM 87-2 (Center for Naval Analysis, January 1987).

10. William S. Cohen, *1998 Annual Report to the President and the Congress* (U.S. Government Printing Office, 1998), p. 142. According to the 1997 Department of Defense Basic Research Plan, biomimetics enable the development of novel synthetic materials, processes, and sensors through advanced understanding and exploitation of design principles found in nature. Nanoscience achieves dramatic, innovative enhancements in the properties and performance of structures, materials, and devices that have controllable features on the nanometer scale (that is, tens of angstroms). Smart structures demonstrate advanced capabilities for modeling, predicting, controlling, and optimizing the dynamic response of complex, multiple-element, deformable structures used in land, sea, and aerospace vehicles and systems. Mobile wireless communications provide fundamental advances enabling the rapid and secure transmission of large quantities of multimedia information (speech, data, graphics, and video) from point to point, broadcast and multicast over distributed networks for heterogeneous C^3I systems. Intelligent systems enable the development of advanced systems able to sense, analyze, learn, adapt, and function effectively in changing or hostile environments until completing assigned missions or functions. Compact power sources achieve significant improvements in the performance (power and energy density, operating temperature, reliability, and safety) of compact power sources through fundamental advances relevant to current technologies (for example, batteries and fuel cells) and the identification and exploitation of new concepts. Director, Defense Research and Engineering, "Basic Research Plan" (U.S. Department of Defense, January 1997).

11. James Adams, *The Next World War: Computers Are the Weapons and the Front Line Is Everywhere* (Simon and Schuster, 1998); John Arquilla and David F. Ronfeldt, eds., *In Athena's Camp: Preparing for Conflict in the Information Age* (Rand Corporation, 1998).

12. U.S. House of Representatives, Committee on Armed Services, "Interim Report of the Committee on Armed Services" (March 30, 1992).

13. Michael R. Gordon and Bernard E. Trainor, *The Generals' War: The Inside Story of the Conflict in the Gulf* (Little, Brown, 1995), pp. 456–57.

14. Perry, "Desert Storm and Deterrence."

15. U.S. Department of Defense, *Conduct of the Persian Gulf War: Final Report to Congress* (U.S. Department of Defense, 1991); Eliot Cohen, *Gulf War Air Power Survey* (Washington, D.C.: Office of the Secretary of the Air Force, 1993).

16. U.S. Chairman of the Joint Chiefs of Staff, *Joint Vision 2010—America's Military: Preparing for Tomorrow,* www.dtic.mil/doctrine/jv2010/jv2010.pdf [accessed November 1999], p. 2.

17. Ibid., pp. 2, 13.

18. Gordon and Trainor, *The Generals' War,* pp. 272–88; Robert H. Scales Jr. and others, *Certain Victory: The U.S. Army in the Gulf War* (U.S. Army, Office of the Chief of Staff, 1993), p. 190ff. Since the Iraqi assault moved over a shorter distance than the redeployment that occurred in September 1994 and since it required a more rapid and more detailed reaction from U.S. forces, the capacity demonstrated in the earlier episode was more advanced than that required in the later one.

19. Alexander Flax, "Implications of Defenses against Tactical Ballistic Missiles," *Arms Control Today*, vol. 24 (May 1994), pp. 6–10; Alexander Flax, "Short- and Medium-Range Ballistic Missiles: Their Historical Roles in Warfare and the Ballistic Missile Defense Response," unpublished paper (National Academy of Sciences, Committee on International Security and Arms Control, May 1998). The rate of fire of the Iraqi missiles did decline over the course of the campaign from forty-nine during the first ten days of the war to an average of only one per day thereafter, suggesting that the operations of the missile launchers may have been suppressed by the interdiction effort. In the final days of the war, however, the rate of missile fire increased again, indicating either that a successful operational adaptation had been worked out or that the lower rate of fire had not been a result of the interdiction effort.

20. U.S. Department of Defense, *Conduct of the Persian Gulf War.*

21. According to U.S. Department of Defense, *Conduct of the Persian Gulf War,* p. 224, within fifteen minutes of launch a mobile Scud launcher could be anywhere within 14.5 kilometers of the launch point (an area of 841 square kilometers)—19.3 kilometers (an area of 1,490 square kilometers) if it traveled on a road.

22. According to Tim Ripley, "Scud Hunting: Counter-Force Operations against Theatre Ballistic Missiles," Bailrigg Memorandum 18 (Lancaster University, Centre for Defence and International Security Studies, 1996), p. 7, by 1990, the Iraqis were able to set up and fire their missiles in less than thirty minutes, "significantly less than the ninety minutes it took the Soviets to fire their own R-17 units." According to Lieutenant Colonel Mark Kipphut, U.S. Air Force, "Theater Missile Defense: Reflections for the Future," *Airpower Journal,* vol. 10 (Winter 1996), pp. 35–52. "A pre–[Gulf] war test, code-named Touted Gleem, demonstrated conclusively that F-111F, F-15E, and LANTIRN-equipped F-16 fighters had less than

a 50 percent chance of acquiring the Scud TEL even when the aircrews had precise target coordinates. TELs proved virtually impossible to find if the missile was not erect. This trend continued during the war when on forty-two separate occasions, pilots visually observed a launch, yet in only eight cases were aircrews able to maintain visual to allow them to employ weapons."

23. See Michael S. Malone, "To Infinity and Beyond," *One Digital Day: How the Microchip Is Changing Our World* (Times Books, May 1998).

24. W. Seth Carus, *Cruise Missile Proliferation in the 1990s* (Westport, Conn.: Praeger, 1992); "Assessing the Cruise Missile Threat," *Strategic Survey 1996/97* (Oxford University Press, 1997), pp. 16–31; multiple articles in *Aviation Week and Space Technology*, vol. 147 (July 14, 1997), pp. 44–57.

25. Steinbruner and Kaufmann, "International Security Reconsidered."

26. Sherman W. Garnett, *Limited Partnership: Russia-China Relations in a Changing Asia,* report of the Study Group on Russia-China Relations, Russian and Eurasian program (Carnegie Endowment for International Peace, 1998), p. 34.

27. The size of these migrations is a matter of dispute. Russian sources claim as many as 2 million, but independent observers consider that to be an exaggeration. Lower-end estimates are on the order of 30,000. Ibid., p. 37.

28. The sortie rates are based on normal aircraft deployment in theater, units capable of rapid response in a crisis situation, and the normal operational rates of the aircraft. The Chinese ground incursion rate is based on units positioned near the border and those capable of relatively rapid mobilization.

29. Alexei G. Arbatov, "A Military Reform in Russia: Dilemmas, Obstacles, and Prospects," *International Security,* vol. 22 (Spring 1998), pp. 129–30.

30. The following discussion of the Russian economy was developed in collaboration with Clifford Gaddy. See also Clifford Gaddy and Barry Ickes, "Russia's Virtual Economy," *Foreign Affairs,* vol. 77 (September/October 1998), pp. 53–67; Clifford Gaddy and Barry Ickes, "An Accounting Model of the Virtual Economy in Russia," *Post-Soviet Geography and Economics,* vol. 40 (March 1999), pp. 79–97. The comparison of economic output would be less stark if material product were compared, but economic value is the relevant measure. Much of the industrial capability that Russia inherited from the Soviet Union produced products of such low economic value that they were in effect a waste of resources and effort.

31. Petr A. Karpov, chairman, "Report of the Inter-Agency Balance Sheet Commission" (Moscow: Inter-Agency Balance Sheet Commission, December 1997).

32. Steinbruner and Kaufmann, "International Security Reconsidered."

33. Alexei G. Arbatov, "Military Reform in Russia: Dilemmas, Obstacles, and Prospects," *International Secutiry,* vol. 22 (Spring 1998), pp. 83–134.

34. This recognition is embedded in the provisions of the nuclear nonproliferation treaty, the central legal and political pillar for agreed restraints on weapons acquisition. Those states that formally renounce national nuclear weapons pro-

grams under the provisions of the treaty do so under the understanding that the nuclear weapons states will restrain both their nuclear and their conventional forces. That principle is stated in categorical terms in Article 6 of the treaty, which commits the signatories to the ultimate goal of general and complete disarmament, but the more immediate practical implication is that continued adherence to the treaty depends on incremental progress in both areas.

35. Treaty on the Non-Proliferation of Nuclear Weapons, "Narrative," www.acda.gov/treaties/npt1.htm [accessed October 1999].

36. Nicholas Johnson, "Monitoring and Controlling Debris in Space," *Scientific American,* vol. 279 (August 1998), p. 64.

37. Ibid., p. 60.

38. Allen Thomson, "Satellite Vulnerability: A Post–Cold War Issue?" *Space Policy*, vol. 11 (1995), pp. 19–30.

39. The earth is an imperfect sphere with a somewhat higher concentration of mass around the equator. That anomaly at appropriate altitude and inclinations, ranging between 200 nautical miles at 97 degrees and 600 nautical miles at 100 degrees, produces the 1 degree per day recession in the orbit that preserves a constant angle to the sun. The inclination is the angle formed in reference to the equator as a satellite intersects it traveling northward. A satellite with 0 degree inclination travels due east along the equator, one with 90 degrees moves due north, and one with 180 degrees moves due west. At mid-altitudes the anomaly has a negligible effect, but it strongly influences the low-altitude transfer orbits necessary to get there; hence there is a strong incentive to adhere to the 63.4 degree inclination where the effect cancels out and orbits are naturally stable. See Charles MacGregor and Lee Livingston, eds., *Space Handbook* (Maxwell Air Force Base, Ala.: Air University Press, 1977); Lieutenant Colonel Alan J. Parrington "Toward a Rational Space-Transportation Architecture," *Airpower Journal,* vol. 5 (Winter 1991), pp. 47–62.

40. Johnson, "Monitoring and Controlling Debris."

41. Ibid., p. 64.

42. NATO, Japan, and the Republic of Korea constitute the U.S. alliance system. UN Population Division, Department of Economic and Social Affairs, "Population (in Thousands) for the Countries of the World: 1998," www.popin.org/pop1998/2.htm [accessed October 1999].

43. Strobe Talbott, "Dealing with the Bomb in South Asia," *Foreign Affairs,* vol. 78 (March/April 1999), pp. 110–22.

44. The image of total warfare unaffected by any constraint whatsoever appears in the literature from time to time, but not in operational history, particularly not since nuclear weapons have been hovering in the background.

45. Weaker conventional forces create a lower threshold of reaction for nuclear operations and also expose those operations to a greater threat of interdiction from opposing conventional forces. In any confrontation involving the United

States and particularly one that is located in the European theater, Russian forces would be exposed to a very serious threat of conventional interdiction, and the internal pressures associated with it would be commensurately severe.

46. Dorn Crawford, "Conventional Armed Forces in Europe (CFE): A Review and Update of Key Treaty Elements" (U.S. Arms Control and Disarmament Agency, January 1998).

47. Republic of Korea, Ministry of National Defense, *Defense White Paper 1996–97*, p. 65, cited in O'Hanlon, "Stopping a North Korean Invasion," p. 147.

48. Garnett, *Limited Partnership,* p. 18ff.

Chapter Four

1. Ruth Leger Sivard, *World Military and Social Expenditures 1996* (Leesburg, Va.: WMSE Publications), p. 8.

2. The estimate is derived from Ruth Leger Sivard, *World Military and Social Expenditures 1993* (Washington, D.C.: World Priorities, 1993), cited in Yahya Sadowski, *The Myth of Global Chaos* (Brookings Institution, 1998), p. 137.

3. The episodes that would have been the logical occasion for assertive international reaction occurred in the Punjab in July and August 1947, when riots and forced displacement killed hundreds of thousands of people. See Stanley Wolpert, *Roots of Confrontation in South Asia: Afghanistan, Pakistan, India, and the Superpowers* (New York: Oxford University Press, 1982). The Truman doctrine had been proclaimed in March of that year, and Secretary of State George Marshall's speech at Harvard University initiating the Marshall Plan occurred in June. In January 1948, the Security Council did adopt Resolution 39 (1948), establishing the United Nations Commission for India and Pakistan to investigate and mediate the dispute, but the commission was given neither the mandate nor the capacity to contain violence directly. The first UN peacekeeping operation did not occur until 1948 and was located in the Middle East, not in South Asia.

4. Sadowski, *Myth of Global Chaos,* pp. 84–85, 131.

5. Ibid., p. 136.

6. Barbara Harff, "Victims of the State: Genocide, Politicides, and Group Repression since 1945," *International Review of Victimology*, vol. 1 (1989), pp. 23–41, as cited in Sadowski, *Myth of Global Chaos,* p. 13.

7. This distinction between the Hutu and the Tutsi is based primarily on cultural history and is not evident from language, appearance, or personal name. The Tutsi were warriors and cattle herders, were favored by the German and Belgian colonial administrators, and became over the course of the colonial period the cultural elite. The Belgians systematically reinforced the distinction through a system of identity cards. The Hutu were farmers and came to power when the country acquired independence in 1962 by virtue of their electoral majorities. See Gérard Prunier, *The Rwanda Crisis 1959–1994: History of a Genocide* (Colum-

bia University Press, 1995); Scott R. Feil, *Preventing Genocide: How the Early Use of Force Might Have Succeeded in Rwanda* (Washington, D.C.: Carnegie Commission on Preventing Deadly Conflict, April 1998), app. B.

8. In retrospect, the timely arrest of less than 100 known individuals would have prevented most of the civilian casualties, since these were inflicted largely by irregular militia gangs organized explicitly for the purpose. Professional assessments also suggest that a single U.S. infantry brigade—the basic unit capable of undertaking all aspects of the required operation—could have provided sufficient reinforcement for UNAMIR to control the situation. See Feil, *Preventing Genocide.*

9. Lynne Duke, "Zaire's Complex Conflict Keeps Refugees in Peril," *Washington Post,* April 2, 1997, p. A13.

10. William Clinton, "Remarks by the President to Genocide Survivors, Assistance Workers, and U.S. and Rwanda Government Officials" (White House, Office of the Press Secretary, Kampala, Uganda, March 25, 1998).

11. As noted in Sadowski, *Myth of Global Chaos,* p. 184, this argument can be traced back to the writings of Aristotle and is a prominent theme in contemporary studies of civil violence as well; see, for example, John Hagan and Ruth D. Peterson, eds., *Crime and Inequality* (Stanford University Press, 1995). Sadowski's own analysis based on a comparison of economic prosperity by country indicates that the more violent conflicts tend to occur in the poorer countries. See Sadowski, *Myth of Global Chaos,* p. 119ff.

12. In his 1999 assessment, Michael Klare notes that there is no authoritative count of the number of small arms and light conventional weapons in worldwide circulation; see Michael Klare, "International Trade in Light Weapons," in Jeffrey Boutwell and Michael Klare, eds., *Light Weapons and Civil Conflict: Controlling the Tools of Violence* (Lanham, Md.: Rowman and Littlefield, 1999). As the best available estimate, he cites the number 500 million provided by Air Commander Jasjit Singh of the Institute of Defense Studies and Analyses in New Delhi in 1995; see Jasjit Singh, "Introduction," in Jasjit Singh, ed., *Light Weapons and International Security* (New Delhi: Indian Pugwash Society and British American Security Information Council, December 1995), p. ix.

13. John Noble Wilford, "Cosmologists Ponder 'Missing Energy' of the Universe," *New York Times*, May 5, 1998, p. F1.

14. See Jan Willem Honig and Norbert Both, *Srebrenica: Record of a War Crime* (Penguin, 1996); David Rohde, *Endgame: The Betrayal and Fall of Srebrenica, Europe's Worst Massacre since World War II* (Farrar, Straus, and Giroux, 1997).

15. There may be some evolutionary basis for the propensity. It appears that with a single exception humans are the only species whose members will conduct organized attacks on each other, as distinct from opportunistic ones conducted to secure food, defend territory, or achieve some other immediate purpose. The single exception is the chimpanzee, to which humans are most closely related in genetic

terms. In the absence of effective defense or organized restraint, some chimpanzees—predominantly males—will band together to attack entire groupings of others, not merely to appropriate their assets but to exterminate them. The implication is that these two species have uniquely been exempted in the process of evolution from a genetic constraint on such behavior. Richard Wrangham and Dale Peterson, *Demonic Males: Apes and the Origin of Human Violence* (Houghton Mifflin, 1996).

16. The view that human nature is inherently violent is usually traced to the philosopher, Thomas Hobbes, who argued the point quite forcefully and maintained that authoritative institutions of the state are required to contain the carnage that human interactions would otherwise produce. See Thomas Hobbes, *Leviathan* (E. P. Dutton, 1931). Jean-Jacques Rousseau argued to the contrary that human nature itself is fundamentally benign and that violence emerges from the social convention of private property and the inequality that it engenders. See Jean-Jacques Rousseau, *The Social Contract and Discourses* (E. P. Dutton, 1920), pp. 200–07. A guru of the American revolution, John Locke, sided with Rousseau, more or less, in arguing that human nature is more reasonable than violent but agreed with Hobbes on the need for the state to contain residual inclinations to violence, protect property, and promote equity. Sir Ernest Barker, ed., *Social Contract, Essays by Locke, Hume, and Rousseau* (Oxford University Press, 1958).

17. Philosophical descendants of Locke hold that the inclination to violence depends on the type of government. Democracies, they contend, do not assault their own citizens, do not fight each other, and do not generally initiate war, whereas authoritarian governments frequently do all of these things. See, for example, Kenneth Benoit, "Democracies Really Are More Pacific (in General)," *Journal of Conflict Resolution*, vol. 40 (December 1996), pp. 636–57. The implication that a general extension of democracy can be counted on to establish global peace is disputed, however, by latter-day adherents of the Hobbesian view. The most popular of these in recent times has been Robert Kaplan, "The Coming Anarchy," *Atlantic Monthly*, vol. 273 (February 1994), pp. 44–65. See also Graham Fuller, *The Democracy Trap: The Perils of the Post–Cold War World* (Dutton Books, 1991). Citing Immanuel Kant for philosophical reference, John R. O'Neal and Bruce Russett have examined the annual incidence of violent conflict between 6,000 pairs of states from 1885 to 1992 and have concluded on statistical grounds that democracy, economic interdependence, and the actions of international organizations have reduced its occurrence. John R. O'Neal and Bruce Russett, "The Kantian Peace: The Pacific Benefits of Democracy, Interdependence, and International Organizations," *World Politics*, vol. 52 (October 1999). Their data set tilts the argument for the period in question, but it does not establish that peace is the inevitable consequence of globalization.

18. See Ted Robert Gurr, Monty G. Marshall, and Anne Pitsch, "The Minorities at Risk Project: Lessons, Limits, New Directions," paper prepared for the annual meeting of the American Political Science Association, Atlanta, September

2, 1999; Paul Collier and Anke Hoeffler, "The Coming Anarchy? The Global and Regional Incidence of Civil War" (Oxford University, Center for the Study of African Economics, January 1998); Peter Wallensteen and Margareta Sollenberg, "Armed Conflict and Regional Conflict Complexes, 1989–97," *Journal of Peace Research,* vol. 35 (September 1998), pp. 621–34.

19. Carnegie Commission on Preventing Deadly Conflict, *Preventing Deadly Conflict: Final Report* (Washington, D.C.: Carnegie Commission on Preventing Deadly Conflict, 1997), p. xvii.

20. As with any argument about how an historical event might have been altered, there is a range of opinion about how decisive a timely intervention in Rwanda would have been. Skeptics argue that controlling the violence would have been difficult and would have required more than a single brigade. Most of the skeptics appear to concede, however, that a meaningfully effective operation could have been undertaken with the level of resources that were reasonably available. See Alan J. Kuperman, "Rwanda in Retrospect," *Foreign Affairs*, vol. 79 (forthcoming, January-February 2000), pp. 94–118.

21. See Robert B. Oakley, Michael J. Dziedzic, and Eliot M. Goldberg, eds., *Policing the New World Disorder* (Washington, D.C.: National Defense University, 1998), provides a good overview of the state of international policing.

22. The following discussion draws on John D. Steinbruner, *Preventing Mass Violence: Toward a Doctrine of Sovereign Responsibility* (University of California-Los Angeles, Center for International Relations, 1998).

23. Simon Duke, "The State and Human Rights: Sovereignty versus Humanitarian Intervention," *International Relations,* vol. 12 (August 1994), pp. 25–48.

24. United Nations, "The Charter of the United Nations," in *The United Nations and Human Rights, 1945–1995,* United Nations Blue Book Series 7 (United Nations, 1995), p. 143.

25. See the following sections in United Nations, *The United Nations and Human Rights 1945–1995*: "The Universal Declaration of Human Rights," pp. 153–55; "The International Covenant on Economic, Social, and Cultural Rights," pp. 229–34; "The International Covenant on Civil and Political Rights," pp. 235–44.

26. Francis M. Deng and others, *Sovereignty as Responsibility: Conflict Management in Africa* (Brookings Institution, 1996); Abram Chayes and Antonia Handler Chayes, *The New Sovereignty: Compliance with International Regulatory Agreements* (Harvard University Press, 1995).

27. John Eriksson, "The International Response to Conflict and Genocide: Lessons from the Rwanda Experience—Synthesis Report" (Steering Committee of the Joint Evaluation of Emergency Assistance to Rwanda, March 1996).

28. Daniel C. Esty and others, *Working Papers: State Failure Task Force Report* (McLean, Va.: Science Applications International Corporation, November 30, 1995); Daniel C. Esty and others, *State Failure Task Force Report: Phase II*

Findings (McLean, Va.: Science Applications International Corporation, July 31, 1998).

29. Fédération Internationale des Droits de l'Homme, Africa Watch, Union Interafricaine des Droits de l'Homme et des Peuples, Centre International des Droits de la Personne et du Développement Démocratique, *Rapport de la Commission Internationale d'Enquête sur les Violations des Droits de l'Homme au Rwanda depuis le 1er October 1990* (New York: Africa Watch, 1993), pp. 62–66; Charles Trueheart, "UN Alerted to Plans for Rwanda Bloodbath," *Washington Post*, September 25, 1997, p. A1.

30. To those who have studied them closely, the relief organizations and other nongovernmental organizations are also quite exasperating in many respects, including especially their contentious relationships with one another. In general they are not systematically prepared to perform early-warning functions, and their coupling with formal governmental institutions for that purpose is poorly developed. They are nonetheless a natural locus of information and assessment, and their performance could be improved with dedicated effort. Thomas G. Weiss, "Nongovernmental Organizations and Internal Conflict," in Michael E. Brown, ed., *The International Dimensions of Internal Conflict* (MIT Press, 1996), pp. 435–59.

31. See Susan L. Woodward, *Balkan Tragedy: Chaos and Dissolution after the Cold War* (Brookings Institution, 1995).

32. Terrence Lyons and Ahmed I. Samatar, *Somalia: State Collapse, Multilateral Intervention, and Strategies for Political Reconstruction* (Brookings Institution, 1995), pp. 17n25, 26.

33. Ibid., p. 17n25.

34. The estimate of deaths in Somalia is derived from Sivard, *World Military and Social Expenditures 1993*, cited in Sadowski, *Myth of Global Chaos,* p. 138.

35. Carnegie Commission on Preventing Deadly Conflict, *Preventing Deadly Conflict,* pp. 69–104.

36. Mark Danner, "Endgame in Kosovo," *New York Review of Books*, vol. 46 (May 6, 1999), pp. 8–11.

37. See Warren Zimmerman, *Origins of a Catastrophe: Yugoslavia and Its Destroyers—America's Last Ambassador Tells What Happened and Why* (Times Books, 1996); Wayne Bert, *The Reluctant Superpower: United States Policy in Bosnia, 1991–1995* (St. Martin's Press, 1997); Laura Silber, *Yugoslavia: Death of a Nation* (TV Books, distributed by Penguin Books, 1997).

38. For the perspective of the lead U.S. negotiator at the Dayton talks, see Richard C. Holbrooke, *To End a War* (Random House, 1998).

39. U.S. Committee for Refugees, *World Refugee Survey 1994* (Washington, D.C.: Immigration and Refugee Services of America, 1994), p. 42.

40. For a good overview of the dissolution of Yugoslavia and the crisis in Bosnia, see a series of nine articles by Mark Danner, which appeared in the *New York Review of Books*, December 1997 through October 1998.

41. See Mohamed Sahnoun, *Somalia: The Missed Opportunities* (Washington, D.C.: U.S. Institute of Peace, 1994).

42. "Population-Based Mortality Assessment—Baidoa and Afgoi, Somalia, 1992," *Morbidity and Mortality Weekly Report,* vol. 41 (December 11, 1992), pp. 913–17.

43. Ibid.

44. Telephone conversation with Public Affairs Office of the Fifteenth Marine Expeditionary Unit in the spring of 1999.

45. The initial intervention led by the United States and organized as UNITAF was terminated in May 1993, and the U.S. forces that had conducted it were withdrawn. UNITAF was replaced by UNOSOM II on May 4. However, 1,500 U.S. combat forces remained in the area under national command, as available reinforcement for UNOSOM II should that be necessary. The hunt for Aideed and the October battle that resulted were conducted by U.S. Army Ranger units assigned to the U.S. national force.

46. United Nations, *The United Nations and Somalia, 1992–1996* (New York: United Nations, 1996), p. 55.

47. Ibid., p. 225.

48. See John L. Hirsh and Robert B. Oakley, *Somalia and Operation Restore Hope: Reflections on Peacemaking and Peacekeeping* (Washington, D.C.: United States Institute of Peace Press, 1995).

49. Karl Vick, "An Anarchic Somalia Lurches toward Another Famine," *Washington Post,* December 27, 1998, p. A23.

50. Kosovo is a border region where sovereign jurisdiction has been contested by the Ottoman Empire, by the Slavic states Bulgaria, Montenegro, and Serbia with frequent Russian involvement, and by the Austro-Hungarian empire. It also has been a point of contentious intersection between Islamic, Orthodox, and Roman Catholic religions. See Noel Malcolm, *Kosovo: A Short History* (New York University Press, 1998); Miranda Vickers, *Between Serb and Albanian: A History of Kosovo* (Columbia University Press, 1998).

51. See Malcolm, *Kosovo,* chaps. 12 and 16.

52. Ibid., p. xxvii.

53. Ibid., pp. 264–66.

54. Governments that are considered to be legitimate victims of terrorist actions generally are given military assistance rather than denied it.

55. U.S. Department of State, "Daily Press Briefing" (March 22, 1999), secretary.state.gov/www/briefings/9903/990322db.html [accessed October 1999].

56. Nick Cook, "War of Extremes: Lessons from Kosovo," *Jane's Defense Weekly* (July 7, 1999), p. 21, as cited in Anthony H. Cordesman, "The Lessons and Non-Lessons of the Air and Missile War in Kosovo" (Center for Strategic and International Studies, September 29, 1999), www.csis.org/kosovo/LessonsText.pdf [accessed October 1999], p. 24.

57. The NATO air campaign directly caused an estimated 1,500 civilian deaths throughout Yugoslavia, and the Serbian rampage in Kosovo is judged to have killed up to 10,000 noncombatants.

58. Yugoslav forces in Kosovo were not capable of defeating a combined-arms offensive by NATO, but difficult routes of access to the province posed a demanding logistical problem that would have translated into substantial risk and inevitable casualties for an invading force.

Chapter Five

1. White House, Office of the Press Secretary, "Executive Order 12938: Proliferation of Weapons of Mass Destruction" (November 14, 1994).

2. Richard Preston, *The Cobra Event* (Random House, 1997) is the novel reportedly read by the president. In his commencement speech at Annapolis in May 1998, President Clinton outlined a series of measures that he presented as a comprehensive strategy to address the threat of biological weapons. They included vaccinating all military personnel against anthrax and preparing military units to assist emergency teams at the state and local levels. See White House, Office of the Press Secretary, "Fact Sheet: Preparations for a Biological Weapons Attack" (May 22, 1998). The measures outlined would be prudent and plausibly effective for modest incidents, but not large ones. The "comprehensive strategy" to address the "scourge of biological weapons" did not include any measures designed for systematic prevention.

3. Ashton Carter, John Deutch, and Philip Zelikow, "Catastrophic Terrorism: Tackling the New Danger," *Foreign Affairs*, vol. 77 (November/December 1998), pp. 80–94.

4. According to the Organisation for the Prohibition of Chemical Weapons, as of June 23, 1999, there were 170 signatories to the Chemical Weapons Convention, 129 of which had ratified it.

5. The following discussion of biological agents draws on John D. Steinbruner, "Biological Weapons: A Plague upon All Houses," *Foreign Policy*, no. 109 (Winter 1997/98), pp. 85–96. See also Joshua Lederberg, *Biological Weapons: Limiting the Threat* (MIT Press, 1999).

6. Joshua Lederberg, Robert E. Shope, and Stanley C. Oaks Jr., eds., *Emerging Infections: Microbial Threats to Health in the United States* (Washington, D.C.: Institute of Medicine, National Academy Press, 1992), pp. 16–19.

7. Joint United Nations Program on AIDS (UNAIDS), "HIV/AIDS: The Global Epidemic, December 1996" (UNAIDS and World Health Organization, November 1996).

8. The history and inherent difficulty of the formal control efforts are well summarized by Robert Kadlec, Allan Zelicoff, and Ann Vrtis, "Biological Weap-

ons Control: Prospects and Implications for the Future," in Lederberg, *Biological Weapons,* pp. 95–111, and by George W. Christopher and others, "Biological Warfare: A Historical Perspective," in Lederberg, *Biological Weapons,* pp. 17–35.

9. Stephen Black, "Investigating Iraq's Biological Weapons Program," in Lederberg, *Biological Weapons,* pp. 159–65.

10. Lederberg, Shope, and Oaks, eds., *Emerging Infections;* National Center for Infectious Diseases (NCID) and Centers for Disease Control and Prevention (CDCP), *Addressing Emerging Infectious Disease Threats: A Preventive Strategy for the United States* (Atlanta, Ga.: CDCP, 1994); Committee on International Science, Engineering, and Technology, Working Group on Engineering and Reemerging Infectious Diseases, *Infectious Diseases: A Global Health Threat* (Washington, D.C.: National Science and Technology Council, September 1995); NCID and CDCP, *Preventing Emerging Infectious Diseases, A Strategy for the 21st Century* (Atlanta, Ga.: CDCP, October 1998).

11. Public health officials in the United States resisted large-scale testing of the Sabin vaccine out of concern that the live viruses might mutate into more dangerous forms as they passed between vaccinated and unvaccinated individuals. Since that possibility could not be tested without conducting large-scale trials, there appeared to be a very significant risk in undertaking the trials. The Soviet results demonstrated that propagation of the live strains in the Sabin vaccine blocked the spread of virulent strains of the virus and reduced the incidence of disease significantly below what had earlier been accomplished with the Salk vaccine, which was based on a killed virus. Albert B. Sabin, "Oral Poliovirus Vaccine," *Journal of Infectious Disease,* vol. 151 (March 1985), pp. 420–36; Albert B. Sabin, "Role of My Cooperation with Soviet Scientists in the Elimination of Polio: Possible Lessons for Relations between the U.S.A. and the USSR," *Perspectives in Biology and Medicine,* vol. 31 (Autumn 1987), pp. 57–61.

12. See, for example, James Crawford and others, "Draft Convention to Prohibit Biological and Chemical Weapons under International Criminal Law," *CBW Conventions Bulletin,* vol. 42 (December 1998), pp. 1–2.

13. James R. Ferguson, "Biological Weapons and U.S. Law," in Lederberg, *Biological Weapons,* pp. 87–90; Jonathan B. Tucker, "Bioterrorism: Threats and Responses," in Lederberg, *Biological Weapons,* p. 309.

14. National Academy of Sciences, Institute of Medicine, and National Research Council, "Controlling Dangerous Pathogens: A Blue-Print for U.S.-Russian Collaboration" (National Academy of Sciences, October 1997).

15. Vladimir M. Shkolnikov and France Meslé, "The Russian Epidemiological Crisis as Mirrored by Mortality Trends," in Julie DaVanzo, ed., *Russia's Demographic Crisis* (Santa Monica, Calif.: Rand Corporation, 1996), tables 4.10 and 4.11.

16. Alex Goldfarb, "TB: Scarier than Nukes," *Moscow Times,* August 19, 1998.

17. A. P. Pomerantsev and others, "Expression of Cereolysine AB Genes in *Bacillus anthracis* Vaccine Strain Ensures Protection against Experimental Hemolytic Anthrax Infection," *Vaccine*, vol. 15 (1997), pp. 1846–50.

18. See, for example, William J. Broad, "Gene-Engineered Anthrax: Is It a Weapon?" *New York Times*, February 14, 1998, p. A4; Laurie Garrett, "Concern over Russia's Anthrax," *Newsday*, February 19, 1998, p. 4; Debora MacKenzie, "Naked into Battle," *New Scientist*, vol. 157 (February 28, 1998), p. 4.

Chapter Six

1. George H. W. Bush, "Address before a Joint Session of the Congress on the Persian Gulf Crisis and the Federal Budget Deficit (September 11, 1990)," *Public Papers of the Presidents of the United States: George Bush,* book 2*: July 1 to December 31, 1990* (U.S. Government Printing Office), p. 1219.

2. For a variety of perspectives on the concept of a new world order, see Graham Allison and Gregory F. Treverton, eds., *Rethinking America's Security: Beyond Cold War to New World Order* (Norton, 1992); Carol Rae Hansen, ed., *The New World Order: Rethinking America's Global Role* (Flagstaff: Arizona Honors Academy Press, 1992); Noam Chomsky, *World Orders, Old and New* (Columbia University Press, 1994); George C. McGhee, *International Community: A Goal for a New World Order* (Lanham, Md.: University Press of America; Charlottesville, Va.: University of Virginia, Miller Center, 1992); Alan K. Henrikson, "How Can the Vision of a New World Order Be Realized?" *Fletcher Forum of World Affairs*, vol. 16 (Winter 1992), pp. 63–79; Robert W. Tucker and David C. Hendrickson, *The Imperial Temptation: The New World Order and America's Purpose* (New York: Council on Foreign Relations Press, 1992).

3. The conceptual basis for the distinction between a deliberate threat and one that emerges from broadly distributed processes is discussed in John Steinbruner, *The Cybernetic Theory of Decision: New Dimensions of Political Analysis* (Princeton University Press, 1974).

4. This point was convincingly argued by the historian Thomas S. Kuhn in one of the more influential monographs of the cold war period, *The Structure of Scientific Revolutions* (University of Chicago Press, 1962). Kuhn argued that the progress of modern science has been substantially determined by seminal conceptual shifts in the assumptions that are used to organize scientific investigation—the insight of Kepler, Copernicus, and Galileo, for example, that the earth orbits the sun rather than the other way around as was previously believed. Despite what appears in retrospect to be the obvious, compelling, and enormously consequential superiority of these conceptual advances, many of the most important were highly controversial in their own time and were consolidated only over the course of a generation or more.

5. In 1997, for example, the Department of Defense undertook what it considered to be a comprehensive review of national security policy, and, in accord with a legislated requirement, the results were reviewed by an independent panel of appointed specialists. Both of the documents that emerged from the exercise—U.S. Department of Defense, *Report of the Quadrennial Defense Review* (May 1997), and National Defense Panel, *Transforming Defense: National Security in the 21st Century* (December 1997)—acknowledged sweeping global changes already experienced and still in progress. Both also discussed technical innovations, adjustments to the configuration of forces, and changes in the design of U.S. military operations that were anticipated as a result of different circumstances of threat. Neither report questioned the continuation of active deterrent operations, however, or preparations for rapid global projection of conventional forces against organized aggressive threats. The official planning document, the quadrennial review, explicitly reiterated the commitment to prepare conventional forces for two simultaneous regional contingencies. The independent panel report accepted that as a planning standard but discounted the actual probability of that type of threat and focused instead on lesser, more widespread, and less predictable forms of violence. Neither contested the confrontational character of established policy.

6. Wolfram Fischer, Herbert Hax, and Hans Karl Schneider, eds., *Treuhandanstalt: The Impossible Challenge* (Akademie Verlag, 1996); Padma Desai, "Russian Privatization: A Comparative Perspective," *Harriman Review,* vol. 8 (August 1995), pp. 1–34.

7. Petr A. Karpov, chairman, "Report of the Inter-Agency Balance-Sheet Commission" (Moscow: Inter-Agency Balance Sheet Commission, December 1997), as elaborated by Clifford Gaddy with Barry Ickes, "An Accounting Model of the Virtual Economy in Russia," *Post-Soviet Geography and Economics,* vol. 40 (March 1999), pp. 79–97.

8. Ibid.

9. Telephone interview conducted April 13, 1999, with Yuri Markov of the International Grains Council, London. David Hoffman, "U.S., Russia Detail Three-Part Food Deal," *Washington Post*, November 7, 1998, p. A17; William Clinton, "Statement by the President" (White House, Office of the Press Secretary, November 4, 1998); Mike Smith, "EU Outlines Food Package for Russia," *Financial Times,* November 10, 1998, p. 2.

10. Paul Blustein, "Rescue of Russian Economy Failing; Experts Predict New Bailout Effort," *Washington Post,* August 14, 1998, p. A1. From the time it was submitted in late October 1997 to July 1998, the Russian Federation's 1998 budget lost $20 billion against its original assumptions due to lower tax receipts, lower energy prices, and higher cost of servicing its domestic debt.

11. In an effort to reduce Soviet concerns about a unified Germany, U.S. interlocutors such as Secretary of State James Baker repeatedly promised the Soviets in the early stages of talks about possible German reunification that NATO would

not expand eastward. See Philip Zelikow and Condoleezza Rice, *Germany Unified and Europe Transformed: A Study in Statecraft* (Harvard University Press, 1995), pp. 176, 182–187, 189; James M. Goldgeier, *Not Whether but When: The U.S. Decision to Enlarge NATO* (Brookings, 1999), pp. 14–17; and Angela E. Stent, *Russia and Germany Reborn: Unification, the Soviet Collapse, and the New Europe* (Princeton University Press, 1999), pp. 141, 225.

12. See, for example, Igor Khripunov, "Moscow Reacts," *Bulletin of the Atomic Scientists,* vol. 55 (July/August 1999), pp. 32–35.

13. Reports to this effect circulating among retired military officers are summarized by Yves Goulet, "MPRI: Washington's Freelance Advisors," *Jane's Intelligence Review,* vol. 10 (July 1, 1998), p. 38. Military Professional Resources (MPRI), a private company based in Arlington, Virginia, was involved in training the Croatian military, under the U.S. Department of State's democracy transition assistance program. The Goulet article acknowledges MPRI's statement that "its contracts with Croatia were limited to classroom teachings and never involved any training in tactics or use of weaponry," but it also records general skepticism about that claim: "Many press reports indicated . . . that MPRI's activities . . . involved much more than academic discussions about democracy. These rumours seemed to be confirmed following the two successful military operations launched by Croatia in 1995, just months after the beginning of MPRI's contracts began." One of these operations—Operation 'Storm'—"defeated the Serbian forces located in the Krajina region within just seventy-two hours . . . The scope of this unprecedented change led to speculations that MPRI tactical thinking had been decisive in the preparation of these military operations. It is also believed that the training of a regular professional army and the development of a competent and professional corps of officers were the result of MPRI's activities. MPRI denies these allegations." Whatever the literal truth of the matter, the speculation fueled Russian suspicions.

14. William Clinton, "Presidential Statement on the National Missile Defense Act" (White House, Office of the Press Secretary, July 23, 1999).

15. White House, Office of the Press Secretary, "Joint Statement between the United States and the Russian Federation Concerning Strategic Offensive and Defensive Arms and Further Strengthening of Stability"(Cologne, Germany: White House, Office of the Press Secretary, June 20, 1999).

16. Nick Wadhams, "Russia Wants Nuclear Arms Upgrade," *Associated Press,* April 29, 1999; Victor Baranets, "Russia Takes Time over Preventive Nuclear Strikes," *Komsomolskaya Pravda,* April 30, 1999; Pavel Felgenhauer, "Defense Dossier: Back to a Nuclear Future," *Moscow Times,* May 27, 1999; Andrei Piontkovsky, "Season of Discontent: Kremlin Keen on Limited Atomic War," *Moscow Times,* May 27, 1999, p. 8.

17. Alexander Babakin, "Our Zapad 99 Is Not against the West," *Moscow Rossiyskaya Gazeta,* June 26, 1999, p. 2 in Foreign Broadcast Information Ser-

vice, *Daily Report: Central Eurasia,* July 28, 1999; Michael Gordon, "Maneuvers Show Russian Reliance on Nuclear Arms," *New York Times,* July 10, 1999, p. A1.

18. Nicholas R. Lardy, "China and the Asian Contagion," *Foreign Affairs,* vol. 77 (July/August 1998), p. 78.

19. Nicholas R. Lardy, *China's Unfinished Economic Revolution* (Brookings Institution, 1998).

20. State Council of the People's Republic of China, Information Office, *China's National Defense* (Beijing, July 1998), p. 9.

21. Ibid., p. 20.

22. Richard A. Bitzinger, "Military Spending and Foreign Military Acquisitions by the PRC and Taiwan," in James R. Lilley and Chuck Downs, eds., *Crisis in the Taiwan Strait* (National Defense University Press, 1997), p. 77.

23. William M. Arkin, Robert S. Norris, and Joshua Handler, *Taking Stock: Worldwide Nuclear Deployments 1998* (Washington, D.C.: Natural Resources Defense Council, March 1998), pp. 45–52; Natural Resources Defense Council Nuclear Program, "Table of Chinese Nuclear Forces, End 1996," China-embassy.org/Cgi-Bin/Press.pl?1972 [accessed October 1999].

24. That is the apparent logic of the episode in 1996 in which China conducted missile tests that fell just short of and just beyond the island.

25. "China Says It Will Not Use Nuclear Weapons against Taiwan," *New York Times,* September 3, 1999, p. A3. The speculation that generated the statement had been inspired by China's announcement two months earlier, in a context of active tension over Taiwan, that it had developed an enhanced radiation weapon. The doctrinal statement, which clearly had been carefully considered and was accepted as authoritative, was made in response to a direct question in the press conference about whether China would use the new weapon against Taiwan.

26. Joint Communiqué of the United States of America and the People's Republic of China, released on February 28, 1972, in Washington and Beijing; Joint Communiqué of the United States of America and the People's Republic of China, released on December 15, 1978, in Washington and Beijing; Joint Communiqué of the United States of America and the People's Republic of China released on August 17, 1982, in Washington and Beijing.

27. Joint Communiqué of the United States of America and the People's Republic of China, released on December 15, 1978, in Washington and Beijing.

28. John Pomfret, "Zhu's Trip to U.S. Ends on Bright Note; Clinton Agrees to Resume WTO Talks," *Washington Post,* April 17, 1999, p. A11. U.S. House of Representatives, Select Committee on U.S. National Security and Military/Commercial Concerns with the People's Republic of China, The Cox Report, www.house.gov/coxreport [accessed October 1999]; President's Foreign Intelligence Advisory Board, *Science at Its Best, Security at Its Worst: A Report on Security Problems at the U.S. Department of Energy* (June 15, 1999), www.whitehouse.gov/WH/EOP/pfiab-report.pdf [accessed November 1999].

"Asia: Taiwan's Unnerving President Does It Again," *Economist*, vol. 352 (July 17, 1999), pp. 35–36.

29. Senate Committee on Governmental Affairs, *The Proliferation Primer: A Majority Report of the Subcommittee on International Security, Proliferation, and Federal Services* (January 1998), www.senate.gov/~gov_affairs/prolifpr.htm [accessed October 1999], p. 33.

30. David Albright, "How Much Plutonium Does North Korea Have?" *Bulletin of the Atomic Scientists*, vol. 50 (September 1994), p. 46.

31. Leon V. Sigal, *Disarming Strangers: Nuclear Diplomacy with North Korea* (Princeton University Press, 1998), p. 75.

32. The thermal output of a reactor, the appropriate measure for assessing its capacity to produce plutonium, is larger than its capacity to generate electricity. The largest of the North Korea reactors would have been able to generate 200 megawatts of electrical power, but 600 to 800 megawatts of thermal output. Albright, "How Much Plutonium."

33. Sigal, "Disarming Strangers," pp. 124–27, 257–59.

Index